T0305467

A Research Agenda for Economic Anthropology

Elgar Research Agendas outline the future of research in a given area. Leading scholars are given the space to explore their subject in provocative ways, and map out the potential directions of travel. They are relevant but also visionary.

Forward-looking and innovative, Elgar Research Agendas are an essential resource for PhD students, scholars and anybody who wants to be at the forefront of research.

Titles in the series include:

A Research Agenda for Global
Environmental Politics
Edited by Peter Dauvergne and Justin Alger

A Research Agenda for New Institutional
Economics
Edited by Claude Ménard and Mary M. Shirley

A Research Agenda for Regeneration
Economies
Reading City-Regions
Edited by John R. Bryson, Lauren Andres and Rachel Mulhall

A Research Agenda for Cultural
Economics
Edited by Samuel Cameron

A Research Agenda for Environmental
Management
Edited by Kathleen E. Halvorsen, Chelsea Schelly, Robert M. Handler, Erin C. Pischke and Jessie L. Knowlton

A Research Agenda for Creative Tourism
Edited by Nancy Duxbury and Greg Richards

A Research Agenda for Public
Administration
Edited by Andrew Massey

A Research Agenda for Tourism
Geographies
Edited by Dieter K. Müller

Research Agenda for Economic Psychology
Edited by Katharina Gangl and Erich Kirchler

A Research Agenda for Entrepreneurship
and Innovation
Edited by David B. Audretsch, Erik E. Lehmann and Albert N. Link

A Research Agenda for Financial Inclusion
and Microfinance
Edited by Marek Hudon, Marc Labie and Ariane Szafarz

A Research Agenda for Global Crime
Edited by Tim Hall and Vincenzo Scalia

A Research Agenda for Transport Policy
Edited by John Stanley and David A. Hensher

A Research Agenda for Tourism and
Development
Edited by Richard Sharpley and David Harrison

A Research Agenda for Housing
Edited by Markus Moos

A Research Agenda for Economic
Anthropology
Edited by James G. Carrier

A Research Agenda for Social
Entrepreneurship
Edited by Anne de Bruin and Simon Teasdale

A Research Agenda for Economic Anthropology

Edited by

JAMES G. CARRIER

Max Planck Institute for Social Anthropology, Halle, Germany and Indiana University, Bloomington, USA

Elgar Research Agendas

Edward Elgar
PUBLISHING

Cheltenham, UK • Northampton, MA, USA

Published by
Edward Elgar Publishing Limited
The Lypiatts
15 Lansdown Road
Cheltenham
Glos GL50 2JA
UK

Edward Elgar Publishing, Inc.
William Pratt House
9 Dewey Court
Northampton
Massachusetts 01060
USA

A catalogue record for this book
is available from the British Library

Library of Congress Control Number: 2019938737

This book is available electronically in the **Elgar**online
Economics subject collection
DOI 10.4337/9781788116107

ISBN 978 1 78811 609 1 (cased)
ISBN 978 1 78811 610 7 (eBook)

Typeset by Servis Filmsetting Ltd, Stockport, Cheshire
Printed and bound in Great Britain by TJ International Ltd, Padstow, Cornwall

Contents

Contributors

James G. Carrier is adjunct professor of anthropology at the University of Indiana and associate of the Max Planck Institute for Social Anthropology. He has done research and written on aspects of economy in Papua New Guinea, the United States and the United Kingdom. His publications include *Wage, trade and exchange in Melanesia* (University of California Press, 1989), *Gifts and commodities: Exchange and Western capitalism since 1700* (Routledge, 1995), and the edited volumes *Meanings of the market* (Berg, 1997), *A handbook of economic anthropology* (Edward Elgar, revised edition 2012), *Anthropologies of class* (Cambridge University Press, 2015, with Don Kalb) and *Economy, crime and wrong in a neoliberal era* (Berghahn Books, 2018).

Jaume Franquesa received his PhD from the University of Barcelona in 2006 and currently is associate professor of anthropology at the University at Buffalo, The State University of New York. His research focuses on the relationship between resource commodification and the making of local livelihoods, paying special attention to the role of state, class and cultural politics in shaping organised and everyday forms of political resistance. His latest book is *Power struggles: Dignity, value, and the renewable energy frontier in Spain* (Indiana University Press, 2018).

Stefan Leins is a senior lecturer at the Department of Social Anthropology and Cultural Studies of the University of Zurich. He works on commodity trading, supply chains, financial forecasting practices, Islamic finance, socially responsible investing and the narrative dimension of finance. His *Stories of capitalism: Inside the role of financial analysts* was published by the University of Chicago Press in 2018. Since January 2017 he has been helping to co-ordinate and conduct research in the project 'Valueworks: Effects of financialization along the copper value chain', funded by the Swiss Network for International Studies (SNIS).

Fabio Mattioli is a lecturer in social anthropology at the University of Melbourne, where he co-ordinates several interdisciplinary research projects on business start-ups. His book manuscript, *Illiquidity and power*, describes the failed construction deals and exploitative financial practices that framed the emergence of authoritarian politics in the Republic of Macedonia. His publications include 'Financialization without liquidity: In-kind payments, forced credit, and authoritarianism at the periphery of Europe' (*Journal of the Royal Anthropological Institute*, 2018) and 'Finance beyond function: Three causal explanations for financialization' (*Economic Anthropology*, 2018, with Aaron Pitluck and Daniel Souleles).

Mark Moberg is a professor of anthropology at the University of South Alabama. Trained as an economic anthropologist, his research has focused on Central America and the Eastern Caribbean, as well as the United States. He has published in the areas of rural development, alternative trade, work and the environment. Among his books are *Myths of ethnicity and nation: Work and identity in the Belize banana industry* (Tennessee, 1997), *Slipping away: Banana politics and Fair Trade in the Eastern Caribbean* (Berghahn, 2008), *Fair Trade and social justice: Global ethnographies* (NYU Press, 2010, with Sarah Lyon) and *Engaging anthropological theory: A social and political history* (Routledge, 2018).

Tom Neumark is a research fellow in social anthropology at the University of Edinburgh. He has previously taught economic anthropology at the University of Cambridge. His current research focuses on data and distributed renewable energy in East Africa. His previous work examined redistribution, charity, ethics, relationality and forms of care in Kenya, and aspects of it have been described in '"A good neighbour is not one that gives": Detachment, ethics, and the relational self in Kenya' (*Journal of the Royal Anthropological Institute*, 2017). His book *Caring cash* is currently under contract with Pluto Press.

Valeria Siniscalchi is a professor of economic anthropology at the École des Hautes Études en Sciences Sociales (EHESS), Centre Norbert Elias, in Marseilles. Her research focuses include the policies of nature, work and industrial districts, food activism and politics. She did research in the south of Italy, the French Alps and in the Slow Food movement. Her publications include *Antropologia culturale: Un'introduzione* (Carocci, 2001, revised edition 2012), the edited collections *Frammenti di economie: Ricerche di antropologia economica in Italia* (Pellegrini, 2002) and *Food activism: Agency, economy and democracy* (Bloomsbury, 2014, with Carole Counihan), and the forthcoming *Slow Food: The economy and politics of a global movement* (Bloomsbury, 2019).

Felix Stein is an economic anthropologist and post-doctoral researcher at the Usher Institute of the University of Edinburgh. For his PhD at the University of Cambridge he wrote an ethnography of German management consultants entitled *Work sleep repeat*. It was a joint winner of the LSE First Book Competition and was published by Bloomsbury Publishing in 2017. He is a founder and managing editor of the *Cambridge Encyclopedia of Anthropology* (www.anthroencyclopedia.com). Presently he is studying the political economy of water and the fight against cholera in Haiti.

Andreas Streinzer is a fellow at the Institute for Social Research in Frankfurt/ Main and PhD candidate at the Department of Social and Cultural Anthropology, University of Vienna. He has held visiting scholarships at the University of Thessaly, the Max Planck Institute of Social Anthropology and the Department of Sociology at the University of Lancaster. His recent publications include 'Stretching money to pay the bills: The temporal modalities and relational practices of getting by in the Greek economic crisis' (*Cambridge Journal of Anthropology*, 2016) and 'Doing economic relations otherwise: Everyday politics of solidarity in the TEM currency network in Volos, Greece' (*Ethnologia Europaea*, 2018).

Greg Urban is the Arthur Hobson Quinn Professor of Anthropology and quondam Chair of the Department of Anthropology at the University of Pennsylvania. A specialist in linguistic and cultural anthropology, Urban studies the processes of cultural motion, with a focus on the forces that impel that motion through space and time. Among his books are *Metaculture: How culture moves through the world* (University of Minnesota Press, 2001), *Metaphysical community: The interplay of the senses and the intellect* (University of Texas Press, 1996), *A discourse centered approach to culture* (University of Texas Press, 1991) and, as editor, *Corporations and citizenship* (University of Pennsylvania Press, 2014).

Introduction to *A Research Agenda for Economic Anthropology*

James G. Carrier

Contemporary anthropological study of economy traces its disciplinary roots back to the first decades of the twentieth century. Early scholars approached people's economic activities as part of their study of social life, practice and organisation as a whole. This work marked out attributes of economic anthropology that remained important until the closing decades of that century.

One of those attributes, already mentioned, is that economic activities were approached as part of people's lives generally, linked with, affecting and affected by religion, kinship, politics and the rest, to form a unity that could be seen as a whole, even if not necessarily a very tidy one. This set that study off from conventional economics, which generally saw economy as a distinct realm that was studied and thought about in isolation from the rest of social life. A second important attribute emerged from the places where those early anthropologists did their research, small societies that lacked the money and market systems that were important in the countries that were home to those anthropologists. Again, this was different from conventional economics, which was concerned primarily with those home countries, large societies characterised by monetary transactions in the market.

In the closing decades of the twentieth century, first the economists and then the anthropologists began to shift their orientation. For the economists, the macroeconomic interest in economic systems, which had been important since the 1930s, gave way to interest in the transactions between autonomous individuals that characterised neoclassical economics. For the anthropologists, the study of small-scale societies, what came to be called grass-hut or mud-hut anthropology, began to give way to the study of people in much larger, monetised and market-oriented places, ranging from small-holders in Central America who grow coffee for international buyers to people in London shopping in supermarkets and people in Muncie, Indiana, celebrating Christmas. The reasons for the change in orientation in both disciplines are complex. However, one consequence was that anthropologists and economists increasingly were concerned with the same sorts of people in the same sorts of societies.

To understand the present state of the sub-discipline, and to understand the significance of the research agendas of economic anthropology that are laid out by the contributors to this volume, it is important to understand how we got to that state. I present a sketch of that journey now.

Economic anthropology in the twentieth century

I said that the foundations of the sub-discipline were laid early in the twentieth century. The two people from that era who are best remembered probably are Bronislaw Malinowski and Marcel Mauss. The former is known for his work on the kula, a regional system of exchange in the islands in the east of what is now Papua New Guinea (Malinowski 1922). The latter is best known for his synthetic description of the ways that gift exchange obligates people to each other in societies where it is important, ranging from Melanesia and the Pacific Northwest through India and ancient Germany (Mauss 1990 [1925]).

Malinowski was an inveterate field worker while Mauss was an analyst and theoretician, and both wrote about societies that were alien to the Western Europe where they lived and worked. It would be wrong, however, to think that the description and analysis of people in alien places and times was their only goal. Certainly they sought that, but in some ways that was a means to a further end. That end was increasing our understanding of the Western societies that were home both to them and to the vast majority of their readers. For Malinowski (e.g. 1921) an important question was how people understand the giving and getting that were central to the circulation of things on Kiriwina, the small island that was the focus of his research. Mauss addressed a similar question, and particularly how those understandings differed in different societies, including (1990 [1925]: chapter 4; see also Parry 1986) how they had changed following the emergence of commercial capitalism in Europe. Neither man, then, was concerned solely with the description of alien societies, practices and cultures, for both used these to reflect in different ways on the West with which they were familiar. For them, that is, the work that they did was concerned with what Michel-Rolph Trouillot (2003) called the Savage Slot, using their descriptions of others to reflect upon themselves.

That reflection entailed a questioning, sometimes implicit and sometimes explicit, of the approach to economic activity that was common in the discipline of economics since the nineteenth century and that has been dominant since the 1970s. That approach had its roots in Adam Smith's *The wealth of nations*. Smith wrote many things in that work, but important among them was that economic activity rests on the decisions of autonomous individuals who calculate what it is among the things on offer that best serves their own interests given the resources that they have at hand. As he (1976 [1776]: 18) put it, 'It is not from the benevolence of the butcher, the brewer, or the baker, that we expect our dinner, but from their regard to their own interest', so that, in our dealings with our fellows, 'We address ourselves, not to their humanity, but to their self-love, and never talk to them of our own necessities, but of their advantages.' This view, of calculating individuals facing choices, came to be extended beyond the realm of market transaction that concerned Smith to life in general. This is explicit in an influential work by a British economist in the 1930s, Lionel Robbins. He said that the focus of the discipline of economics is economic reasoning: 'Economics is the science which studies human behaviour as a relationship between ends and scarce means which have alternative uses' (Robbins 1945 [1932]: 16). Moreover, he was clear that this reasoning is by no means restricted to buying and selling, giving and getting: 'The distribution of time between prayer and good works has its economic aspect equally with the distribution of time between orgies and slumber' (1945 [1932]: 26).

Thus it was that most anthropologists, concerned with people's thoughts and actions in their economic lives, studied something different from most economists, concerned with economic reasoning. The two approaches were thrashed out in the only time when economists and anthropologists confronted each other intellectually in a sustained way. That was the formalist–substantivist debate around the 1960s, each side touting the virtues of its own approach and criticising the shortcomings of the other. The debate took its name from the distinction that Karl Polanyi (1957: 243) drew between two meanings of 'economic'. The one that he called 'formal' is concerned with 'the logical character of the means–ends relationship', Robbins's concern with allocating scarce resources among alternative ends. The one that he called 'substantive' is concerned with how people acquire 'the means of material want satisfaction', the processes, activities and relationships through which people secure their livelihoods. The debate, of course, ultimately was sterile because the two sides largely were talking past each other. Though both sides invoked 'economy', the word meant different things to them, so different that resolution was impossible (Carrier 2009).

While the debate may have been sterile, commonly the formalists, with their economistic approach, were seen to have won, and perhaps because of that a decline in economic anthropology followed. Rather, it might be more accurate to say that the sub-discipline was reoriented, for many became interested in economic processes that were of larger scale and more systemic than what had interested earlier researchers. For the Marxists this meant things like the structure of capitalism (e.g. Althusser and Balibar 1970) and the articulation of modes of production (e.g. Wolpe 1980). For others it meant things like world-systems theory (Wallerstein 1974) and the question of underdevelopment (Frank 1966). None of these placed much stress on detailed ethnographic description of the sort that characterised older work in the sub-discipline.

The declining visibility of economic anthropology occurred around the same time as important changes in the discipline as a whole. One of these is the Cultural Turn of the 1970s and its consequences, which resulted in anthropologists being decreasingly concerned with social organisation and practice. Instead, they attended more and more to meaning, increasingly to what things mean to smaller and smaller sets of people; not just the X people, but small subsets of them, such as those of the same gender, age, marital status, religion, economic position, and so on and so forth. Associated with this, increasingly they denied themselves a place on which to stand, one that would provide them with an analytical perspective on what they observed. That is because they saw their job increasingly as recording people's culture, the way that they saw meaning in their world, rather than analysing it or relating it to the social organisation and practice in which the people they studied found themselves. In this reluctance to engage in more than description, many in the discipline rejected one of the two legs on which, A.R. Radcliffe-Brown (1952) said, anthropology stood. One of these he called ethnography, the description of what the researcher sees in the particular place and time of field work. The other he called comparative sociology, producing reasonably valid generalisations about aspects of social life in a range of settings and societies. Finally, anthropology became more overtly a moral discipline, as Trouillot's Savage Slot came to be replaced by the Suffering Slot (Robbins 2013). That is, many in the discipline saw their task as representing the voice of the downtrodden, particularly when those downtrodden seemed to hold or represent views that accorded with the dominant moral and political orientations in anthropology (see Carrier 2016: chapter 3).

This situation began to change as the world changed in the 1980s and especially in the 1990s and afterward. Globalisation became insistent, communism ended, free-market capitalism seemed triumphant not only in economies but also in government policies and public debate. These large-scale events that had clear economic effects, combined with events in anthropology generally, seem to have led to a resurgence of anthropological interest in economy. In the discipline generally, and for a number of reasons, anthropologists were abandoning conventional research in villages and instead were studying parts of Western societies. As well, many were motivated to investigate the practical consequences of changes that appeared to be the result of globalisation and what came to be called neoliberalism.

These tendencies in the sub-discipline became more powerful with the financial crisis of 2008 and the Great Recession and waves of austerity that followed. While anthropologists may have remained focused on the downtrodden, a growing number of them were paying attention to structures and processes, especially in the financial sector in different countries. These shaped people's lives but were likely to be invisible to them and so not part of their culture and universe of meanings in any obvious way. Moreover, the rising nationalism and Right-wing protest that was associated with that austerity made a growing number of anthropologists question the wisdom of the disciplinary tendency to focus on those who accorded with anthropological sensibilities. Researchers may not have liked supporters of Le Pen in France, the Northern League in Italy, Orbán in Hungary, Trump in the United States or Pegida and the AfD in Germany. Increasingly, though, they realised that if they were to understand what was going in the world, much less in those countries, they could not dismiss such people as distasteful aberrations who safely could be ignored, however comforting that methical ignorance might have been.

The result was that economic anthropologists were studying what economists studied, people in large social systems that were dominated by capitalist free markets.

They did so, however, in very different ways. Economics continued to concern itself with the analytical models of what Robbins described in the 1930s, calculating individuals deciding how to allocate their scarce resources among alternative ends. On the other hand, economic anthropologists continued their old substantivist concern with the economic systems through which people secured, or sought to secure, their subsistence: what they are, how they work and how they reflect and affect people's lives, circumstances and aspirations.

This does not mean, of course, that the economic anthropology of the opening decades of the twenty-first century is the same as it was in the opening decades of the twentieth. I have already mentioned one difference, that economic anthropologists are more likely to study people who live in cities, have jobs, shop in supermarkets and use computers than they are to study subsistence agriculturalists who live in villages full of grass huts.

Another difference is less obvious but is perhaps more important. Early scholars were concerned with building economic anthropology, and anthropology more generally, as a recognisable and fairly coherent intellectual field. The consequence of this was that their orientations and the questions that they asked were likely to be shaped in significant ways by what was going on within their discipline and sub-discipline. This is most striking in another of the founders, though one who attracts less attention than hitherto, Emile Durkheim. As illustrated most clearly in *The division of labour in society* (Durkheim 1984 [1893]), he was concerned with arguing for the existence of society as a thing and with trying to describe its nature: not this society or that society, but society itself. However, beginning late in the twentieth century and insistently since the financial crisis, economic anthropologists' orientations and the questions that they ask increasingly have been shaped by events in the world: globalisation, the spread of neoliberalism, the financial crisis, turmoil in the housing market in various countries, austerity.

Increasingly, that is, we seem more concerned with responding to and describing what is going on in the world than with developing and extending the analytical models and theoretical frames that make up our way of thinking about and making sense of the world. Certainly, a study of the effects of government austerity in central Italy is likely to attract more interest than an analysis of forms of circulation in a small society in Papua New Guinea. It will take some time, however, to tell if the result is to make economic anthropology a better discipline.

About this volume

I have described some of the recent events and trends in the world, the discipline and the sub-discipline, and they are the background that helps explain the focus and significance of the chapters that follow. It is worth explaining how those chapters came to be.

Once I decided to accept the invitation to put together a volume on a research agenda for economic anthropology I started to communicate with anthropologists, economic and other. I explained the nature of the project and asked them for suggestions of topics that might be included in it. Even though several topics were suggested by many people, the result was well over a hundred different ones. Reluctant to approach the publisher with a request to turn this into a multi-volume work, I set about trying to reduce that mass of different and fairly detailed suggestions into a more manageable set of more general topics, each intended to incorporate a number of specific suggestions.

I then approached the more knowledgeable people I knew and asked if they wanted to write on one or another topic, and if they knew of other people whom I might approach. The result was a set of topics and people who were competent to write chapters on them and were willing to do so. Collective exercises like this one are always somewhat chancy. In this case one person dropped out and I recruited another person to write on a different topic. The result is what you see here, some chapters written by senior scholars and some by those earlier in their academic careers.

As will become obvious in the paragraphs that follow, those chapters are not intended to survey work on topics in economic anthropology. Of course they refer to such work, but their orientation is different. That is because the authors are telling us what we should be doing, whether by identifying topics that have not attracted the interest they deserve or by describing new ways to approach existing topics. They are not, then, surveys of where we are, but are suggestions about where we ought to go.

I do not intend to describe the chapters in detail, but a few comments seem in order.

To begin with, in view of what I said about the tendency to focus on the downtrodden provided that they accord with anthropological sensibilities, it is worth pointing to two chapters that express unease with this tendency. They are the last two chapters, one by Andreas Streinzer and the other by Mark Moberg. Streinzer's chapter is concerned with ethics and consumption, and he argues that if we are to learn how people's values shape their consumption choices, we must not restrict ourselves to those who have values of which we approve. Moberg's is concerned with our approach to the world more generally, and he illustrates his arguments with the dismissive view that many anthropologists had of supporters of Donald Trump during the campaign for the US presidency in 2016. That view echoed a comment by Trump's opponent in the campaign, Hillary Clinton, who called them deplorable. Of course this led to bumper stickers and T-shirts with slogans like 'Proud to be deplorable'. In their different ways, then, both chapters say that our research on and analysis of the world would benefit if we adopted something like the value neutrality that Max Weber (e.g. 1949) long ago advocated for the social sciences. Of course we have our values and political orientations, but we should not let them blind us to the world that we study.

Some of the authors in this volume suggest that there is much to be gained from pursuing topics that have attracted relatively little attention in the sub-discipline. Greg Urban, for instance, urges us to study what is central to modern capitalism, for-profit corporations, which he approaches as collective economic actors. As he notes, we make many assumptions about corporations on the basis of relatively little knowledge, and he says that our understanding of the economic world around us is impoverished as a result. A second chapter that urges research on a topic that we generally have ignored is by Jaume Franquesa and is concerned with resources. For him, those are aspects of our natural surroundings that humans appropriate for their use. As he presents it, the study of resources covers a range of things, from the appropriation of nature through the social and economic organisation of that appropriation to the creation of wasteland and scrub once the resources in a place have been exhausted. The third of these chapters is by Stefan Leins, who says that we should heed Laura Nader's (1972) famous injunction to study up, and investigate management of various sorts, whether managing people in an organisation, objects in a supply chain or other people's money in the financial sector. We may think that managers do little work and that the little that they do is not real. He says, however, that we need to overcome this prejudice if we are to understand what managers do and how the economy works.

The remaining chapters suggest new ways of approaching existing topics in economic anthropology. So, in his chapter on the relationship between states and markets, Felix Stein observes that, perhaps stimulated by globalisation and the spread of neoliberalism, much recent work has seen them as standing opposed to each other in important ways. However, he argues that this view has a cost, for it diverts attention from features that are common to both. One is financialisation, a term that he extends to include the technologies of financial accounting and representation, down to the level of the ubiquitous Excel spreadsheets and PowerPoint presentations. The other is ritual, an old anthropological topic, which he uses to identify activities that strengthen and express collective entities in both state and market, and the values that justify them. Tom Neumark's chapter considers how we might approach inequality. He says that the dominant anthropological view directs our attention to production, while it would be useful to look at how surplus is appropriated and distributed, whether through informal arrangements or through mechanisms like taxation. In addition, that dominant view tends to ignore the morality of inequality. As he notes, people's objections to inequality often are concerned not with the inequality itself, but with the failure of parties to the unequal relationship to treat each other as they ought.

Fabio Mattioli's chapter, on debt, argues that much research on the topic has attended to the place of debt in everyday lives and its effects on those lives. He urges us to look beyond this, to attend as well to the ways that debt can take many different forms and so is not all of a piece, and to investigate the institutions and processes, often enough invisible to people in their everyday lives, that are part of the national and international system of loaning and borrowing money. Finally, Valeria Siniscalchi says in her chapter that we should extend our attention to social movements beyond the values that they hold and the ways that they advocate them.

In addition, we should attend to the organisations in those movements, how they are structured and financed, and the ways that these organisational nuts and bolts can reflect and affect the lives and orientations of adherents and can shape the future of the organisation.

Conclusion

In this Introduction I have sketched the development of economic anthropology, shaped by changes in the world and in the larger discipline, and have described briefly some of the important points in the chapters that follow.

As that sketch indicated, the sub-discipline has changed in substantial ways since the 1990s and especially since the financial crisis of 2008. The restrictive focus on the culture of sets of people, at the expense of the organisation of their societies and the factors that affect it, seemingly has been losing its appeal, and it would be hard to justify its continued embrace in the face of the effects on those people's lives of institutions and practices occurring far away from, and probably invisible to, them. After all, no one but a specialist or a devoted reader of business news was likely to have heard of collateralised debt obligations, their relationship with the housing market in many countries and what their effects were likely to be if the widespread boom in housing prices turned sour.

This does not mean that we have abandoned interest in culture, in beliefs, values and how people see and think about their world. Indeed, several of the contributors to this volume pay close attention to it. However, theirs is not the task that many anthropologists seem to have assigned themselves in the heyday of the Cultural Turn and the associated wave of postmodern anthropology. That task was rendering people's culture as fully as possible while refraining from seeking to analyse or account for it in any sustained way. Instead, for the contributors to this volume, culture and its effects are things to be analysed and understood, including the culture of anthropologists themselves.

The chapters in this volume are, to an important degree, idiosyncratic, reflecting assessments of what is going on in the sub-discipline that I have made and that have been made by those from whom I sought advice, as well as reflecting the specific interests and ideas of chapter authors. To repeat a point that I have made already, this volume is no handy compendium of where the sub-discipline is headed, nor is it intended to be one. Rather, readers should treat it as a collection of stimulating ideas about topics that have not attracted attention but deserve to do so, about familiar topics that we could approach in new ways and, as I have noted, about our own predilections as we look at the world around us.

If readers are stimulated, even excited, by what they read in one or more of the chapters that follow, then this volume will have justified the effort and attention that the chapter authors and I have devoted to it.

References

Althusser, Louis and Étienne Balibar 1970. *Reading Capital*. London: New Left Books.

Carrier, James G. 2009. Simplicity in economic anthropology: Persuasion, form and substance. In *Economic Persuasions* (ed.) Stephen Gudeman, pp. 15–30. Oxford: Berghahn Books.

Carrier, James G. (ed.) 2016. *After the Crisis: Anthropological Thought, Neoliberalism and the Aftermath*. London: Routledge.

Durkheim, Emile 1984 (1893). *The Division of Labour in Society*. London: Routledge and Kegan Paul.

Frank, Andre Gunder 1966. The development of underdevelopment. *Monthly Review* 18 (4): 17–30.

Malinowski, Bronislaw 1921. The primitive economics of Trobriand Islanders. *The Economic Journal* 31 (121): 1–16.

Malinowski, Bronislaw 1922. *Argonauts of the Western Pacific: An Account of Native Enterprise and Adventure in the Archipelagoes of Melanesian New Guinea*. London: Routledge.

Mauss, Marcel 1990 (1925). *The Gift: The Form and Reason for Exchange in Archaic Societies*. W.D. Halls, trans. London: Routledge.

Nader, Laura 1972. Up the anthropologist: Perspectives gained from studying up. In *Reinventing Anthropology* (ed.) Dell Hymes, pp. 284–311. New York: Pantheon Books.

Parry, Jonathan 1986. *The Gift*, the Indian gift and the 'Indian gift'. *Man* 21 (3): 453–73.

Polanyi, Karl 1957. The economy as instituted process. In *Trade and Market in the Early Empires: Economies in History and Theory* (eds) K. Polanyi, Conrad M. Arensberg and Harry W. Pearson, pp. 243–70. Glencoe, IL: The Free Press.

Radcliffe-Brown, A.R. 1952. Introduction. In *Structure and Function in Primitive Society*, A.R. Radcliffe-Brown, pp. 1–14. London: Routledge and Kegan Paul.

Robbins, Joel 2013. Beyond the suffering subject: Toward an anthropology of the good. *Journal of the Royal Anthropological Institute* 19 (3): 447–62.

Robbins, Lionel 1945 (1932). *An Essay on the Nature and Significance of Economic Science*. London: Macmillan.

Smith, Adam 1976 (1776). *An Inquiry into the Nature and Causes of the Wealth of Nations*. Edwin Cannan, ed. Chicago: University of Chicago Press.

Trouillot, Michel-Rolph 2003. Anthropology and the savage slot: The poetics and politics of otherness. In *Global Transformations: Anthropology and the Modern World* (ed.) M.-R. Trouillot, pp. 17–44. New York: Palgrave Macmillan.

Wallerstein, Immanuel 1974. *The Modern World System: Capitalist Agriculture and the Origins of the European World-Economy in the Sixteenth Century*. New York: Academic Press.

Weber, Max 1949. *The Methodology of the Social Sciences*. Edward A. Shils and Henry A. Finch, eds and trans. New York: The Free Press.

Wolpe, Harold (ed.) 1980. *The Articulation of Modes of Production*. London: Routledge and Kegan Paul.

1 Collective economic actors

Greg Urban

A case can be made that the for-profit business corporation is the central institution of the modern capitalist economic system. Stock exchanges, another key institution, presuppose the existence of companies with share-holders. It is true that shares in collective ventures antedate the development of the great joint-stock companies of the seventeenth century, which formed the legal models for the publicly traded corporation from the nineteenth century onwards (Licht 2014: 145 ff.). A deed for transfer of shares in the Swedish copper mining company at Stora Kopparberg (Great Copper Mountain), for example, was issued in 1288 (Business Historical Society 1929: 7–8; Rydberg 1979: 12–13). Still, formation of the joint-stock companies of the seventeenth century, such as the English East India Company (later the British East India Company) and the Dutch East India Company, accelerated the growth and expansion of stock exchanges, along with the financial systems and occasional speculative fever associated with them. Hence, the corporation as cultural form is arguably an essential component, possibly *the* essential one, of modern capitalism. Yet it has until recently received relatively little ethnographic or theoretical scrutiny within anthropology (exceptions include Foster 2017; Urban and Koh 2013).

Looked at from an anthropological point of view, the economically productive corporation is a social group. It can be studied not just as the manifestation of a legal concept, although it is that in some measure, nor just as a voluntary association of individual rational economic actors, although it is that in some measure as well. It can also be seen as a collectivity, indeed, as a culture-bearing social group. It is amenable to the kind of anthropological research done in small- and medium-scale societies and local communities, although global corporations often require multi-sited research (e.g. Garsten 1994; Oliveira 2013; Røyrvik 2013; Stull 2017). The possibility of using anthropological research from community ethnographies to understand corporations did not escape the attention of popular business writers (Deal and Kennedy 1982; see also Ouchi 1981; Pascale and Athos 1981). Still, recognition of the communal character of corporations failed to produce substantial new theorisation within anthropology, despite the growth of business anthropology and its in-depth ethnographies (e.g. Ho 2009; Krause-Jensen 2010).

From an anthropological perspective, the for-profit business corporation (hereinafter 'business corporation'), publicly traded or not, can be seen as a communal form onto which has been grafted a legal form. Evidence for this view can be found in the historical record. The joint-stock companies of seventeenth-century Europe grew out of the earlier medieval corporation, which was the legal form of towns, guilds, monasteries and universities (Davis 2000 [1905]). Eli Heckscheler (1934: volume 1, 397, quoted in Eklund and Tollison 1980: 718) observed: 'In the joint stock companies, too, the members were "brethren" . . . just like the members of the innumerable medieval corporations, including the municipalities.' A key characteristic of the economic organisations out of which the later companies developed is their family or family-like basis. This is in keeping with Max Weber's (1968 [1925]: 375–84) argument that capitalist forms of economic organisation, including the great joint-stock companies, grew out of the decline of the household as the principal economically productive unit. Of early capitalist partnerships, such as the maritime firm (*societas maris*) and the *commenda* that gave rise to the idea of limited liability that is characteristic of modern corporations, Fernand Braudel (1982: 438) remarked: 'It is worth insisting on the family or near-family atmosphere which characterised them (even when there was no actual family concerned).' Many, even most, small privately held corporations in the US today continue to be based on families or operate in a family-like manner, including some that I have had the opportunity to get to know first-hand.

One key goal for future research in economic anthropology should be the ethnographic analysis and theorisation of the communal character of modern business corporations, including those of the large publicly traded variety. Development of that research agenda will be the main focus of this chapter. The internal cultural processes and patterns of other collective actors, including regulatory bodies such as central banks (Holmes 2009) and advisory organisations like the World Economic Forum at Davos (Garsten and Sörbom 2019), are also necessary for attempts to advance an anthropological understanding of modern capitalism.

In this chapter, I put forth a series of questions that are designed to articulate an anthropological agenda for research on business corporations and other collective economic actors. In what measure are companies internally organised around market (versus communal) principles? To what extent does the profit motive suppress other considerations inside the corporation and other collective actors? How do laws pertaining to the corporate form affect the productive potential of a company as well as communal well-being both inside and outside the productive group? What role does diffusion, in addition to internal transmission, play in shaping corporations and their products as cultural forms?

Market versus communal principles

Perhaps the most fundamental question anthropologists can ask about business corporations is why they exist. The normative variant would be: should they exist, and if so in what form? Since those questions have been asked and answered in different ways in other disciplines and intellectual traditions, a starting point for providing an anthropological answer is to probe the differences between an anthropological approach, oriented to culture and ethnographic research, and others. In this section, I begin with the most obvious starting point, the view from economics.

With its conceptualisation of the economy as consisting of rational individual human beings engaged in self-interested transactions with one another, the existence of collective actors as culture-bearing social groups seems to make little sense. At least, this was the view of Ronald Coase (1937), who posed the question of why firms exist. Coase took as his point of departure what today is known as the efficient-market hypothesis, the idea that market transactions are the best way to price assets. The idea is often associated with Eugene Fama's (1965) research on the pricing of stocks, but it has deep roots in economic thought, its outlines discernible perhaps even in Adam Smith's (1994 [1776]: 485) invisible hand, the idea that individuals engaged in self-interested activity often end up promoting collective interest more effectively than if they consciously tried to do so. From this vantage point, one might well ask why we need corporations. Would it not be better if production were carried out through individuals transacting with one another, rather than through corporate communities? As Coase (1937: 387) noted of the economic thought of his time, 'It is often considered to be an objection to economic planning that it merely tries to do what is already done by the price mechanism.'

Anthropologists will recognise in this line of reasoning the concept of neoliberalism, to which so much scholarly attention has been devoted in the past quarter-century (Harvey 2005). The concept as understood within anthropology, according to Tejaswini Ganti (2014: 91), refers to both a structural force within capitalism and an ideology. As a normative position, neoliberalism asserts that it is desirable that all of social life should be made to resemble market-like transactions. Hence, the role of government should be minimised and governmental functions privatised insofar as is possible. Here we find an ideological position compatible with the objection to economic planning observed by Coase among his colleagues. While much research has been done within anthropology on neoliberalism as a structural phenomenon and also on government policies and procedures, as well as NGOs, bureaucrats and even media representations (Ganti 2014), little ethnographic research has focused on the inner workings of corporations. Indeed, the word 'corporation' is absent altogether from Ganti's review of the anthropological literature on neoliberalism. In what measure do company boards, managers and employees espouse neoliberal ideas and ideals? How aware are they of such ideals? In what ways are they affected by the circulation of neoliberal ideology or by the structural forces of neoliberalism? These are questions ripe for ethnographic investigation.

Coase, however, was not concerned with normative matters. Rather, he was preoccupied with economic theory, especially a blind spot in it. That is, the theory concerns itself with transactions between self-interested individuals while ignoring the empirical existence of collective actors (companies or firms) as key market players. So, his question was: why should such collective actors exist? Could their existence be explained from within economic theory? His efforts, that is, were directed at shoring up economic theory, not undermining it.

The explanation that he proposed is that transactions are not free but are costly. A moment's reflection reveals how unrealistic it would be to think that complex production tasks would arise spontaneously out of transactions where individuals could choose to negotiate every aspect of the work involved. How much will you pay me to flip this switch, call this individual, write this report? Production would bog down in transactional negotiation, if it ever started in the first place. As Coase (1937: 390–91) put it, 'The costs of negotiating and concluding a separate contract for each exchange transaction which takes place on a market must also be taken into account.' Hence, his solution: firms exist to reduce transaction costs.

The solution contains a significant insight that opened up economic research on a range of issues, such as the conditions under which firms tend to be larger or smaller. Importantly also, the insight gave birth to the New Institutional Economics, which has been influential especially in economic history (North 1990; North and Thomas 1973). This development has stimulated some anthropologists, such as Jean Ensminger (1990, 1992) and David Guillet (2001), while being roundly criticised by others, such as F.G. Bailey (2003: esp. chapter 2). Still, virtually nothing in the way of ethnographic research within corporations deals with such transactional issues.

The idea that firms reduce transaction costs allows economic theory to make sense of the existence of corporations. Simultaneously, it provides an opening for anthropological theory, for it allows us to ask about the kinds of situations that might lead people not to treat tasks and interactions as market negotiations. An obvious answer would be in communal endeavours. People work together to accomplish a common goal. Indeed, in many instances it is not even a question of working together towards a goal, but simply of being together with others. In short, it is possible to treat firms or enterprises, whether legally registered as corporations or not, as communities, even if communities of a peculiar sort. What light can anthropological theory shed on business corporations as communities?

In her doctoral research, Madeline Boyer (2018) found that for some people at least, working together, or rather working in the presence of others with whom they interact, is preferable to working alone. These people want to be part of a working community. Boyer did a long-term ethnographic study of co-working spaces. Those are places in which people who might otherwise be working alone – consultants, individual entrepreneurs or those who are required or allowed to work away from their employers' premises – choose to work in a space along with others, even though they may be working towards entirely different and unrelated economic ends. Co-working spaces are part of a worldwide movement and, as Boyer (2018: 19) explains, they are distinct from 'business incubators and accelerators, hackerspaces and makerspaces, office parks, and corporate office-sharing'. They are different in at least one important respect: their main goal is to build community. In co-working spaces, 'financial sustainability' is largely 'a means to an end rather than the end itself' (2018: 21).

Arguably, Boyer's research confirms what business anthropologists have been finding over the past several decades. Even business corporations can be viewed as operating in some measure in accord with communal principles. Life within corporations is not only built around work. In addition, it is built around rituals, including the ritual elements of meetings (Kunda 1995; Sandler and Thedvall 2017; Schwartzman 1989) and workshops (Wilf 2015), around symbols such as corporate motivational videos (Urban 2015), myths and other narratives (including their role in anchoring legitimacy, Ho 2009), around constructing gendered identities (Fisher 2012) and around transmitting information (Orr 1996) (for a broader review, see Urban and Koh 2013). Much ethnographic work waits to be done in these areas. The principal question to be explored is: what is social life like inside of firms and other collective economic groupings? In particular, how does social life articulate with economic interest?

At the same time, anthropologists should not lose sight of the fact that business corporations are also necessarily about economics. Although Coase saw himself as solving a problem within economic theory, Michel Callon (1998: 2) proposes that 'economics, in the broad sense of the term, performs, shapes and formats the economy, rather than observing how it functions'. While he may overstate the point, the empirical question remains of the degree to which corporations are organised around economic principles and around communal and other principles. Ethnographic research is needed to determine the extent to which economics infuses talk inside the firm and other collective economic entities, and especially what kind of economics talk gets circulated, since economic theory changes, is contested and is subject to some extent to fad-like enthusiasms.

Profit versus other considerations

The starting point for thinking about business corporations is entirely different within political economy. Rather than individual rational actors engaged in market transactions and maximisation, for Marx the starting point for the analysis of existing societies was the mode of production, especially the relationship between classes. For Marxists, the business corporation is primarily the place where capitalists are pitted against workers and the central relationship is one of exploitation. Malcolm Dunn (1992: 193), in launching his critique of Coase, quotes Eva Bössman (1981: 667) to the effect that political economists 'presuppose the existence of "economic units", be these households or enterprises, as self-evident'. They require 'no further economic explanation'. Put differently, we might say that the political economist focuses on the broader social relationships in which businesses operate. Consequently, the question asked by Coase of why firms exist does not even arise. Business enterprises are a product of class relations and are the key mechanism through which one class exploits another.

The difference between the orientations of political economy and economics is important not only because of the taken-for-granted status of the firm within political economy. It is important, too, because Coase's formulation purports to derive hierarchical social relations within the firm from the costs associated with forming longer-term contracts with employees versus the costs associated with transacting in the marketplace. In contrast, political economy, and Dunn (1992) in particular, wants to derive the internal hierarchical relations within firms from the external power relations within society. That is, political economy, following Marx, wants exploitative class relations to be seen as the driving force behind those internal relations, with labour denied its proper reward.

In contrast with both economics and political economy, a genuinely anthropological approach to the social relations within firms, and other collective economic entities, would be one grounded in culture. Especially when it comes to productive units such as business corporations and other firms, an anthropological approach directs attention to the culture within the organisation, as well as to the relationship between the organisation's culture and the larger culture outside of it. The relationship between these two cultures has been a focus of business-anthropological research for some time. Examples include the classic monograph by Choong Soon Kim (1992) on the South Korean Poongsan Corporation, including the role of Confucianism within it; Tamoko Hamada's (1991) work on Japanese–American joint ventures, where the differing cultural orientations to management come into focus; and accounts of McDonald's in East Asia (Watson 1997).

The theoretical agenda for an anthropological perspective on culture may be differentiated from that of economics and political economy, in fact, by looking at inside–outside relations. For the economist, Coase in particular, the relation is defined as firm versus market, resting on the point that it would be unrealistic to try to carry out production only through market-based transactions. For the political economist, Dunn in particular, the issue is the power relations in the broader society, especially class relations, and their role in shaping processes within the firm, which itself is taken as given. From the perspective developed in business anthropology, the focus is on the relationship between the culture inside the firm and the culture outside of it, including the culture of other firms, a relationship that is reciprocal and that results in a mutual shaping. Implicit in this is the point that the boundaries of the firm are both created and traversed, a key feature of a distinctive anthropological approach to business.

Indeed, the creation, maintenance and crossing of the boundaries around enterprises may prove the key to the future development of an anthropological theory of collective economic actors. Enterprises must be analysed in terms of their genesis and internal cultural transformations over time, as well as in terms of their relations to external culture, including surrounding rules and laws, as well as broader circulating views of their role in social life. Collective economic actors develop internally as entities in their own right, as culture-bearing social groups. In some cases, African or Native American social groups transform in the direction of business enterprises (Comaroff and Comaroff 2009), as has happened during the recent neoliberal period. An example from the US in the nineteenth century is the Oneida community in New York State, which changed from a religious experiment in communal living into a joint-stock company (Cooper 1987). Other enterprises germinate out of invention and innovation, guided by entrepreneurship, or by finding a niche not yet served by existing firms. In any case, the culture of each business enterprise tends to be in some measure distinct, while also resembling that of other corporations. One goal for future ethnographic research in economic anthropology ought to be to chart the nature and distinctiveness of firms' cultures and the processes of internal transformation that produce them.

Here the possibility of more far-reaching theoretical development emerges. The concept of business enterprises taking shape as social groups characterised by internal cultures suggests a refinement of the labour theory of value associated with Marx and political economy (Urban 2016: 324–27). In that theory, enterprises generate profit through exploitation of workers, where the value of commodities on the market results from the labour time that has gone into them. This is presumed to be true whether we are dealing with tangible objects such as clothing and automobiles or the less tangible, such as financial instruments or skills and know-how (as, for example, in the case of medical services). The idea of a firm's internal culture suggests that commodities are produced not via labour time alone, but by culturally guided activity. That culture is one source, albeit not the only source, of value. The culture of business firms takes place first and foremost around the socially transmittable learning contained within them that is necessary for the production of marketable commodities. In this view commodities are, in effect, congealed culture.

In the case of business corporations, a key part of that congealed culture is the firm's internal culture. There are two key ways in which the distinctive culture within a given enterprise matters: it can manifest itself in the commodity produced, resulting in a product that is perceived to be distinctive, or it can manifest itself in the processes through which it is produced. Where the distinctiveness of the commodity makes little or no difference there is effectively nothing of what Edward Chamberlin (1933: 71 ff.) called 'product differentiation'. In this case the cost efficiency of its production, based on the internal culture of the company, becomes a deciding factor in the competitive market. In this situation, Marx's argument becomes relevant. That is because one way to lower production costs is to pay employees less, and Marx (1990 [1867]: 797–99) holds that in capitalist systems there is inevitably pressure to lower wages, resulting in the immiseration of the working class. (The extent to which business corporations and other enterprises necessarily succumb to the immiserating forces of domination Marx described is, of course, an empirical matter.)

A task for economic anthropology, therefore, is to assess the circulating worldviews within enterprises as culture-bearing communities. Does profit in fact trump all other considerations, even if it can be achieved only at the expense of employee or customer well-being? Alternatively, to what degree do firms focus on making commodities that potential customers need and want? How much consideration is given to the well-being of employees and customers or of broader polities, including the country? Are there other goals? My own experience suggests that differing worldviews compete with one another within any given large corporation.

Effects of laws about the corporate form

It is important to distinguish between the anthropological corporation (clasically Maine 1917 [1861]; also Fortes 1969; Radcliffe-Brown 1952) and the legal corporation (Urban 2016). The former is a culture-bearing social group; the latter is an abstract legal fiction. It is important for anthropologists to make this distinction, since they often assume that 'corporation' refers to a social group when it is used in its legal sense. In many countries one individual can create and own many legal corporations, each of which is a fictitious entity rather than a social group and none needs have any relationship to a social group. A key task for anthropology is to tease the two concepts apart, in order to encourage lawyers, economists, politicians and the general public to use the anthropological concept as the measure in reasoning about the legal concept. Doing so could bring about a shift in orientation to corporations.

John Davis (2000 [1905]: volume II, 215 n1), in his comprehensive survey of the corporation since the early Middle Ages in Europe, concludes: 'The analogy, in legal contemplation, between a family and a corporation seems to have been discovered by Sir Henry Sumner Maine.' An example of the corporation that Maine (1917 [1861]) used, which was taken up by later anthropologists, is the clan, a social group that could live on despite the death of its individual members. As Maine (1917 [1861]: 76) put it, 'corporations never die'. For him, as for later anthropologists, what made a social group a corporation is this temporal durability. That quality gives the clan a substance that resonates with the legal notion, especially as it developed in the late nineteenth and early twentieth centuries in the US.

Reflecting upon a collection of papers concerned with corporate personhood, Ira Bashkow (2014: 296) grapples with the theory of the corporation from the perspective of the classic *e pluribus unum* problem that has informed so much of the anthropological theorising of community: 'How does a collectivity, comprising numerous individuals, come to count as but one?' Bashkow appropriately focuses on the anthropological corporation, though he is aware of the legal corporation, which he tends to dismiss: 'how could such an awesome feat – the creation of an artificial person – be accomplished by the mere filing of a simple form, the "articles of incorporation"?' (2014: 297). From the perspective of the anthropological corporation he is right to pose this question, yet numerous legal corporations are created every day by such performative acts. Understanding the contribution of the legal corporation to the anthropological one is crucial to both our ethnographic and our theoretical task.

As a thought experiment, we might contemplate what the effect would be of sub-tracting the legal from the anthropological corporation. We would still have the productive community, with its internally circulating culture of know-how, beliefs, values, rituals and the like. The *e pluribus unum* question would remain, but some-thing important would be missing. Take, for example, the case of the tobacco industry that Peter Benson (2014) discusses in the collection on which Bashkow comments. Regarding the industry's participation in campaigns to prevent 'the ille-gal sale of tobacco to underage purchasers', Bashkow (2014: 298) observes: 'What drops away in all these campaigns is the coercive nature of addiction and the industry's role in promoting it.' Fair enough. At the same time, however, we might ask what would happen if it were illegal to produce and sell tobacco. The situation could well resemble the era of Prohibition in the US, when making and selling alcohol were illegal. Because they were illegal, the government lacked the ability to set quality standards for what those who wanted alcohol were drinking. That is because the legal part of the anthropological corporation subjects such corpora-tions to legislation and the courts. The company could be sued if it failed to comply with government regulations. And in being subjected to the law, legal corporations are subject to collective supervision. Theorisation of the business corporation as an anthropological entity, then, must take account of its existence as a legal entity.

Taking that legal side into account is likely to be done best by business anthropolo-gists who, as employees or consultants, have an insider's view of the corporation, ideally in legal departments and grappling with the kinds of issues with which business enterprises must deal. Anthropological researchers in such positions would be able to develop answers to important questions. Do corporations see laws simply as external obstacles to be negotiated in the pursuit of profit, as some of the recent legal scandals involving corporations suggest? Are those laws seen as resources? In what measure and for what purposes do anthropological corpora-tions, as collective actors, employ fictive legal corporations? In what measure and under what circumstances do corporate leaders see themselves as contributing to broader societal goals, where complying with national laws may be viewed as part of good citizenship, as opposed to seeing their organisations as independent of any national polity?

The roles of diffusion and internal transmission

A key factor in theorising modern business corporations is the ease with which the internal culture and the products of an organisation can be copied (Urban 2016: 330–36). A good ethnographic account of such copying is Michael Prentice's (2015) insider's description of a Korean firm in which individuals regularly borrowed documents, such as PowerPoint presentations, from other firms, modifying the traits that were characteristic of the source firm. There is a dearth of ethnographic accounts of corporate diffusion, though a fair amount of research on the topic has been done based on externally accessible data. An example of such work is by N. Venkatraman, Lawrence Loh and Jeongsuk Koh (1994), who look at the diffusion of organisational structures and the spread of joint ventures, or Ilir Haxhi and Hans van Ees (2010), who study the diffusion of codes of good corporate governance. The bulk of these studies have come out of business schools. Many other business anthropologists, myself included, have observed the critical role consultants play in such diffusion, especially the major consulting firms, which spread organisational ideas from company to company.

Such studies have demonstrated that corporations as social groups have internal cultures that can be copied by other corporations. However, corporations are also producers of culture. The idea of the commodity as congealed culture discussed earlier modifies the political-economic labour theory of value, in which commodities are 'quantities of *congealed labour-time*' (Marx 1990 [1867]: 130). In that theory, the amount of labour time that goes into producing a commodity accounts for its exchange value, which means that any profit taken out of the market price of the commodity comes at the expense of labour. In the commodity-as-culture approach, in contrast, the question is what forces drive the movement of the commoditised culture, and a critical force appears to be people's interest in the culture that the commodity carries: in the language of economic theory, demand. It is that interest that requires detailed anthropological investigation (see Wilk and Arnould 2016), since the culture carried by the commodity ultimately articulates with the broader culture in which the commodity circulates.

From the point of view of diffusion, another key consideration for anthropological theory is that commodities as congealed culture also participate in inter-corporate copying. This is crucial because the possibility of making a profit depends on the corporation's ability to capture the cultural flow. In other words, in order to realise a profit a corporation must be able to satisfy an interest in or demand for the commodity as culture that is not met by the commodities of other corporations. One way it can do so, as postulated in Marx's theory, is by paying workers less, for example by outsourcing and thereby lowering the cost of production, but this is only one way. Additionally, it can do so by providing what other corporations do not. This happens when there is sufficient interest in the corporation's commodity that customers are willing to pay more than the cost of its production, whether the commodity is desirable because of some aspects of the corporation's internal culture that cannot be readily copied or because of the corporation's control over some necessary constituent of the desired commodity. Many corporations endeavour to make their commodities distinctive and desirable by cultivating loyal followings through brands (Foster 2014; Manning 2010). Without such distinctiveness the desire for profit, to the extent that it is unchecked by other motives, will tend to force employee compensation down, as the labour theory of value implies.

Put differently, corporations can produce profit without exploiting employees by capturing a cultural flow, by having desirable commodities that other corporations cannot produce. This possibility seemingly stands in direct opposition to the ease with which commodities can be copied. Anthropological research and theory can make a significant contribution by exploring this apparent opposition. For example, I (Urban 2016: 334–36, based on results in Urban et al. 2007) looked at the perceived similarities and differences between the faces, the grills and headlights of sports-utility vehicles as they change over time. I found that the changes introduced by manufacturers resembled the changes being made by other manufacturers, which means that manufacturers were copying each other. However, companies also made sure to introduce differences in the copy so that the corporation-specific characteristics of the commodity could be readily detected. The interest of consumers in some commodities as opposed to others, including the affective charge those commodities seem to have, may also be linked to the similarities and differences mapped out by the field of inter-corporate relations as it evolves over time, thereby beginning to address the kinds of questions raised by Richard Wilk and Eric Arnould (2016) about diffusion and demand.

Maintaining the distinctiveness of a corporation's commodities, despite the ease of inter-corporate copying, depends in some measure on the corporation's legal status and, in particular, on its capacity to own intellectual property, including patents and copyrights (see Coombe 1998; Moore 2003). A number of anthropological studies deal with the relationship between the legal capture of the cultural characteristics of a corporation's commodities and the status of small-scale producers in other countries, for example Kedron Thomas's (2016) research on the 'criminalization of brand piracy' by independent clothing producers in Guatemala and Constantine Nakassis's (2012, 2013, 2016) work on brand counterfeiting in South India. The legal capture of cultural flow has also come under scrutiny in the pharmaceutical industry, where drugs can be readily reverse engineered, which means that what is needed to produce them can be figured out by analysing the finished product. An important instance of this is Brazil's successful struggle with multinational pharmaceutical companies to reduce the price of HIV medications (Biehl 2004). While anthropologists have been especially concerned with the relationship between the legal corporation's commodities and the copies produced extra-legally, the copying and differentiating relationship among legal producers themselves promises to provide insight into the nature of demand itself, since that relationship appears to map the social fields in which demand unfolds.

Whether the similarities between commodities produced by two different companies are legal or not depends on recognition of the producers by the state. That is, it depends on state recognition of the corporation in the anthropological sense as a legal corporation. Examination of inter-corporate copying, with or without the introduction of significant difference, thus raises theoretical questions about the nature of community in the modern world. The legitimate use of force today is understood as the province only of states, with corporations engaging instead in state-sanctioned competition in the marketplace. At the same time, and as I noted previously, modern business corporations grew out of early chartered joint-stock companies, and originally those were arms of the state and, in many cases, they had their own armies and routinely employed military force in co-operation with state armies (e.g. the British East India Company, Bryant 1978). Of course, major companies these days employ security services, and the distribution of the use of coercive force between states and private corporations is an empirical question. However, corporate security forces are not authorised to use coercion in policing the copying that goes on between corporations with regard to the commodities that they produce or even with regard to their internal culture. Enforcing the legal limits of inter-corporate cultural borrowing falls upon the state. Anthropologists can play a role in assessing how variations around the world in state regulatory and enforcement regimes, as well as in broader local, national and regional culture, affect the fields of commodities in which the forces of interest (as demand and desire) operate. What commodities are legally available on markets? What commodities circulate in extra-legal environments? In what measure is the internal culture of a corporation shaped by the legality or illegality of inter-corporate copying?

The future

Economic theory has approached the inner worlds of business corporations and their relations with the external world from the starting point of individual rational actors. For political economists, drawing inspiration from the Marxist tradition, the starting point is domination, exploitation and power relations. While ethnographic research justifies these approaches in some measure, a third perspective, the one developed in this chapter, is a possible course for future research in economic anthropology. That is to examine corporations as culture-bearing social groups, which means to examine them as communities. This in turn leads to the possibility of theorising the relations between corporations and other collective and individual actors, including families and households, and also states and regulatory bodies, as aspects of large-scale community that can be understood as bearing complex and dynamic cultures.

From this perspective, economic theory appears as part of circulating metaculture (Urban 2001) that can diffuse through the world, penetrating the boundaries of corporations and other collective social actors and shaping the activity within them (Mackenzie et al. 2007). In what measure do business corporations conform to models contained in economic theory? In what measure do they operate like non-economic communities, built around internal cultural practices, rituals and symbols, as well as non-economic values? Similarly, political-economic perspectives also circulate as metaculture, especially in such arenas as union organising, strikes and broader antipathy to capitalism and capitalist practices. In what measure do these circulating ideas and normative orientations help to shape community in the modern world?

From the starting point of for-profit corporations as forms of communal association that contribute to broader bases of markets and communities, the commodities that they produce appear as congealed bits of culture that participate in and help to shape social and cultural fields (Bourdieu 1984). From this perspective, demand for commodities amounts to the desire for the culture that those commodities carry. Simultaneously, the ease of copying, a form of cultural motion, contributes to the creation of a broader culture that has patterns that shift over time. A task for economic anthropology is to chart those patterns and investigate the regulatory and power relations that shape them and their changes. We can even peer into the future and try to sketch the kinds of community that might be born out of our present culture and social formations.

References

Bailey, F.G. 2003. *The Saving Lie: Truth and Method in the Social Sciences*. Philadelphia: University of Pennsylvania Press.

Bashkow, Ira 2014. Afterword: What kind of person is the corporation? *PoLAR* 37 (2): 296–307.

Benson, Peter 2014. Corporate paternalism and the problem of harmful products. *PoLAR* 37 (2): 218–30.

Biehl, João 2004. The activist state: Global pharmaceuticals, AIDS and citizenship in Brazil. *Social Text* 22 (3): 105–32.

Bössmann, Eva 1981. Weshalb gibt es Unternehmungen? Der Erklärungsansatz von Ronald H. Coase. *Journal of Institutional and Theoretical Economics* 137: 667–74.

Bourdieu, Pierre 1984. *Distinction: A Social Critique of the Judgment of Taste*. Richard Nice, trans. Cambridge, MA: Harvard University Press.

Boyer, Madeline 2018. *Working Alone, Together: Coworking, Community, and Cultural Flow*. PhD Dissertation, Department of Anthropology, University of Pennsylvania.

Braudel, Fernand 1982. *Civilization and Capitalism, 15th–18th Century*, Vol. II: *The Wheels of Commerce*. Siân Reynolds, trans. New York: Harper & Row.

Bryant, Gerald 1978. Officers of the East India Company's army in the days of Clive and Hastings. *The Journal of Imperial and Commonwealth History* 6 (3): 203–27.

Business Historical Society 1929. The oldest joint-stock company. *Bulletin of the Business Historical Society* 3 (1): 7–8.

Callon, Michel 1998. Introduction: The embeddedness of economic markets in economics. In *The Laws of the Markets* (ed.) M. Callon, pp. 1–57. Oxford: Blackwell Publishers.

Chamberlin, Edward 1933. *The Theory of Monopolistic Competition: A Re-orientation of the Theory of Value*. Cambridge, MA: Harvard University Press.

Coase, Ronald H. 1937. The nature of the firm. *Economica* 4 (16): 386–405.

Comaroff, John L. and Jean Comaroff 2009. *Ethnicity, Inc.* Chicago: University of Chicago Press.

Coombe, Rosemary J. 1998. *The Cultural Life of Intellectual Properties: Authorship, Appropriation, and the Law*. Durham, NC: Duke University Press.

Cooper, Matthew 1987. Relations of modes of production in nineteenth century America: The Shakers and Oneida. *Ethnology* 26 (1): 1–16.

Davis, John P. 2000 (1905). *Corporations: A Study of the Origin and Development of Great Business Combinations and of Their Relation to the Authority of the State*. Two volumes. Washington, DC: Beard Books.

Deal, Terrence E. and Allan A. Kennedy 1982. *Corporate Cultures: The Rites and Rituals of Corporate Life*. Reading, MA: Addison-Wesley.

Dunn, Malcolm H. 1992. Firms, markets and hierarchies: A critical appraisal of Ronald Coase's contribution to the explanation of the 'nature of the firm'. *Jahrbuch für die Ordnung von Wirtschaft und Gesellschaft* 43: 193–204.

Eklund, Robert B., Jr. and Robert D. Tollison 1980. Mercantilist origins of the corporation. *The Bell Journal of Economics* 11 (2): 715–20.

Ensminger, Jean 1990. Co-opting the elders: The political economy of state incorporation in Africa. *American Anthropologist* 92 (3): 662–75.

Ensminger, Jean 1992. *Making a Market: The Institutional Transformation of an African Society*. New York: Cambridge University Press.

Fama, Eugene 1965. The behavior of stock market prices. *Journal of Business* 38 (1): 34–105.

Fisher, Melissa S. 2012. *Wall Street Women*. Durham, NC: Duke University Press.

Fortes, Meyer 1969. *Kinship and the Social Order: The Legacy of Lewis Henry Morgan*. Chicago: Aldine Publishing.

Foster, Robert 2014. Corporations as partners: 'Connected capitalism' and the Coca-Cola Company. *PoLAR* 37 (2): 246–58.

Foster, Robert 2017. The corporation in anthropology. In *The Corporation: A Critical Multidisciplinary Handbook* (eds) Grietje Baars and André Spicer, pp. 111–33. New York: Cambridge University Press.

Ganti, Tejaswini 2014. Neoliberalism. *Annual Review of Anthropology* 43: 89–104.

Garsten, Christina 1994. *Apple World: Core and Periphery in a Transnational*. Stockholm studies in social anthropology 33. Stockholm: Department of Social Anthropology, Stockholm University.

Garsten, Christina and Adrienne Sörbom 2019. His master's voice: Conceptualizing the relationship between business and the World Economic Forum. *Journal of Business Anthropology* 8 (1). (forthcoming)

Guillet, David 2001. Reconsidering institutional change: Property rites in northern Spain. *American Anthropologist* 102 (4): 713–25.

Hamada, Tamoko 1991. *American Enterprise in Japan*. Albany: State University of New York Press.

Harvey, David 2005. *A Brief History of Neoliberalism*. New York: Oxford University Press.

Haxhi, Ilir and Hans van Ees 2010. Explaining diversity in the worldwide diffusion of codes of good governance. *Journal of International Business Studies* 41 (4): 710–26.

Heckscheler, E.F. 1934. *Mercantilism*. Two volumes. Mendel Shapiro, trans. London: George Allen and Unwin.

Ho, Karen 2009. *Liquidated: An Ethnography of Wall Street*. Durham, NC: Duke University Press.

Holmes, Douglas R. 2009. Economy of words. *Cultural Anthropology* 24 (3): 381–419.

Kim, Choong Soon 1992. *The Culture of Korean industry*. Tucson: University of Arizona Press.

Krause-Jensen, Jakob 2010. *Flexible Firm: The Design of Culture at Bang & Olufsen*. New York: Berghahn Books.

Kunda, Gideon 1995. Engineering culture: Control and commitment in a high-tech corporation. *Organization Science* 6 (2): 228–30.

Licht, Walter 2014. The rise and embedding of the corporation: Considerations for American democracy and citizenship. In *Corporations and Citizenship* (ed.) Greg Urban, pp. 143–64. Philadelphia: University of Pennsylvania Press.

Mackenzie, Donald, Fabian Muniesa and Lucia Siu (eds) 2007. *Do Economists Make Markets? On the Performativity of Economics*. Princeton, NJ: Princeton University Press.

Maine, Henry Sumner, Sir 1917 (1861). *Ancient Law: Its Connection with the Early History of Society, and its Relation to Modern Ideas*. London: Dent.

Manning, Paul 2010. The semiotics of brand. *Annual Review of Anthropology* 39: 33–49.

Marx, Karl 1990 (1867). *Capital: A Critique of Political Economy*, Vol. 1. Ben Fowkes, trans. London: Penguin.

Moore, Robert E. 2003. From genericide to viral marketing: On 'brand'. *Language and Communication* 23 (3): 331–57.

Nakassis, Constantine 2012. Counterfeiting what? Aesthetics of brandedness and BRAND in Tamil Nadu, India. *Anthropological Quarterly* 85 (3): 701–22.

Nakassis, Constantine 2013. The quality of a copy. In *Fashion India: Spectacular Capitalism* (ed.) Tereza Kuldova, pp. 142–65. Oslo: Akademika.

Nakassis, Constantine 2016. *Doing Style: Youth and Mass Meditation in South India*. Chicago: University of Chicago Press.

North, Douglass C. 1990. *Institutions, Institutional Change and Economic Performance*. New York: Cambridge University Press.

North, Douglass C. and Robert P. Thomas 1973. *The rise of the Western world*. New York: Cambridge University Press.

Oliveira, Pedro 2013. *People-Centered Innovation: Becoming a Practitioner in Innovation Research*. Columbus, OH: The Educational Publisher/Biblio Publishing.

Orr, Julian E. 1996. *Talking about Machines: An Ethnography of a Modern Job*. Ithaca: Cornell University Press.

Ouchi, William 1981. *Theory Z: How American Business Can Meet the Japanese Challenge*. Reading, MA: Addison-Wesley.

Pascale, Richard Tanner and Anthony G. Athos 1981. *The Art of Japanese Management: Applications for American Business*. New York: Simon and Schuster.

Prentice, Michael M. 2015 Managing intertextuality: Display and discipline across documents at a Korean firm. *Signs and Society* 3 (S1): S70–94.

Radcliffe-Brown, A.R. 1952. *Structure and Function in Primitive Society*. London: Routledge and Kegan Paul.

Røyrvik, Emil A. 2013. Incarnation Inc.: Managing corporate values. *Journal of Business Anthropology* 2 (1): 9–32.

Rydberg, Sven 1979. *Stora Kopparberg: 1000 Years of an Industrial Activity*. Stockholm: Gullers International AB.

Sandler, Jen and Rita Thedvall (eds) 2017. *Meeting Ethnography: Meetings as Key Technologies of Contemporary Governance, Development, and Resistance*. New York: Routledge.

Schwartzman, Helen B. 1989. *The Meeting: Gatherings in Organizations and Communities*. New York: Plenum Press.

Smith, Adam 1994 (1776). *An Inquiry into the Nature and Causes of the Wealth of Nations*. New York: Random House.

Stull, Donald D. 2017. Cows, pigs, corporations, and anthropologists. *Journal of Business Anthropology* 6 (1): 24–40.

Thomas, Kedron 2016. *Regulating Style: Intellectual Property Law and the Business of Fashion in Guatemala*. Oakland: University of California Press.

Urban, Greg 2001. *Metaculture: How Culture Moves Through the World*. Minneapolis: University of Minnesota Press.

Urban, Greg 2015. Symbolic force: A corporate revitalization video and its effects. *Signs and Society* 3 (S1): S95–124.

Urban, Greg 2016. Corporations in the flow of culture. *Seattle University Law Review* 39 (2): 321–51.

Urban, Greg and Kyung-Nan Koh 2013. Ethnographic research on modern business corporations. *Annual Review of Anthropology* 42: 139–58.

Urban, Greg, Ernest Baskin and Kyung-Nan Koh 2007. 'No carry-over parts': Corporations and the metaculture of newness. *Suomen Antropologi* 32 (1): 5–19.

Venkatraman, N., Lawrence Loh and Jeongsuk Koh 1994. The adoption of corporate governance mechanisms: A test of competing diffusion models. *Management Science* 40 (4): 496–507.

Watson, James L. (ed.) 1997. *Golden Arches East: McDonald's in East Asia*. Stanford: Stanford University Press.

Weber, Max 1968 (1925). *Economy and Society*. Guenther Roth and Claus Wittich, eds. Berkeley: University of California Press.

Wilf, Eitan 2015. Ritual semiosis in the business corporation: Recruitment to routinized innovation. *Signs and Society* 3 (S1): S13–40.

Wilk, Richard R. and Eric J. Arnould 2016. Why do the Indians wear Adidas? Or culture contact and the relations of consumption. *Journal of Business Anthropology* 5 (1): 6–36.

2 Research directions on states and markets

Felix Stein

Which research trends promise to make the anthropology of states and markets particularly interesting during the years to come? What do these trends tell us about the nature of economic anthropology at a time when more and more of our scholarship is conducted within bureaucracies rather than local communities? In this chapter I attempt to answer both of these questions. I begin with a brief sketch of insights that result from treating states and markets as essentially different, albeit related, entities, drawing especially on recent work on the nature of neoliberalism and global inequality. The bulk of this chapter, however, will focus on those aspects of state and market institutions that show them to be largely collaborative, similar social formations. In doing so, I mean to suggest that future anthropological research should be more explicitly concerned with aspects that cut across the state–market division, including the study of financialisation and ritual.

For each of the themes explored here, the methodological message is the same: economic anthropologists should continue their concern for disenfranchised social groups, continue to carry out research marked by long-term physical engagement and continue to develop concepts that can be applied across differences of time and space. This will allow us to provide analyses of states and markets that promise to be both distinctive to our discipline and relevant for society at large.

States and markets as different entities

For more than a decade, anthropologists approaching states and markets as fundamentally different have tended to describe their relationship with reference to neoliberalism. Drawing on a recent review by Tejaswini Ganti (2014: 91), we can distinguish at least four different meanings of neoliberalism. Firstly, it refers to a model of development with specific roles for labour, capital and the state, and since capital tends to be privileged in this model some have described neoliberalism as a class-based project (Harvey 2005). Secondly, the term denotes historically-situated economic policies including fiscal prudence, the privatisation of state-owned enterprises, trade liberalisation, precarious work regimes and privileging lenders over borrowers in times of debt default. Thirdly, it refers to treating notions linked to market exchange as central to interpreting and evaluating human action. Lastly, it denotes a mode of governance that fosters market-based values such as competition, flexibility, individual responsibility and self-interest throughout society generally. The anthropological literature on neoliberalism often has focused on the shrinking of the welfare state and the rise of market logics and institutions, including charities and NGOs, the associated reconfiguration of life worlds and subjects, and people's modes of adaptation and resistance to these trends (e.g. Gershon 2016; Muehlebach 2012).

Given that range, it is not surprising that neoliberalism has been criticised for being too broad a concept, as it refers simultaneously to paradigms and policies, interpretative grids, moral convictions and intimate systems of governance. Moreover, some (e.g. Kipnis 2008; Venkatesan 2015) have argued that often it is assigned excessive and quite economistic explanatory power, with the result that it defines intellectual approaches too narrowly and tends to predetermine researchers' analytical conclusions. Further, the concept frequently comes with strong negative connotations, which risks turning anthropological writing into a denunciatory project that offers few constructive conclusions about what we ought to do (Ferguson 2010).

However, if we approach neoliberalism as a fairly well-defined set of macroeconomic policies, it is useful for directing our attention to the shifting boundary between states and markets as well as to the interlinked reconfigurations of their power. This means that it is likely to retain analytical value for economic anthropologists during the years to come, especially when they apply it to new developments in contemporary economic activity. For example, anthropologists might want to ask how the concept of neoliberalism could illuminate the redrawing of state–market boundaries in spheres as diverse as internet governance (Golub 2017), the ways in which virtual employment platforms reconfigure labour regimes (Duff Morton 2018) and ongoing changes of global health governance (Stein and Sridhar 2017a). In each of these, testing whether the relationships between state and market may best be described as neoliberal (rather than, say, liberal, nationalist, capitalist or imperialist) will continue to be useful.

In any event, neoliberalism is likely to stay with us because its spread as a set of policies during the 1970s and 1980s and its rise as an academic and popular concept since the early 1990s has turned it into a widespread notion that is used in social movements and NGOs and by individual activists (e.g. Ferguson 2015). As such, there will be analytic value in investigating it as a meaningful category through which people describe and criticise their positions as economic actors or as citizens.

This points to a second guiding theme concerning states and markets that will remain important for future anthropological scholarship, the rise of inequality. In 2018, Crédit Suisse estimated that 42 men owned roughly the same amount of wealth as half of the world's population (Oxfam 2018), mainly because of stagnant real wages, tax evasion by the very wealthy and increasing corporate power over salaries and legislation. This is not new. Over the past quarter-century, the top 1 per cent of global income earners had a greater share of income than the bottom 50 per cent (Oxfam 2017), and the richest 1 per cent of the world's population received over 80 per cent of all wealth created in 2017 (Oxfam 2018). The striking rise of global inequality since the 1980s and the associated life-style changes among the world's super-rich have led observers to call ours a new Gilded Age (Krugman 2014), in which corporate managers have greater power than before in setting their own remuneration. Of course, Thomas Piketty (2014) has argued that a tendency for increasing inequality lies at the core of capitalism, as the rate of return on capital exceeds rates of income and output growth, in spite of rising skill and employment levels that expand the amount of wealth going to labour, if not the proportion.

In order to make sense of this increasing inequality, anthropologists have recently returned to the idea of class, though they have moved away from the old Marxian link between it and the exploitation of labour in production (Carrier 2015). Instead, they use it in politically engaged comparative analyses of people's economic lives generally under extremely unequal economic conditions (Kalb 2015), which can be studied with reference to the organisation of production, exchange or consumption. So, class now is used in a way that highlights socio-economic differences more widely, enabling us to analyse a series of relevant and potentially related phenomena, such as ongoing processes of socio-economic dispossession (Carbonella and Kasmir 2015), the links between concrete labour and speculative activity (Bear 2015), mounting accusations of corruption (Sanchez 2016) and the possibility that the world's poorest may not get incorporated into a wage-based economy any time soon (Ferguson 2015). It is important to find out whether and how these phenomena are linked, and class can offer new insights about this, in two ways. One is as an analytical tool that can help us to understand social relations and processes and the ways that they change. The other is as an emic category that we can investigate to help us to understand the circumstances under which different sets of people come to see themselves in class terms.

Rediscovering class raises questions about the respective roles of states and markets in the creation, reproduction and growth of inequality. According to Keith Hart's *The memory bank*, its origins lie in the historic rise of the state. He argues that inequality came about through state capitalism, a conjunction of machine-based production and the institutions of agrarian civilisation, such as territorial states, landed property and racism (Hart 2000: 65). Machine-based production meant that, starting in the nineteenth century, humans harnessed steam, electricity and information processing for almost all aspects of economic life, leading to a vast increase in economic productivity. At the same time, the institutions of agrarian civilisation made redistribution of the resulting wealth more difficult. Hart (2000: 135) holds that the state is instrumental for upholding inequality, for example in that it facilitates the separation of groups into areas with very different standards of living. Passports, borders, police and the military hold people in low-wage economies in place, thereby ensuring that the goods and services produced by their labour remain cheap. The citizens of high-wage countries are physically separated yet economically linked to people in poor areas through the provision of those cheap goods and services.

In this analysis, monetary transactions are potentially egalitarian. That is because money is a communicative and relational technology, a means of human interaction across time and space as well as across ethnic, religious and national divides. In the past it helped the European middle classes to seize power from the landed aristocracy, and today the ascent of new currencies and online payment systems allow larger groups of people than ever before to transact from afar. Moreover, new payment systems and the rapid spread of the internet could allow people to bypass state institutions altogether and to minimise the cut taken on each payment by banks and corporate intermediaries. This is particularly true for citizens of post-colonial states, who often do not have access to established forms of banking and who use digital technology in the pursuit of greater economic autonomy (Maurer 2015), though it is not clear if these new technologies will in fact end up supporting, rather than undermining, that autonomy.

Other scholars have approached the state as a potential force for equality, as illustrated by the way that many of the more virulent attacks on neoliberalism and the associated expansion of the market sphere contain a vision, even if only implicit, of a just and redistributive state. Similarly, Piketty (2014: 471) ended his analysis of rising inequality with a call for a progressive global tax on capital, aiming at exposing wealth to democratic scrutiny, redistributing it and enabling an effective regulation of the banking system and international capital flows. That said, Piketty (2014: 473) observes that state intervention in the economy before the financial crisis of 2007–08 had been much greater than during the Depression of the economically liberal 1930s. So, it seems that the question of when and under what historical, cultural and institutional circumstances states or markets foster or undermine inequality remains unanswered, and it is one of the important issues that anthropologists may want to investigate.

The importance of studying both the relationship of states to markets and the sources, forms and effects of inequality foreground a significant methodological point. Economic anthropologists are today more than happy to 'study up' (Nader 1972; Moberg this volume) as they work with people across the class spectrum, from waste pickers and low-level bureaucrats in developing countries to affluent white-collar employees in the world's financial centres. At the same time, their guiding concern should remain marginalised people. Such people need not always be the object of study, but their presence ought to continue to shape the analytic frames and concepts that we use to make sense of economic life. Whether it is out of an attempt to place our analyses in the broadest possible context, out of the discipline's historic connection to the disenfranchised or out of the realisation that scholarly work itself is socially embedded, anthropologists should retain a heightened sensitivity to economic injustice, regardless of whom they study at any given moment.

States and markets as fundamentally similar

I have described some of the ways that economic anthropologists have approached states and markets as being fundamentally different. I noted, however, that there is also work that points to their similarities. I turn to that now, beginning with work on financialisation.

Financialisation

To speak about the relationship between states and markets and their connection to socio-economic inequality requires attention to financialisation, the increasing role of financial motives, logics, actors and institutions in the operation of domestic and international economies (Epstein 2005: 3; Mattioli this volume). This can be observed on a small scale when we consider the growth of consumer debt, microcredit, savings clubs and debt collection agencies (James 2015). It can also be seen in the increasing frequency, size and profitability of financial transactions as compared to non-financial ones for many companies (Krippner 2005). Financial activities play a more and more important part in business profits, stock markets increasingly determine production and shareholder value has become the primary indicator of corporate success (Ho 2009; Lazonick 2011). Further, the importance of financialisation for states has become highly visible, indicated by the increasing importance of capital markets and credit-rating agencies for national economies and the importance of central banks and multilateral institutions when markets do not provide the capital that national governments require. Financialisation also drives the transformations of multilateral institutions such as the World Bank, which increasingly acts as a broker and facilitator for private investors rather than continuing to be a lender to developing countries (Stein and Sridhar 2017b).

The rise of finance shows how useful it is to see states and markets as distinct entities. Their distinction may enable us to consider financialisation as an aspect of neoliberalism. Since the 1970s, after all, states have been unable or unwilling to tax or regulate the financial sector, which has drastically expanded, increasing its political influence and its sway over diverse aspects of people's lives, ranging from their relation to the natural environment to the kind of housing, education and healthcare available to them. Economic anthropologists might thus want to ask whether a thoroughly financialised version of neoliberalism differs from its less financialised beginnings.

At the same time, we can see that there is much more to financialisation than just a continuation of past neoliberal patterns. I turn to that 'much more' now, and in doing so will show the limitations that come from seeing states and markets as radically distinct. In fact, they have much in common, especially in the ways that they approach the world and the technology they use to record and process their understandings of it.

Financialisation is a particularly abstract phenomenon. Sovereign bond yields, the price of shares and the value of currency derivatives depend on the labour involved in agriculture and manufacturing, yet the two rarely meet. Workers in the financial sector are white-collar labour, which does not get its hands dirty. Futures traders make sure that the lean hogs and cocoa beans that they trade never actually end up on their doorstep. Thereby, they remain at least one step removed from engaging with the concrete nature of the objects that they exchange. More evidence of this abstraction is that the financial sector also links and makes commensurable vast sets of disparate people, products and activities via spreadsheet models, Bloomberg terminals and broadly reported speech acts that present authoritative narratives to itself and to the public (Holmes 2014). This virtualised environment cuts across state and market institutions, and in it the fluctuations of the value of sovereign bonds, corporate shares and new financial instruments depend largely on the changing nature of the dominant narratives that exist around them.

The abstract nature of financial activity does not preclude the ongoing presence of the concrete, but rather reconfigures it. Caitlyn Zaloom (2006) has shown this in her study of the material carriers of financial knowledge, recent forms of which increasingly are common in states as well as financial institutions. She shows how different sets of technologies, such as open-pit trading floors, computer screens and yield curves, influence their users' judgements (Zaloom 2009). Field work at the Chicago Board of Trade as a runner and clerk, recording orders on paper and delivering them with hand signals to brokers, exposed her to the embodied aspects involved in derivatives trading. There, transactions depended on the general atmosphere of the pit as much as on market information on the screen. Traders were constrained by whether and how shouted orders and offers were heard. Pit architecture put competing traders side by side, shoving and pushing each other, while collaborating traders relied on body language, eye contact and personal relations to come to agreements. On the other hand, at a London futures-trading firm using screen-based technologies, traders were less reliant on the myriad of stimuli around them. Instead they did a lot of interpretative work, trying to contextualise and decipher the limited market information that they saw on their screens. Zaloom's work usefully illustrates how narratives and financial knowledge depend on their material carriers. These carriers take different forms, and I turn now to those that are a point of similarity between state and market institutions.

In my own research on German management consultants who work for both governments and private companies, narrative and knowledge frequently were created and transmitted with Microsoft Excel and PowerPoint (Stein 2017). Both are pervasive in state and commercial institutions, and in their appearance on screen and on paper they combine descriptive and aesthetic features that mix rhetoric with the creation and transmission of knowledge in peculiar ways. Excel's design encourages the use of quantitative data, since it reaches its full calculative potential only when it is used to put large amounts of numbers into relation with one another. At the same time, it encourages seeing the entities that it describes in terms of a managerial ideal, in which employees can be understood and manipulated as discrete and passive entities. PowerPoint slides, on the other hand, often are written to have an immediate, affectively charged learning effect in the viewer. In my field site, slide message, main graph and side description were supposed to be harmonised to make the slide's content 'jump at' the reader, and slides that did not have this effect were considered to be of poor quality and often had to be rewritten. At the same time, PowerPoint presentations resembled cartoons in various ways. As mixtures of word and image they had the effect of being polysemic and often were of only limited use when read in hindsight. In other words, while they were useful in meetings, they rendered consulting projects opaque for people who tried to understand them later on. These observations regarding Excel and PowerPoint support Anthony Pickles's (2017) suggestion that we approach technologies such as spreadsheets by drawing on the body of anthropological work on literacy and the nature of writing (e.g. Goody 1977). This is likely to be particularly promising for the study of highly financialised state and market entities, where emails, memos, presentations, text messages, spreadsheets and graphs are produced almost frantically.

Even if much of finance itself is abstract, personal trajectories, informal relationships and local values continue to matter in its workplaces and business centres, as they do in states. Karen Ho's (2009) analysis of Wall Street investors has shown this, describing how the recruitment policies of investment banks focus on only a handful of prestigious US universities, facilitating the creation of old-boy networks of mostly White American men who subsequently have substantial influence in the corporate world. At the same time, Ho (2009: 36) has argued that investment evaluations are mission driven rather than purely abstract and rational. Thus, Wall Street investors do not approach the allocation of capital in purely rational-economic terms. Instead they pursue the culturally specific goal of unifying the ownership and control of corporations by shareholders, as well as fostering a culture of smartness, elitism, job uncertainty and hard work. Wall Street's dominant value set, closely bound to the value sets of those prestigious universities, encourages those who work on the Street to believe that they live in a meritocracy, a stance that facilitates recurring mass layoffs. One of the questions that remain for economic anthropologists is whether alternative forms of interplay between personal habitus and cultural values are possible in financialised settings, whether in markets or states, and how they might come about.

Finally, an important role for economic anthropology in financialised states and markets is to witness the concrete effects that high finance has on the disadvantaged. The bursting of the bubble in the US housing market around 2008 led millions of Americans to lose their homes, often by forced eviction, which had catastrophic effects that touched every aspect of their lives. This is shown in Matthew Desmond's *Evicted* (2016), grounded in long-term field work in Milwaukee and documenting how Americans who lose their homes often see their entire existence thrown into disarray. Desmond traces how poor healthcare provision, drug abuse, reduced educational opportunities and high crime rates are linked to US housing policies. His work demonstrates how the abstract narratives of finance markets end up being turned into concrete reality, occasionally accompanied by the threat of physical violence. The same is true for highly financialised states such as Greece, whose crass reliance on the international bond markets before the 2011 sovereign debt crisis eventually forced it to adopt radical austerity. This resulted in increased unemployment and homelessness, as well as the collapse of the country's healthcare system and the rise of the Greek far Right. The effects of financialisation thus reverberate throughout social life, and it is up to anthropologists to describe and analyse how this affects configurations of power, labour, health, education and housing.

Economic anthropology conventionally has focused on small-scale societies domi-nated by subsistence activities, and many in the sub-discipline have been wondering what they might have to offer in multi-sited research projects focused on well-educated people doing abstract work (e.g. Holmes and Marcus 2006). It seems to me that participant observation, a long-term and embodied research method, can provide unique insights in such projects. As long as abstract market activity and people's concrete existences intersect, anthropologists are in a position to study their interplay. While a deluge of published corporate market models, government policy documents, reports and memos leads us to engage increasingly with digital technology, the concrete and embodied nature of long-term field work continues to promise insights of the sort offered by Ho, Zaloom and Desmond, which are often unique and unmatched in their qualitative depth.

Ritual

Another potentially fruitful avenue of research for the study of states and markets is the use of analytical categories that have very broad comparative scale as well as concrete application, the sort of categories that are uncommon in sociology and economics. Modern economics remains based on an individualistic approach and the assumption that people maximise their utility in economic activity, which the discipline describes in quantitative terms (Earle et al. 2017). This view of utility-maximising individuals has spread from economics into the quantitative social sciences, while the rise of 'big data' (Boellstorff 2013) and audit culture (Shore and Wright 1999; Strathern 1996, 2000) have gradually turned it into a dominant approach to the world, stretching from corporate reliance on audit and metrics to increasingly quantified notions of the self.

The anthropological study of states and markets should continue to resist this reductionist trend. Let me outline what I mean by this, with reference to ritual. Broadly following Victor Turner (1969), the term denotes an expressive activity of considerable social seriousness and importance that includes a host of objects and actions that are representative of or transformative for social values and relations. With reference to markets, anthropologists have long established that ritual activ-ity matters, mostly by focusing on small-scale, face-to-face economic systems (e.g. Gudeman and Hann 2015). However, the study of ritual in economy could go much further than it currently does. It can fruitfully be applied to even the most abstract and diversified capitalist institutions, and ethnographic work shows that ritual is not subordinated to logics of efficiency and profit maximisation, but instead is woven through capitalist work and institutions and remains a key driver of them (LiPuma 2017).

Economic and political analysts often present market activity as a rational response to objective levels of supply and demand, yet Max Weber (1958 [1904–05]) told us long ago that the idea of economic rationality rests on non-rational and even metaphysical considerations (Rudnyckyj 2009). In telling us that, he raised the general matter of the degree to which the means and ends of economic life are social and cultural rather than only objective and rational. In a similar vein, Marshall Sahlins (1972) argues that scarcity is not a natural fact of life, but instead is a relationship between collectively defined means and ends. Such work suggests that capitalism's incessant drive for accumulation and its concomitant desire for speed, busy-ness and change are not the ultimate expression of some inherent predisposition to truck, barter and exchange one thing for another, as Adam Smith (1976 [1776]) put it. Rather, they reflect a substantive, non-rational drive that is present in both state and market institutions.

This is where the study of ritual comes in. For capitalism to reproduce itself, its values need to be reproduced by expressive activity that remains inexplicable within the frameworks of neoclassical economics and much quantitative social science. Such activity can in fact be found everywhere and one might even argue that every monetary transaction is part of it, in the way that Christina von Braun (2012) shows that payments have symbolic aspects that hark back to notions of guilt and sacrifice. She considers money to be an instrument that binds people together by expressing relations of mutual indebtedness. She also has highlighted the interplay of fertility and sacrifice in monetary payments, one that is symbolised by images of the bull, by currency signs and by economic concepts that imply fertility, such as capital, stock and economic growth. David Graeber (2011: 98), on the other hand, argues that money is socially corrosive, especially when used in debt relations, as it breaks with the foundational social principle of what he calls baseline communism: 'from each according to their abilities, to each according to their needs'. Though von Braun and Graeber come to different conclusions about money, both see it as having ritual aspects, each payment expressing and altering a web of meanings, even if those meanings are contested and may be the subject of important misunderstandings (Peebles 2012; Ssorin-Chaikov 2000).

At the same time, payment can also be a trenchant social definition of competing understandings of value. Rather than being the natural outcome of supply and demand, or merely the expression of faith in a central bank, prices often express and shape understandings of labour, nature, the human body and metaphysical entities (Gudeman and Rivera 1990). The co-existence of these competing understandings means that nobody exactly knows what the price of anything should be, a topic that Robert Foster (2014) has recently explored. In his ethnographic study of the valuation of Coca-Cola, he shows that in the eyes of corporate analysts half of the company's market capitalisation resides in its brand. This is to say that Coca-Cola is worth roughly twice as much as a company of similar size and profitability, simply because it elicits strong and positive associations with millions of people around the globe. For corporate investors, this intangible asset, the sort of thing that companies like McDonald's and Disney have, can be worth more than the material entities that make up a company's production, distribution and sales networks. Foster's work shows how market analysts, corporate investors, consumers and marketing departments heatedly struggle over meaning when they try to estimate or increase brand value. While advertising can affect brand value, to a significant degree it rests on how consumers think about and deal with the branded objects and services, and Foster argues that when people pay a premium for a product or a share of the company that makes it, they are thus paying extra for a value that they themselves have helped to create. In this capitalist forest of symbols, it seems that payment is at least in part a ritual activity that is not just symbolically expressive but also socially effective. Harking back to the points that Weber and Sahlins made, one might consider the possibility that at least in contexts of great affluence economic activity may even be more ritualistic than utilitarian.

Ritual also is important for creating the conceptual boundaries around state and market actors. Concerning market actors, recent scholarship in the study of corporate forms has shown that central banks, state treasuries, mining companies, consulting firms and NGOs are heterogeneous (e.g. Welker et al. 2011), each one combining many competing sets of ideas, actors, locations and technologies. Those in these entities, as well as those who deal with them and the analysts who study them, constantly need to turn that heterogeneity into a meaningful whole, a task that gets more difficult as production processes and corporate structures become more complex, outsourcing increases and value chains become longer. The rise of project-based work in the consulting sector and the growth of the gig economy challenge the nature and rigidity of external corporate boundaries even further.

Concerning classic state institutions, the problem of boundaries is raised in Benedict Anderson's argument that the nation-state is an imagined community that cannot directly be observed. Anderson (1991: 53) says that if we are to understand how nation-states become real to their citizens we have 'to look at the ways in which administrative organisations create meaning', ranging from the idea of simultaneity to notions about the nature of truth and language. Alexei Yurchak's study of people's relation to the state during late Soviet socialism pursues that creation, showing that Soviet citizens related to the discourse of the state via their participation in rituals and events like May Day and Revolution Day marches and Komsomol meetings. Over time, people's attention to the content of these rituals waned but their participation became more fervent, which Yurchak explains in terms of the distinction between what he calls (following Austin) their constative and performative dimensions. Yurchak illustrates that distinction with regard to voting, for which the former includes the opinion that the vote expresses, while the latter includes the way that voting reflects rules and norms that are considered legitimate (Yurchak 2005: 23). He then describes moments of 'performative shift', in which the performative dimension, the concrete ritualised form of discourse such as the act of voting, grows in importance, and does so relatively independently of its constative significance. Yurchak's close attention to the ritualistic nature of citizen engagement with the state allows him to explain why the unexpected end of the seemingly endless Soviet socialism was handled quite well by large parts of Soviet citizenry. Mikhail Gorbachev's reforms unravelled existing discursive regimes during the second half of the 1980s, but Soviet citizens had long been developing new forms of life, notions of temporality and understandings of person-hood, partially by drawing on cultural production from abroad. Because of that, the break with the Soviet regime quickly felt logical and manageable to them, even if it had been drastic and unforeseen.

Alex Golub has taken up the problem of corporate boundary-making even more explicitly, in his study of the Porgera gold mine in Papua New Guinea. National law requires that the mining company deals with local Ipili-speaking landowners, and Golub is concerned with how these two sets of people produce a semblance of unity among themselves and in relation to each other. As Golub (2014: 3) observes, understanding the production of that unity entails addressing one of 'the oldest questions about human social life: How do individuals come to represent groups?' Golub describes how eighteen months of difficult, and ultimately unsuccessful, negotiations between mine and landowners had to be condensed into an authorita-tive and anonymous account of about 400 words, which was published as part of a sustainability report. The plans of the main groups involved in the negotiation that culminated in that account had to be represented by single individuals whose personal background mattered for negotiation outcomes. Moreover, the ability to speak and act as one was unequally distributed among mine, state and landowners, and depended on infrastructure as much as on regional kinship patterns and the area's colonial history. Golub's account points to the ritual activities that make meaning and that are likely to exist whenever entities like companies and owners have to present themselves as unitary wholes.

Ritual is only one of many categories that are of potential use for the analysis of states and markets. Witchcraft (James 2012), divination (Zeitlyn 2012), hierar-chy (Sahlins 1963) and rhetoric (Holmes 2014) are others. This observation does not, however, mean that every classic anthropological concept can be applied to contemporary political and economic life. For example, popular references to eco-nomic tribes do give modern capitalism a somewhat archaic feel but promise little in terms of analytic insight (Sneath 2016). However, as long as the concepts we use arise from our efforts to join wide applicability and concretely grounded meaning, economic anthropology will continue to be both a distinctive and a highly revealing approach in the study of states and markets.

Conclusion

I have argued that the anthropology of states and markets will remain exciting over the years to come. When taken as essentially different albeit related entities, states and markets may teach us more about the nature and development of neoliberalism and about life under the condition of extreme and increasingly financialised socio-economic inequality. We can try to find out the degree to which states, markets or both drive that inequality, whether and how class identity comes about and how technological change in things like employment, payment systems and tracking consumers will affect people's lives as both market actors and as citizens.

That said, this chapter has emphasised that interesting work can arise from focusing on the similarities between states and markets. As increasingly financialised and essentially corporate entities, state and market institutions reconfigure the interplay of the abstract and the concrete. This is true for the technologies of knowledge that they employ, for the informal social bonds that exist within and between them and for the cultural values that underlie them. Like others, the anthropological concepts that I described in this chapter emerged out of the discipline's desire to produce comparative generalisation from a body of research immersed in local, emic terms. Drawing on the conceptual apparatus of classic anthropology will help us to tease out aspects of states and markets that are likely to be invisible to disciplines like economics or quantitative sociology, such as the ritual activities that intertwine their existence and interplay.

For all of these reasons, orthodox anthropological concerns and research methods continue to have a lot to offer. By combining a concern for disadvantaged people with long-term, embodied participant observation and a clear sense of what makes the concepts that anthropologists develop distinctive, our study of states and markets can help us to think outside the box – provided, of course, that relentless calls for immediate practical research impact and increasing pressure to publish do not stifle these efforts.

Acknowledgement

I would like to thank Sebastian Stein for improving the text in both content and style.

References

Anderson, Benedict 1991. *Imagined Communities: Reflections on the Origin and Spread of Nationalism*. London: Verso.
Bear, Laura 2015. *Navigating Austerity: Currents of Debt along a South Asian River*. Stanford: Stanford University Press.
Boellstorff, Tom 2013. Making big data in theory. *First Monday* 18 (10). http://firstmonday.org/article/view/4869/3750 (accessed 1 October 2018)
Carbonella, August and Sharryn Kasmir 2015. Dispossession, disorganization and the anthropology of labor. In *Anthropologies of Class: Power, Practice and Inequality* (eds) James G. Carrier and Don Kalb, pp. 41–52. Cambridge: Cambridge University Press.

Carrier, James G. 2015. The concept of class. In *Anthropologies of Class: Power, Practice and Inequality* (eds) J.G. Carrier and Don Kalb, pp. 28–40. Cambridge: Cambridge University Press.

Desmond, Matthew 2016. *Evicted: Poverty and Profit in the American City*. New York: Crown Publishers.

Duff Morton, Gregory 2018. Neoliberal eclipse: Donald Trump, corporate monopolism, and the changing face of work. *Dialectical Anthropology* 42 (2): 207–25.

Earle, Joe, Cahal Moran and Zach Ward-Perkins 2017. *The Econocracy: The Perils of Leaving Economics to the Experts*. Manchester: Manchester University Press.

Epstein, Gerald 2005. *Financialization and the World Economy*. Cheltenham, UK and Northampton, MA, USA: Edward Elgar.

Ferguson, James 2010. The uses of neoliberalism. *Antipode* 41 (S1): 166–84.

Ferguson, James 2015. *Give a Man a Fish: Reflections on the New Politics of Distribution*. Durham, NC: Duke University Press.

Foster, Robert 2014. Corporations as partners: 'Connected capitalism' and the Coca-Cola Company. *PoLAR* 37 (2): 246–58.

Ganti, Tejaswini 2014. Neoliberalism. *Annual Review of Anthropology* 43: 89–104.

Gershon, Ilana 2016. 'I'm not a businessman, I'm a business, man': Typing the neoliberal self into a branded existence. *Hau* 6 (3): 223–46.

Golub, Alex 2014. *Leviathans at the Gold Mine: Creating Indigenous and Corporate Actors in Papua New Guinea*. Durham, NC: Duke University Press.

Golub, Alex 2017. Beyond open access, net neutrality: Cultural anthropology takes action. SCA News, *Cultural Anthropology*. https://culanth.org/fieldsights/1171-beyond-open-access-net-neutrality-cultural-anthropology-takes-action (accessed 1 October 2018)

Goody, Jack 1977. *The Domestication of the Savage Mind*. Cambridge: Cambridge University Press.

Graeber, David 2011. *Debt: The First 5000 Years*. New York: Melville House.

Gudeman, Stephen and Chris Hann 2015. Introduction: Ritual, economy, and the institutions of the base. In *Economy and Ritual: Studies of Postsocialist Transformations* (eds) S. Gudeman and C. Hann, pp. 1–30. Oxford: Berghahn Books.

Gudeman, Stephen and Alberto Rivera 1990. *Conversations in Colombia: The Domestic Economy in Life and Text*. Cambridge: Cambridge University Press.

Hart, Keith 2000. *The Memory Bank: Money in an Unequal World*. London: Profile Books.

Harvey, David 2005. *A Brief History of Neoliberalism*. Oxford: Oxford University Press.

Ho, Karen 2009. *Liquidated: An Ethnography of Wall Street*. Durham, NC: Duke University Press.

Holmes, Douglas R. 2014. *Economy of Words: Communicative Imperatives in Central Banks*. Chicago: University of Chicago Press.

Holmes, Douglas R. and George E. Marcus 2006. Fast capitalism: Para-ethnography and the rise of the symbolic analyst. In *Frontiers of Capital: Ethnographic Reflections on the New Economy* (eds) Melissa S. Fisher and Greg Downey, pp. 33–57. Durham, NC: Duke University Press.

James, Deborah 2015. *Money from Nothing: Indebtedness and Aspiration in South Africa*. Stanford: Stanford University Press.

James, Erica Caple 2012. Witchcraft, bureaucraft, and the social life of (US)AID in Haiti. *Cultural Anthropology* 27 (1): 50–75.

Kalb, Don 2015. Introduction: Class and the new anthropological holism. In *Anthropologies of Class: Power, Practice and Inequality* (eds) James G. Carrier and D. Kalb, pp, 1–27. Cambridge: Cambridge University Press.

Kipnis, Andrew B. 2008. Audit cultures: Neoliberal governmentality, socialist legacy, or technologies of governing? *American Ethnologist* 35 (2): 275–89.

Krippner, Greta R. 2005. The financialization of the American economy. *Socio-Economic Review* 3 (2): 173–208.

Krugman, Paul 2014. Why we're in a new Gilded Age. *The New York Review of Books* (8 May). www.nybooks.com/articles/2014/05/08/thomas-piketty-new-gilded-age/ (accessed 1 October 2018)

Lazonick, William 2011. Innovative business models and varieties of capitalism: Financialization of the U.S. corporation. *Business History Review* 84 (4): 675–702.

LiPuma, Edward 2017. *The Social Life of Financial Derivatives: Markets, Risk, and Time*. Durham, NC: Duke University Press.

Maurer, Bill 2015. *How Would You Like to Pay? How Technology is Changing the Future of Money*. Durham, NC: Duke University Press.

Muehlebach, Andrea 2012. *The Moral Neoliberal: Welfare and Citizenship in Italy*. Chicago: University of Chicago Press.

Nader, Laura 1972. Up the anthropologist: Perspectives gained from studying up. In *Reinventing Anthropology* (ed.) Dell H. Hymes, pp. 284–311. New York: Vintage.

Oxfam 2017. An economy for the 99%. Oxford: Oxfam. www.oxfam.org/sites/www.oxfam.org/files/file_attachments/bp-economy-for-99-percent-160117-en.pdf (accessed 1 October 2018)

Oxfam 2018. Reward work, not wealth. Oxford: Oxfam. www.oxfam.org/en/research/reward-work-not-wealth (accessed 1 October 2018)

Peebles, Gustav 2012. Filth and lucre: The dirty money complex as a taxation regime. *Anthropological Quarterly* 85 (4): 1229–55.

Pickles, Anthony J. 2017. To Excel at bridewealth, or ceremonies of Office. *Anthropology Today* 33 (1): 20–23.

Piketty, Thomas 2014. *Capital in the Twenty-First Century*. Arthur Goldhammer, trans. Cambridge, MA: Harvard University Press.

Rudnyckyj, Daromir 2009. Spiritual economies: Islam and neoliberalism in contemporary Indonesia. *Cultural Anthropology* 24 (1): 104–41.

Sahlins, Marshall 1963. Poor man, rich man, big-man, chief: Political types in Melanesia and Polynesia. *Comparative Studies in Society and History* 5 (3): 285–303.

Sahlins, Marshall 1972. *Stone Age Economics*. Chicago: Aldine-Atherton.

Sanchez, Andrew 2016. *Criminal Capital: Violence, Corruption and Class in Industrial India*. London: Routledge.

Shore, Cris and Susan Wright 1999. Audit culture and anthropology: Neo-liberalism in British higher education. *Journal of the Royal Anthropological Institute* 5 (4): 557–75.

Smith, Adam 1976 (1776). *An Inquiry into the Nature and Causes of the Wealth of Nations*. Chicago: University of Chicago Press.

Sneath, David 2016. Tribe. In *The Cambridge Encyclopedia of Anthropology* (eds) Felix Stein, Sian Lazar, Matei Candea, Hildegaard Diemberger, Joel Robbins, Andrew Sanchez and Rupert Stasch. www.anthroencyclopedia.com/entry/tribe (accessed 1 October 2018)

Ssorin-Chaikov, Nikolai 2000. Bear skins and macaroni: The social life of things at the margins of a Siberian state collective. In *The Vanishing Rouble: Barter Networks and Non-Monetary Transactions in Post-Soviet Societies* (ed.) Paul Seabright, pp. 345–62. Cambridge: Cambridge University Press.

Stein, Felix 2017. *Work, Sleep, Repeat: The Abstract Labour of German Management Consultants*. London: Bloomsbury.

Stein, Felix and Devi Sridhar 2017a. Health as a 'global public good': Creating a market for pandemic risk. *The British Medical Journal* 358: 1–4.

Stein, Felix and Devi Sridhar 2017b. The World Bank reinvents itself – and puts poverty reduction at risk. *The Conversation*. https://theconversation.com/the-world-bank-reinvents-itself-and-puts-poverty-reduction-at-risk-79403 (accessed 1 October 2018)

Strathern, Marilyn 1996. From improvement to enhancement: An anthropological comment on the audit culture. *The Cambridge Journal of Anthropology* 19 (3): 1–21.

Strathern, Marilyn (ed.) 2000. *Audit Cultures: Anthropological Studies in Accountability, Ethics and the Academy*. London: Routledge.

Turner, Victor 1969. *The Ritual Process: Structure and Anti-Structure*. Chicago: Aldine.

Venkatesan, Soumhya (ed.) 2015. Debate: 'The concept of neoliberalism has become an obstacle to the anthropological understanding of the twenty-first century'. *Journal of the Royal Anthropological Institute* 21 (4): 911–23.

von Braun, Christina 2012. *Der Preis des Geldes: Eine Kulturgeschichte*. Berlin: Aufbau.

Weber, Max 1958 (1904–05). *The Protestant Ethic and the Spirit of Capitalism*. New York: Charles Scribner's Sons.

Welker, Marina, Damani J. Partridge and Rebecca Hardin 2011. Corporate lives: New perspectives on the social life of the corporate form: An introduction to Supplement 3. *Current Anthropology* 52 (S3): 3–16.

Yurchak, Alexei 2005. *Everything Was Forever, Until It Was No More*. Princeton, NJ: Princeton University Press.

Zaloom, Caitlin 2006. *Out of the Pits: Traders and Technology from Chicago to London*. Chicago: University of Chicago Press.

Zaloom, Caitlin 2009. How to read the future: The yield curve, affect, and financial prediction. *Public Culture* 21 (2): 245–68.

Zeitlyn, David 2012. Divinatory logics: Diagnoses and predictions mediating outcomes. *Current Anthropology* 53 (5): 525–46.

3 Inequality

Tom Neumark

Since the onset of the Great Recession, a concern for economic inequality has taken on a renewed urgency as scholars, activists and ordinary citizens seek to grapple with a world in which the gap between the rich and the poor, the stable and the precarious, the 1 per cent and the 99 per cent, appears to have grown larger and more entrenched. With this concern, a growing body of literature on inequality has emerged, with contributions from a range of disciplines, including history, archaeology, political science and economics. Because of the complexity of the phenomenon, a better understanding of how it is generated and experienced, as well as the ways in which it might be challenged or supported, will require the combined efforts of scholars possessing a diverse set of theoretical, substantive and methodological backgrounds. This chapter explores what economic anthropology might have to offer in this endeavour and sets out a potential research agenda for the sub-discipline.

Economic inequality refers to differences concerning the relationship between 'human beings and the human-produced world' of both material and immaterial things (Cliggett and Wilk 2007: 36), but, importantly, only those differences that can be measured and compared using a common standard (Humphrey 2012). This broad understanding of inequality allows for an extensive and diverse set of ideas about its shape and texture. That said, certain measurement criteria have become widely accepted and can usefully be employed to help sketch an outline of inequality's historical contours.

If we take one criterion, income inequality, we can observe that within the Anglo-Saxon countries it has formed a U-shaped curve over time: high at the beginning of the twentieth century, dipping in the middle, rising again from the 1970s (Piketty 2014). With regard to global income inequality, the situation is more complicated, although it is still possible to obtain a general idea of its shape. Particular countries, including India and China, have moved closer to the more affluent ones, while others, many of them in sub-Saharan Africa, are poorer than they were in the middle of the twentieth century (Deaton 2015: 234–35). In this way, specific regions seem to have grown apart, even if the vast population size and economic growth of China in particular means that global economic inequality as a whole might have fallen or remained steady (Deaton 2015: 262).[1]

This economic inequality, anthropologists have routinely argued, does not arise from the law-like forces that are commonly identified by neoclassical economists. Instead, it emerges out of specific constellations of social relationships and institutions. The research agenda that I set out will continue to feature this approach, and I begin the chapter by outlining it. However, I propose that an agenda will also involve enquiring into inequality as a moral phenomenon. This is to say that within specific social landscapes there are specific ideas about what is right or fair in relation to economic disparities. For instance, people have, and debate, ideas about the form these disparities should take, about how people should behave within them and about who owes what to whom. Moreover, this moral aspect should not be seen merely as a reflection upon inequality, but as an integral part of the way that it is shaped. Therefore, running through this chapter is an urge for scholars to investigate the ways in which social relationships and institutions, moral values and ethical practices shape the contours of economic inequality.

I argue that a research agenda for economic inequality may fruitfully examine the sociology and morality of income inequality through attention to the concept of surplus. Surplus is most commonly understood in the Marxian sense, where it refers to either the labour or the product of labour that is in excess of that which is required to sustain the producer. For Marx (1990 [1867]), this producer may be the slave, the serf and, in capitalism, the worker. In capitalist political economies, he argued, the surplus produced by the working class is appropriated by the capitalist class. The focus on surplus generated in capitalist production by Marx and those who followed him is important, but it diverts attention from another important question: how surplus may be distributed. In contrast, I suggest that anthropologists studying inequality may find it helpful to examine how surplus is produced, appropriated *and* distributed. I finish the chapter by suggesting that a further strategy for anthropologists interested in economic inequality would be to extend this focus on surplus to a consideration of historical and contemporary radical alternatives that may serve to help challenge inequality and the social relationships and moral values that underpin it.

The sociology of inequality

In the study of economic inequality, anthropology has conventionally joined other social sciences by setting itself apart from the discipline of economics, particularly the neoclassical school. Here, economics finds itself accused of treating inequality solely as a result of law-like forces. The textbook case for global economic inequality is a good example of this. It argues that owing to the law of supply and demand, higher-educated workers producing things with higher prices have been able to demand higher wages. With technological progress, particularly in information and communication technologies, there has been a further favouring of those more educated workers, leading to a growing income disparity both within and between countries (Atkinson 2015: 86). Economists, of course, consider such descriptions as a useful simplification rather than an actual representation of economic reality.

Despite this, their apparent usefulness has come under sustained attack, even from economists.

Branko Milanović, for instance, dismisses as '[n]aive "economism"' those attempts to explain inequality exclusively through the 'forces of supply and demand' (Milanovic 2016: 73). Others, notably Thomas Piketty (2014), have emphasised the importance of historical events, such as the world wars, in explaining economic inequality. Nevertheless, for anthropologists there still remain certain problematic assumptions in the work of these economists. For instance, Piketty takes for granted the concept of capital as well as the idea that rents accrue to it naturally (Ralph 2015), and thereby ignores much of the historical violence, such as colonialism and slavery, that allowed some countries' and people's capital to increase.

In contrast to this mainstream economic approach, anthropology has frequently emphasised social relationships, including the violent historical and political ones. This approach is particularly evident in the anthropological variant of the political-economic approach that has shaped the discipline's understanding of economic disparity. From the 1960s through the 1980s, political economy, particularly the Marxian version, held significant sway in economic anthropology. Then, many writers extended Marx's ideas, applying them to non-Western societies. While these studies all understood economic life as essentially constituted by relationships, for instance between classes, it was not until the work of Sidney Mintz (1985) and Eric Wolf (1982) that there was a recognition of the historical and global scale of these relationships. Wolf found inspiration in Immanuel Wallerstein's (1974) world-systems theory, which explored the exploitative relationship between core countries and peripheral ones. Global economic inequality, it was argued, was built into the global system. This heavily Marxian approach to inequality soon came under criticism itself, with some claiming that it required the anthropologist to adopt a set of beliefs and assumptions that did violence to those of their informants (Strathern 1988). While anthropology subsequently shifted away from its close adherence to Marxian ideas, a broad interest in political economy remained and has perhaps grown in recent years (e.g. Carrier and Kalb 2015).

The morality of inequality

It remains crucial for us to continue considering the social relationships and institutions that generate and sustain economic inequality. However, I argue that we should complement that consideration with attention to the moral domain. This would recognise that economic models, as well as actually existing economies, are saturated with moral ideas, values, attitudes and debates concerning how people should behave in their economic dealings with each other, what kind of person they could be, as well as about the public good, justice and who owes what to whom.

The observation that economic phenomena are intertwined with the moral domain is not new. Since Aristotle, and continuing through to the classical political economists, the study of economic life has always also been a moral enquiry. Adam Smith (1982 [1776]) famously thought that the greater public good would emerge out of everybody's self-interest, but he also saw this self-interest as balanced by sympathy for others (Smith 1984 [1759]), an argument that was generally ignored by economists in the twentieth century. However, it is crucial to note that both aspects of his argument refer to the moral domain.

For instance, while economists might be accused of treating the economy as an amoral sphere of exchange, their theories are based upon fundamental moral assumptions. This is most notable in their model of personhood, which elevates self-interest to an especially prominent position. Moreover, neoclassical economists have used this particular model of personhood to construct wider moral and political arguments. Friedrich von Hayek, for instance, wrote about the public good and the dangers posed when 'expert administrators' take over the responsibility of defining it, and he urged instead that we see the expression of self-interest by market actors as defining the common good (Hayek 2011: 378). So while the discipline of economics has, until recently, largely neglected the topic of inequality, this was not because it had no interest in issues such as poverty, but because it has its own understanding of the value of economic growth to the common good (Atkinson 2015: 14–15). Unfortunately, with the growing influence of economic thought this particular disciplinary construction of the moral nature of the free market got turned into an ahistorical universal.[2]

Anthropologists have sought to avoid understanding economic behaviour as produced through such restricted motivations and conceptions of personhood, and instead have considered them within their wider social and moral contexts (Parry and Bloch 1989). Particularly important has been a recognition of those social relationships that we may call political. For instance, it has been shown that certain economic subjectivities with restricted motivations may be produced within certain historically and politically constituted economic discourses. Most recently these have included the sorts of subjectivities that are produced through what have been called neoliberal economic policies. In addition, anthropologists have been involved in charting how people may resist the workings of powerful economic actors or collectivities by drawing on their own moral economic traditions. As E.P. Thompson (1971) showed with regard to the riots of urban weavers and artisans in nineteenth-century England, this might not necessarily reflect opposition to inequality per se, but to the absence of right moral behaviour within certain forms of inequality. Thompson, as well as the substantivists within anthropology (e.g. Bohannan and Dalton 1962: 4), pitted local, traditional, moral economies against markets that were either amoral or possessed an impoverished form of morality that was internal to them rather than arising from the values of the wider society.

As I have suggested, anthropologists today consider all economies as moral, even those economic models that obscure this morality behind their universal reasoning, mathematical formulae and statistical analyses (Bear 2015: 18). We therefore do not want to restrict our understanding of the moral to only certain economies, for instance of the marginalised who may or may not stand up against other power-ful economic regimes. However, we will want to retain the focus on inequality that is evident in the aforementioned works. People do not only inhabit different moral systems that include ideas about the shape and quality of social relationships that constitute inequality. In addition, they are differently positioned within social relationships and institutions that not only shape moral systems but also influence what or whose moral values are allowed to be heard. This is one place where the sociology and morality of inequality meet.

People regularly reflect on their economic position relative to others as well as the behaviours that they believe should be exhibited in such relationships. At the same time, people often envisage, dream about and try to bring into being better economic worlds, including new arrangements of social relationships. Yet these reflections, as well as these dreams, are shaped by existing moral ideas and sensi-bilities that inhabit certain relationships and institutions. Moreover, as I noted, this social landscape opens and closes spaces for differently positioned actors to have their moral reflections heard and subsequently reflected in, for instance, public policy. Therefore, while a variety of empirical phenomena including labour, tax and welfare, and their relation to economic inequality, might be debated in strongly moral terms, there remains inequality in the possibility for debate itself.

In the remainder of this chapter I explore a path that economic anthropologists may be able to follow in seeking to better understand this sociology and morality of inequality. What I have charted so far, then, should be seen as presenting one pos-sible framework that opens up questions around inequality. In other words, it is a toolkit that may be carried by anthropologists as they explore aspects of the path. In the next section, I present this path, exploring the way that it is orientated around the production and the handling of surplus.

States, markets and surplus

I have suggested that a research agenda for economic anthropologists interested in inequality will need to focus on the way different economic systems create and move surplus. As I mentioned, surplus can be described as that labour, or product of labour, which is above what is required to sustain the producer. This means, for instance, that a study of the creation and circulation of surplus could feasibly include a study of the way in which meat is produced and acquired through hunt-ing in hunter-gatherer societies; the way that slaves produce for slave-owners; the production of agricultural products by serfs and the demand for tribute in feudal societies; the way in which capitalists make profits from their workers' production or a rentier class acquires rents in capitalist societies.

While all these economic systems can be, and have often been, examined through attention to surplus, here I focus on the most important contemporary one – capitalism. Anthropologists have often viewed the market with suspicion, seeing it as eroding other forms of economic life. In addition, the market has regularly been equated with capitalism, even though markets are present in a range of economic systems. Nevertheless, capitalist systems and their variants, including those described as neoliberal, post-neoliberal and rentier, have gained a global, even hegemonic, status. Across the social sciences, these particular economic ideas and practices have been shown to have contributed to a sharpening and deepening of inequality. For instance, the deregulation of finance as part of neoliberal economic policies has made it possible for particular individuals to dramatically increase their wealth while pushing others into precarity, with low wages and a welfare system that often has become punitive. Even academia has not been able to escape neoliberalising processes that have led to situations where the production of research outputs relies upon an increasingly precariously employed workforce. It may be accurate to describe these sorts of situations, following John Maynard Keynes, as a form of rentier capitalism, where certain populations are increasing their wealth through the rents paid by others (Standing 2016).

For Marx, under capitalism surplus is produced by workers and appropriated by capitalists. As George DeMartino (2003) argues, however, this Marxian focus on the production and appropriation of surplus largely ignores its distribution. DeMartino suggests that we should consider economic justice in a broader sense, seeing its possibility not just in the production and appropriation of surplus, but also in its distribution. In the sections below, I outline each of these processes in more detail. While my ambitions in this chapter are not normative, I find the three economic processes helpful in pointing to where anthropologists might dedicate their efforts in thinking about the different ways in which economic inequality might be generated and sustained.

Obviously, these economic processes are constituted by specific social relationships between groups of people. The production, appropriation and distribution of surplus take place across a range of interacting domains, from the household to the community to the market. Anthropologists are well placed to explore these processes across these domains, particularly as they can draw on disciplinary work that has shown how social relationships and moralities considered to belong to one domain frequently operate in others. An example is the way in which kinship and its concomitant obligations doggedly endure in the realm of the market.

I think it particularly important for anthropologists to draw on their analysis of the way in which political communities, most significantly those that involve the state, play an essential role in surplus and economic inequality.[3] The state, James Holston (2007: 21) has argued, 'is an association [but] it is also an association of associations that establishes the rules of other associations and regulates their membership'. Seeing the state in this way allows us to examine the relationship between it and other domains, such as the household, the community and the market, particularly the ways that legislation and state policy set rules that shape inequality.

These rules are also related to moral visions that political communities have about what constitutes a good life for their citizens (Jiménez 2007: 15), including ideas about the distribution of economic resources. The visions themselves emerge from political processes and moral debates among a broad set of associations within and between states, including trade unions and other social movements, corporations and their shareholders as well as political parties. Some of these seek to serve the interests of economic elites and so are interested in protecting specific aspects of political equality, such as rights surrounding private property, rather than being interested in reducing economic inequality (McGill 2016: 65). However, other associations envision ways in which society might be remade in order to curb or reverse economic inequality. In all of these areas, people reflect upon what is just or fair and upon the sorts of obligations that should surround this production, appropriation and distribution of surplus.

Producing and appropriating

As I have said, the Marxian approach considers workers in capitalist societies as producing surplus through their labour, which is subsequently appropriated by the capitalist class. Anthropologists influenced by this approach have shown the processes through which people are brought into capitalist systems and required to produce a surplus for new entities, such as banks. Julia Elyachar (2005), for instance, has used David Harvey's (2003) concept of accumulation by dispossession to show the way in which NGOs and banks running microcredit programmes in Cairo dispossessed urban craftsmen of their market culture in order to bring these workers into the formal economy and generate economic growth.

A research agenda for economic anthropologists should continue to examine the increasing financialisation of the global South that those Cairo microcredit schemes illustrate, particularly as it seeks to incorporate the poorest people on the planet. Much of this financialisation has gained momentum through the late C.K. Prahalad's (2006) now popular idea of the entrepreneurial potential of those at the bottom of the pyramid. This idea itself tapped into existing arguments that the market can bring significant swathes of the global population out of poverty (de Soto 2000). Future anthropological research should examine the way in which these notions and programmes can generate new forms of inequality, for instance between those deemed to have entrepreneurial potential and those who lack it and are consequently relegated to the status of surplus population (Li 2010). This population is surplus in a sense different from the way that I have used the term: they are surplus because they are not even valued sufficiently to be exploited.

These processes of financialisation remain a vital area for anthropologists to explore, particularly because of the way in which they have become part of what has been called rentier capitalism. Stephen Gudeman (2015), for instance, has argued that increasingly abstract financial spheres are extracting rent from the spheres of the household and community. Others have shown how debt has changed over time and has increasingly become akin to a business deal that requires repayment regardless of any other moral obligations that might exist in society (Bear 2015; Graeber 2011; see also Mattioli this volume). In this way, surplus accrues to the owners of capital, and does so at the expense of the workers who produced it. In these studies of debt, anthropologists have incorporated the way in which debt, as a particular social relationship, is surrounded by moral ideas and debates.

Also central to the study of the production and appropriation of surplus is the corporation (see also Urban this volume). Anthropologists have criticised the corporation for its narrow pursuit of shareholder value, but this criticism applies most appropriately only to the Anglo-American corporate model. Such a blanket approach to corporations precludes a careful analysis of models that may recognise a broader array of stakeholders. More work could be done to analyse other corporate forms, both old and new, such as the Benefit Corporation movement in the US. In doing this, we will be able to examine the changing and competing ways in which the corporation is viewed as doing good (Rajak 2011).

However, we may also wish to analyse economic collectivities other than the corporation that members or adherents, or even anthropologists, believe are less associated with inequality. One example is workers' co-operatives, where surplus may be appropriated and distributed on behalf of the workers in ways that might be deemed fairer than dividends distributed to owners. Another example is the new forms of digital communities, for instance those that have emerged around bitcoin and the underlying blockchain technology. Advocates of these see, often in utopian ways, the lack of centralised authority as paving the way for a more equitable economic system. Yet here the anthropologists' critical attitude will, of course, keep them alert to the possibilities for new forms of surplus and inequitable distribution in those communities.

Finally, I suggest that economic anthropologists should also consider how the state appropriates surplus, whether from the existing stock of resources or borrowed from the future. It does this through taxation, debt cancellation, sovereign wealth funds and bonds, as well as new types of state money creation, most notably quantitative easing. We might study all these forms of appropriation, but I believe that we should carefully examine the topic of taxation. Tax has been the central way in which a surplus is appropriated by the state, and it has played a central role in the formation of the modern state and its subjects (Tilly 1993). Yet despite its importance and, as the popular saying goes, its certainty, anthropologists have paid little attention to taxation (but see Abelin 2012; Cantens 2018; Carrico 2013; Roitman 2007). This lack of disciplinary attention is especially noteworthy given that anthropologists concerned to reduce inequality frequently urge reforming the tax system.

Research on taxation should involve a variety of entities at different scales, including things like the mechanisms and social relationships through which the global elite and corporations escape tax regimes (Shaxson 2012). Corporations, which have taken on the legal status as persons, have been able to accumulate and control tremendous amounts of wealth, putting them in conflict with states as well as global institutions, a conflict in which corporations often seem to have the upper hand. Moreover, understanding the growing power of corporations may also involve exploring the role of other actors, such as accountants, who have played an integral part in the devising of strategies through which corporations and individuals can navigate through regimes of appropriation by taxation. Historians, economists and those in accounting studies have already recognised the historical role of accountancy and its tools, such as double-entry bookkeeping, in the development of capitalism. Anthropologists can build upon this knowledge to examine what accountancy means for the shape of capitalism and of the inequalities it produces in the contemporary era. Furthermore, we may want to explore the way in which accounting, in both its historical and contemporary forms, has been a moral as well as an economic technology (Quattrone 2004).

Distributing

We can now turn to the distribution of appropriated resources. Distribution includes various things, from market exchange to gifts to state welfare payments. For example, a capitalist may take profit and invest it in a company, exchange it for something in a market transaction or give it to another person, commonly a family member. Of particular significance here, however, is what is known as redistribution, a process through which resources are appropriated by a central authority and subsequently redistributed.

Redistribution can take many forms, from institutionalised charity to corporate social responsibility to state welfare. It also often involves the interaction of the private realm of charities and corporations and the public realm of the state. For instance, in many countries in sub-Saharan Africa welfare activities normally associated with the state have come to be operated by transnational charities (there called NGOs), even though these organisations often rely upon the tax receipts of wealthier states. Furthermore, charities as well as corporations increasingly are forming public–private partnerships with the state. The state is therefore not necessarily the only entity to be examined with regard to welfare. Yet it is perhaps the entity that is most commonly seen as holding significant potential to shape inequality. Indeed, important work in economic anthropology, such as that of Karl Polanyi (2001 [1944]) and Marcel Mauss (2002 [1925]), sees state welfare as a challenge to liberal models of the economy. For Polanyi it marked the re-embedding of the economy, while for Mauss it heralded a return to the logic of the archaic gift.

In contemporary anthropology, welfare has mostly been approached in terms of its relationship to neoliberal economic policies. Anthropologists have explored the way in which social relationships and institutions structure welfare, but also the way in which welfare is a highly moralised domain. For instance, Andrea Muehlebach (2012) has argued that neoliberal political economy in Italy involves an attempt in the welfare sector to create citizen-volunteer moral subjectivities that involve motivations beyond the narrow one of self-interest. Others have shown how welfare construes deserving recipients as those who are willing to take responsibility for their own and their families' well-being. These recipients are then expected to use the minimal welfare resources available to them to escape from the dependency they have upon the state or charity (see Fraser and Gordon 1994). In a related argument, anthropologists have argued that there has been a shift from ideas of solidarity and justice towards a more minimal humanitarian logic of charity that concentrates on the bare and biological, rather than the biographical, lives of people (Redfield 2005).

As the above description of anthropological studies of welfare might indicate, anthropologists have generally joined other scholars in condemning neoliberalism and its own brand of welfare. At certain times, this argument seems to come at the expense of one that is more ethnographically informed. As a result, some anthropologists have sought to temper this blanket denunciation (e.g. Ferguson 2010; Jean-Klein and Riles 2005). Stephen Collier (2011), for instance, has shown that in Russia older notions of what the state owes to its citizens endure even through processes of economic liberalisation. Neoliberalism, he argues, in both thought and practice, cannot automatically be denounced by anthropologists without careful study. In fact, our old language of a Polanyian double movement of social protection against the liberalisation of the market may not be appropriate if we find that social protection is an integral part of, rather than a reaction against, some forms of liberal economic thought. In other words, it can be that a liberal moral economy does not simply reflect the idea of the sovereign individual but can instead exhibit moral attitudes towards solidarity and social security that seek to reduce economic inequality. The crucial question is whether anthropologists approach these efforts as simply a moral fig leaf that covers social relationships of capitalist exploitation or, in contrast, as potentially progressive arrangements of social relationships.

In considering this question, I follow those who suggest that we need to pay more attention to our critical attitude (Fassin 2017; Latour 2004). In doing so, I suggest that research on the distribution of economic wealth should remain curious, but not naïve, about new forms of welfare that are emerging across the world. One such model is Universal Basic Income, an idea that has its origins in the eighteenth century and that is receiving support across the political spectrum. For some anthropologists, the proposals and experiments concerning new forms of welfare offer opportunities to explore a different form of social assistance that might contribute to a reduction in economic inequality (see Ferguson 2015). That form differs from conventional forms of welfare, which routinely make moral judgements by dividing populations into the deserving and the undeserving. It is also one that rejects the paternalism of conventional welfare, by stripping away the normal surveillance of grant recipients. Anthropologists have the opportunity to explore both the ideas and their politics, as James Ferguson (2015) has recently done, but also to use ethnographic-related methodologies to explore the associated lived realities

(Neumark 2017). What divergences and continuities, for instance, might there be in this welfare? How might it interact with the more conventional forms? In what ways might it be transforming what it means to be a citizen?

Challenging inequality: Alterity and intellectual resources

I have suggested that economic anthropologists may find it fruitful to explore the ways in which surplus is produced, appropriated and subsequently distributed. Exploring these processes may provide useful opportunities to better understand not only the generation and maintenance of inequality, but also the debates about its fairness and legitimacy that surround it. The findings produced by such research may help to contribute to efforts to challenge certain forms of economic inequality. In this section, I turn to a further strategy in which anthropologists may contribute to a challenge to inequality. This involves producing new intellectual resources by examining certain things that can unsettle assumptions concerning inequality and the systems that produce it (see also Englund 2011: 88).[4]

One place to search for new intellectual resources is the past. Indeed, mining the past has been a common strategy for those wishing to imagine alternatives to our current situation of inequality. Perhaps the most common approach has been to imagine inequality as arising from humanity's move from small-scale hunter-gathering to large-scale settled agriculture. With this approach, hope for a more equitable contemporary world seems to rely on dreams of a return to local, small-scale societies.[5] Recently, however, David Graeber and David Wengrow (2018) have argued that there is little evidence to justify this view of the past. They claim that the evidence shows that inequality and egalitarianism are social forms that do not necessarily characterise a particular society at one point in time, but instead can characterise the same society at different points in time, most notably during different seasons (Wengrow and Graeber 2015). Of course, the idea of a society being capable of shifting between different social forms was first pointed out over half a century ago by Edmund Leach (1964), who described the Kachin of Highland Burma as oscillating between structures and principles of hierarchy and egalitarianism. Taken together, these arguments point to the way in which we might imagine, or even recognise around us, more flexible, fluid, as well as plural, social and economic systems (see also Gibson-Graham 1996), including ones that may exhibit less inequality.

To generate new intellectual resources, anthropologists can also, of course, look to more contemporary phenomena. Social movements are a particularly fertile area. These may offer economic and political models that differ, sometimes radically, from dominant ones, which may help contribute to the building of more equitable economies. Historically, Latin America has exhibited striking levels of inequality (Scheper-Hughes 1993) and has proved to be particularly productive for examining radically different political, economic, cultural and even ontological alternatives to Western liberalism and capitalism. For instance, Arturo Escobar (2010) has argued that the MAS movement in Bolivia, which led to the election of Evo Morales, facilitated greater economic equality through redistribution, as well as allowing new economic and political ideas to be enshrined in the constitution in a way that displaced the singular pursuit of economic growth.

However, Escobar thinks that there is the potential for a more radical restructuring of society in the ideas and practices of indigenous social movements. These movements, he argues, have a relational ontology. This broadly means that people, environment, places and so on have to be understood not as prior to their relationships but as being constituted by them. Here, then, relationships are thought of not simply in the analytical sense familiar to anthropology, to which I have referred throughout this chapter, but in the sense that they exist in people's specific views about how the world is made up. This sort of worldview may challenge the possessive individualism (Macpherson 1962) that characterises forms of liberalism that, many argue, lead to and even encourage the self-interested pursuit of wealth. That challenge arises from the assertion that you are constituted by your relationships with others, which implies that you are obligated to them. Recognising those obligations may nurture economies that place greater emphasis on a more equitable distribution of wealth.

Social movements are not the only place to look for ideas that might contribute to a challenge to inequality, for such ideas may exist in the larger public sphere. One interesting example of this is Harri Englund's (2011) study of a Chichewa-language radio talk show in Malawi in which people share stories of exploitation and impoverishment. Englund argues that these stories express understandings of moral obligations and conceptions of equality that differ from the liberal political philosophies that inform discourses of human rights. Those understandings express how the aim of many Malawians is not to flatten hierarchical relationships and their differences, but to ensure that figures of authority fulfil their obligations towards their subordinates. This shows how particular forms of difference may be considered legitimate and that people can make claims within, rather than against, such disparities.

While an individualist conception of equality often tends to celebrate each person's capacity to be different (Robbins 1994), it also works to reduce existing inequalities in order to offer equal opportunities. But as I showed earlier, people often desire not that those disparities be extinguished, but that they work as they ought (see also Thompson 1971). In other words, it is not always inequality that people see as the problem, but the *quality* of inequality. In their consideration of the ways that people think about their relationships with others, anthropologists have the chance to see the strength of relations of inequality that may offend liberal sensibilities. Such an approach may provide fresh avenues for thinking about how injustices across the world are subject to moral debate in languages and aesthetics that differ to the dominant ones, such as human rights (Englund 2011). It might also offer us opportunities to enter into debates about our own obligations to tackle global poverty and inequality (Englund 2012).

The lesson here for a research agenda in economic anthropology is that any study of inequality must remain open-minded about how people think about and legitimate economic inequality. Furthermore, in looking for challenges to inequality we may be required to cast our net wide and attend to areas that might reveal alternatives to liberal ideas of equality, particularly those individualist ones that stress people's rights but that often offer them few ways to improve their material conditions. Moreover, we must also seek to bring together this fine-grained ethnographic analysis of local, moral ideas with an analysis of the broader social relationships and institutions within which they are situated.

Conclusion

Anthropology has already made a number of significant contributions to our understanding of economic inequality. This chapter has sketched ways in which we might build upon these contributions, particularly by bringing together the understanding that inequality is constituted by social relationships and institutions with the recognition that it is also steeped in moral understandings, attitudes and values. As I have argued, informants and their anthropologists alike regularly engage in debates about surplus, how it is produced and appropriated, about what is a fair distribution of it, about what they or others should do with it and about how things can or should change. Furthermore, these debates take place through political processes that shape institutions, legislation and policies, which people may adopt or challenge. I have suggested that examining how surplus is handled might be useful if we want to understand the way in which inequality is produced and sustained, and the sorts of moral debates that surround it; debates that may reflect moral and ontic bases radically different from our own. By better grasping what counts as justice for people in the production, appropriation and distribution of surplus, anthropologists may themselves be part of a wider conversation concerning economic inequality and its future.

NOTES

1 This relatively rosy picture of global disparities is perhaps on shaky ground. That is because it relies on the percentage of income increase in poor and rich countries rather than on the actual amount of increase (Wade, in Hickel 2017: 2211).

2 Advocacy of self-interest emerged in the eighteenth century, presented as a way of keeping other unruly passions in check (Hirschman 1977).

3 In this chapter I focus on the state, because it is largely within their states that people make their claims, even if it is to entities that have a global reach.

4 Regrettably, there is not enough space in this chapter to discuss the crucial issue of how those intellectual resources may be subsequently appropriated and distributed.

5 Equally, those who consider a much shorter time-scale look back to the Keynesian pact of the mid-twentieth century to generate hope for a less unequal economy.

References

Abelin, Mireille 2012. Entrenched in the BMW: Argentine elites and the terror of fiscal obligation. *Public Culture* 24 (2 67): 329–56.

Atkinson, Anthony B. 2015. *Inequality: What Can Be Done?* Cambridge, MA: Harvard University Press.

Bear, Laura 2015. *Navigating Austerity: Currents of Debt along a South Asian River.* Stanford: Stanford University Press.

Bohannan, Paul and George Dalton 1962. Introduction. In *Markets in Africa* (eds) P. Bohannan and G. Dalton, pp. 1–26. Evanston: Northwestern University Press.

Cantens, Thomas 2018. Of taxation, instability, fraud and calculation. In *Economy, Crime and Wrong in a Neoliberal Era* (ed.) James G. Carrier, pp. 116–39. Oxford: Berghahn Books.

Carrico, Kevin 2013. Towards an anthropology of taxation. *Anthropology News* 54 (5), 16–18.

Carrier, James G. and Don Kalb (eds) 2015. *Anthropologies of Class: Power, Practice, and Inequality.* Cambridge: Cambridge University Press.

Cliggett, Lisa and Richard R. Wilk 2007. *Economies and Cultures: Foundations of Economic Anthropology*, 2nd edition. Boulder, CO: Westview Press.

Collier, Stephen J. 2011. *Post-Soviet Social: Neoliberalism, Social Modernity, Biopolitics.* Princeton, NJ: Princeton University Press.

Deaton, Angus 2015. *The Great Escape: Health, Wealth, and the Origins of Inequality.* Princeton, NJ: Princeton University Press.

DeMartino, George 2003. Realizing class justice. *Rethinking Marxism* 15 (1): 1–31.

Elyachar, Julia 2005. *Markets of Dispossession: NGOs, Economic Development, and the State in Cairo.* Durham, NC: Duke University Press.

Englund, Harri 2011. *Human Rights and African Airwaves: Mediating Equality on the Chichewa Radio.* Bloomington: Indiana University Press.

Englund, Harri 2012. Poverty. In *A Companion to Moral Anthropology* (ed.) Didier Fassin, pp. 283–302. Hoboken: Wiley-Blackwell.

Escobar, Arturo 2010. Latin America at a crossroads. *Cultural Studies* 24 (1): 1–65.

Fassin, Didier 2017. The endurance of critique. *Anthropological Theory* 17 (1): 4–29.

Ferguson, James 2010. The uses of neoliberalism. *Antipode* 41 (S1): 166–84.

Ferguson, James 2015. *Give a Man a Fish: Reflections on the New Politics of Distribution.* Durham, NC: Duke University Press.

Fraser, Nancy and Linda Gordon 1994. A genealogy of dependency: Tracing a keyword of the U.S. welfare state. *Signs* 19 (2): 309–36.

Gibson-Graham, J.K. 1996. *The End of Capitalism (As We Knew It): A Feminist Critique of Political Economy.* Cambridge, MA: Blackwell.

Graeber, David 2011. *Debt: The First 5,000 Years.* Brooklyn: Melville House.

Graeber, David and David Wengrow 2018. How to change the course of human history. *Eurozine.* www.eurozine.com/change-course-human-history/ (accessed 6 April 2018)

Gudeman, Stephen 2015. Review article: Piketty and anthropology. *Anthropological Forum* 25 (1): 66–83.

Harvey, David 2003. *The New Imperialism.* New York: Oxford University Press.

Hayek, F.A. 2011. *The Constitution of Liberty* (ed.) Ronald Hamowy. Chicago: University of Chicago Press.

Hickel, Jason 2017. Is global inequality getting better or worse? A critique of the World Bank's convergence narrative. *Third World Quarterly* 38 (10): 2208–22.

Hirschman, Albert O. 1977. *The Passions and the Interests: Political Arguments for Capitalism before Its Triumph.* Princeton, NJ: Princeton University Press.

Holston, James 2007. *Insurgent Citizenship: Disjunctions of Democracy and Modernity in Brazil.* Princeton, NJ: Princeton University Press.

Humphrey, Caroline 2012. Inequality. In *A Companion to Moral Anthropology* (ed.) Didier Fassin, pp. 302–19. Hoboken: Wiley-Blackwell.

Jean-Klein, Iris and Annelise Riles 2005. Introducing discipline. *PoLAR* 28 (2): 173–202.

Jiménez, Alberto Corsin 2007. Introduction: Well-being's re-proportioning of social thought. In *Culture and Well-Being: Anthropological Approaches to Freedom and Political Ethics* (ed.) A.C. Jiménez, pp. 1–32. London: Pluto Press.

Latour, Bruno 2004. Why has critique run out of steam? From matters of fact to matters of concern. *Critical Inquiry* 30 (2): 225–48.

Leach, Edmund R. 1964. *Political Systems of Highland Burma: A Study of Kachin Social Structure.* London: The Athlone Press.

Li, Tania Murray 2010. To make live or let die? Rural dispossession and the protection of surplus populations. *Antipode* 41 (S1): 66–93.

McGill, Kenneth 2016. *Global Inequality: Anthropological Insights.* Toronto: University of Toronto Press.

Macpherson, C.B. 1962. *The Political Theory of Possessive Individualism: Hobbes to Locke.* Oxford: Oxford University Press.

Marx, Karl 1990 (1867). *Capital: Critique of Political Economy Vol. 1.* London: Penguin Classics.

Mauss, Marcel 2002 (1925). *The Gift: The Form and Reason for Exchange in Archaic Societies.* W.D. Halls, trans. London: Routledge.

Milanovic, Branko 2016. *Global Inequality: A New Approach for the Age of Globalization.* Cambridge, MA: Harvard University Press.

Mintz, Sidney W. 1985. *Sweetness and Power: The Place of Sugar in Modern History.* New York: Viking.

Muehlebach, Andrea 2012. *The Moral Neoliberal: Welfare and Citizenship in Italy.* Chicago: University of Chicago Press.

Neumark, Tom 2017. 'A good neighbour is not one that gives': Detachment, ethics and the relational self in Kenya. *Journal of the Royal Anthropological Institute* 23 (4): 748–64.

Parry, Jonathan and Maurice Bloch (eds) 1989. *Money and the Morality of Exchange.* Cambridge: Cambridge University Press.

Piketty, Thomas 2014. *Capital in the Twenty-First Century.* Arthur Goldhammer, trans. Cambridge, MA: Harvard University Press.

Polanyi, Karl 2001 (1944). *The Great Transformation: The Political and Economic Origins of Our Time.* Boston: Beacon Press.

Prahalad, C.K. 2006. *The Fortune at the Bottom of the Pyramid: Eradicating Poverty through Profits.* Upper Saddle River: Prentice Hall.

Quattrone, Paolo 2004. Accounting for God: Accounting and accountability practices in the Society of Jesus (Italy, XVI–XVII centuries). *Accounting, Organizations and Society* 29 (7): 647–83.

Rajak, Dinah 2011. *In Good Company: An Anatomy of Corporate Social Responsibility.* Stanford: Stanford University Press.

Ralph, Michael 2015. The concept of *capital. Hau* 5 (1): 501–08.

Redfield, Peter 2005. Doctors, borders, and life in crisis. *Cultural Anthropology* 20 (3): 328–61.

Robbins, Joel 1994. Equality as a value: Ideology in Dumont, Melanesia and the West. *Social Analysis* 36 (October): 21–70.

Roitman, Janet 2007. The right to tax: Economic citizenship in the Chad Basin. *Citizenship Studies* 11 (2): 187–209.

Scheper-Hughes, Nancy 1993. *Death Without Weeping: The Violence of Everyday Life in Brazil.* Berkeley: University of California Press.

Shaxson, Nicholas 2012. *Treasure Islands: Tax Havens and the Men who Stole the World.* London: Vintage.

Smith, Adam 1982 (1776). *An Inquiry into the Nature and Causes of the Wealth of Nations.* London: Penguin Classics.

Smith, Adam 1984 (1759). *The Theory of Moral Sentiments*. Indianapolis: Liberty Fund.

de Soto, Hernando 2000. *The Mystery of Capital*. Chatham House, London: NP.

Standing, Guy 2016. *The Corruption of Capitalism: Why Rentiers Thrive and Work Does Not Pay*. London: Biteback Publishing.

Strathern, Marilyn 1988. *The Gender of the Gift: Problems with Women and Problems with Society in Melanesia*. Berkeley: University of California Press.

Thompson, E.P. 1971. The moral economy of the English crowd in the eighteenth century. *Past & Present* 50: 76–136.

Tilly, Charles 1993. *Coercion, Capital and European States, AD 990–1990*. Cambridge, MA: Wiley-Blackwell.

Wallerstein, Immanuel 1974. *The Modern World-System*. New York: Academic Press.

Wengrow, David and David Graeber 2015. Farewell to the 'childhood of man': ritual, seasonality, and the origins of inequality. *Journal of the Royal Anthropological Institute* 21 (3): 597–619.

Wolf, Eric R. 1982. *Europe and the People Without History*. Berkeley: University of California Press.

4   Debt, financialisation and politics

Fabio Mattioli

As a form of delayed reciprocity that allocates wealth, resources and value between the present and the future, debt and credit have fascinated anthropologists since the emergence of the discipline in its modern form. Scholars such as Boas, Malinowski and Mauss spent considerable energy trying to decode and explain the obligation to reciprocate transfers among non-Western populations, where debt and credit were crucial for binding social groups together. This produced refined analyses of non-monetary gift economies that explain the delay between the gift and its reciprocation in terms of cultural and social mechanisms. Often, these early discussions highlighted the moral meaning of exchanges that, on their surface, appeared incompatible with Western, self-interested economic rationality.

Over time, however, the technologies, modalities and forms of debt in the societies that anthropologists have studied changed considerably. Instead of ritual exchanges of necklaces, researchers found people entangled with mortgages, credit-card debt and economic crises that stemmed from debts accrued by distant entities such as corporations and states. By and large, after the Second World War debt was not a direct relation between people in the way that it had been. Instead, it was quantified in national currencies and followed the ebb and flow of ever-expanding financial products and markets, what scholars understood as a general process of financialisation of the economy.

These changes call for a different kind of anthropological enquiry, better suited to explaining the increased complexity of debt. In the first part of this chapter, I trace the evolution of anthropological approaches to debt and credit. Focused on issues of exchange between individuals, as I noted, early anthropological studies of debt explored the moral norms that regulated reciprocal and delayed transactions, offering a framework that remained influential in later studies of finance. As this part shows, morality constituted a crucial category through which anthropologists understood debt, among both financial elites and ordinary people, contributing to a copious literature on what came to be called the 'financialisation of the everyday' that included both a cultural and a political-economic perspective.

The second part of this chapter develops a research agenda that seeks to overcome that 'everyday' to tackle directly the complexity of financialised debt. Rather than focusing on the moral negotiations deployed by people and communities in their encounters with debt, I suggest that anthropologists should study the political dimensions of debt. Financialised debt connects different actors and organisations who often utilise multiple forms and means of exchange, in social formations that come to modify their political orientation both locally and internationally. To explore this complexity, the chapter identifies three angles of enquiry: examining conjunctures and disjunctures across different layers of financial debt, exploring the multiple forms taken by financial debt transactions, and retracing the struggles over the management of financial debt.

Considering the work of ethnographers together with that of other social scientists, the chapter encourages us to engage in interdisciplinary, collaborative studies that examine the dynamics of debt and credit. Anthropologists who embrace this multi-scale and interdisciplinary approach, instead of focusing on the morality of everyday debt, can produce useful and influential work. In the current, confused political conjuncture, policy-makers and the public are particularly receptive to anthropological insights, which can help the discipline to recover its practical, public role.

Debt and *homo moralis*

Even before the invention of modern fiat money, the anthropological archive detailed multiple forms of exchange that allocated wealth, resources and value over time, what we would call credit and debt. Delayed exchanges, reciprocities and other economic relations figured as essential axes for understanding non-Western societies in the work of anthropologists such as Marshall Sahlins (1972), Bronislaw Malinowski (1922) and Marcel Mauss (1990 [1925]), who understood debt as an expression of face-to-face and enduring social relationships.

Malinowski's famous *Argonauts of the Western Pacific* is one of these influential early explorations of credit and debt relations. In their sparsely populated archipelago in what is now Papua New Guinea, people of the Trobriand Islands travelled from island to island to give armbands and necklaces made of cowries and beads to members of other communities. Exchanged in ceremonies known as *kula*, these gifts would not be reciprocated immediately. Instead, indebted partners would wait to repay their debt until they could find an item of equal or greater prestige than what they had received. The delay in reciprocating gifts, which is to say the duration of the debt relation, added an historical depth to the exchange that enhanced the value of objects that moved in every transaction.

The theme of delayed reciprocity was subsequently examined by Mauss, who analysed gifts as the primary vehicle for understanding debt and credit relations. For him, gifts, debts and other exchanges involving delayed reciprocity were motivated by a combination of self-interest and cultural value. As Gustav Peebles (2010: 278) stressed, this approach gave anthropologists a language to articulate how 'the movement of economic resources through time and space via the mechanism of credit/debt cannot be merely reduced to "economic rationality" or "self-maximization". Anthropologists consistently seek out the flow of credit/debt in modalities outside the standard market for such instruments.' In other words, Mauss's work inspired anthropologists to formulate explanations of exchange, credit and debt that highlight the interplay between economic forces and morality, an approach that understands credit and debt as productive (see Roitman 2005).

Maussian insights have been widely applied in anthropology. Scholars noted that debt repayments are often framed in moral terms. This includes, for instance, the common assumption that 'one has to pay one's own debt', the leitmotiv of David Graeber's (2011) description of the historical origins of debt. Other historically salient debates include the moral distinction between legitimate and odious debt, which took place in Salamanca in the fourteenth century (Wennerlind 2003) and which was resurrected in the context of decolonisation (Bonizzi 2013; Cox 2014). These moral debates about debt could be very technical, as in arguments about mortgages and interest in Islamic finance (Pitluck 2009). However, they also implied a certain dissonance between discussion and praxis. Bill Maurer (2006), for instance, found that Islamic bankers present their mortgage lending as moral because it allows them to constitute an alternative economic domain not focused on interest. In practice, however, those who produce alternative forms of credit and debt proceed tentatively, often feeding off lending practices indistinguishable from or dependent on standard finance.

Other anthropologists, however, understood the morality of debt and credit as directly linked to the organisation of social ties. Greg Yudin and Ivan Pavlyutkin (2015), in their study of debts contracted in grocery stores in a small town in Russia, argue that debt constitutes a moral space in which local communities face their own internal tensions and try to face the larger economic issues that affect their livelihood (see also Herzfeld 2009). Conversely, other scholars suggest that debt and credit relations strengthen or (re)generate ties between the worlds of the living and the dead (Chu 2010; Kwon 2007; Schuster 2016; Shipton 2009).

From debt to financialisation

The exponential growth of financial markets and their increased influence in society, a process generally called financialisation (Epstein 2005; Krippner 2005), has radically transformed debt relations. Today, we deal with debts that are often connected to larger financial dynamics. We routinely pay for things with credit cards and contract loans to finance our consumer purchases, educations and homes. The social life of those debts, however, is not restricted to borrowers and lenders. Instead, loans travel far, often being repackaged into new products and sold to distant investors.

Even if we do not contract loans, financial debt and credit find other ways to become part of our lives. For one thing, even the most routine financial transactions commonly have a lending component. More broadly, the companies we work for, the cities we live in, the states whose citizens we are – each of these owns and issues debt, whose value and interest rates directly affect our livelihoods.

My point is that contemporary debt is increasingly complex, protean and connected with financial processes. It is not constituted by sequences of delayed exchanges between people of the sort that interested Mauss and his contemporaries. Instead, financial debt generally has many owners and is mediated by layers of institutions such as banks, lending agencies, even national bureaucracies. Moving through these different spaces transforms debt and its attributes. Sometimes, for instance, monetary debt can turn into non-monetary obligations (Mattioli 2018; Truitt 2018). Also, financial debt can be transformed into a capital asset, parcelled out and sold on financial markets, ultimately creating additional wealth for some and undesirable effects for others. In other words, the speed, connections and space through which financial debt moves cannot be understood by focusing on its moral dimension alone.

The old disciplinary approach to debt, then, is no longer adequate, and anthropologists have been slow to recognise this. Until now, those who explored the increasing complexity of financial debt have tended to focus on the meaning and impact of finance on specific, localised communities, the 'financialisation of the everyday' that I mentioned previously (e.g. Langley 2008; Martin 2002). Generally, these approaches follow two parallel paths. Influenced by the work of Michel Callon (1998; see also Knorr Cetina and Preda 2012; MacKenzie 2008), some scholars suggest that the economy, and especially debt, is shaped by knowledge accumulated by social actors. Economic ideas about debt do more than allow individuals to negotiate locally the economic forces that originate outside of their community, as argued by studies on the morality of debt. Rather, scholars such as Caitlin Zaloom (2006) contend that entire financial markets are shaped by processes of human and non-human valuation (see Stein, this volume). Together with their material and moral infrastructures, which can range from credit scores to bodily experiences, economic and moral ideas about debt and credit become 'market devices' (Muniesa 2014; see also Çalişkan and Callon 2009) that generate networks of distributed economic agency that go beyond local communities.

Anthropologists who embraced these perspectives have been particularly effective in understanding the hidden social meanings that lend credence to economic ideas such as the efficient-market hypothesis (Polillo 2018) and theories about shareholder value (Ho 2009). In fact, as William O'Barr and John Conley (1992) and, more recently, Kimberly Chong and David Tuckett (2014), have pointed out, economic actions such as trading, contracting and evaluating financial debt routinely have an affective dimension, especially when those involved are faced with the volatility and uncertainty of financial markets (see also Pixley 2004).

While scholars who focus on valuation provide insights into the lives of those who manipulate and create financial debt and credit, their analyses often relegate broader issues of power and inequality to the background. Especially in the aftermath of the financial crisis of 2008, however, it has become increasingly clear that it is impossible to understand financial debt without considering its capacity to enhance the forms of precariousness embedded in advanced capitalism. In dialogue with critical political economists such as David Harvey (2003), Giovanni Arrighi (1996) and Costas Lapavitsas (2013), a second group of anthropologists has focused on the impact of financial complexity and debt on vulnerable communities. Ana Flavia Badue and Florbela Ribeiro (2018), for instance, find that devices of credit inclusion such as microcredit and cash-transfer programmes contribute to the marginalisation of their targeted populations (see also Ferguson 2015). Others stress that replacing direct investment and welfare provision with entrepreneurship programmes supported by financial credit or investments schemes (Erikson 2015; Kehr 2018) accentuates the dependency of the marginalised, ill and disabled, who become exposed to new, privatised and often unpredictable forms of care (Han 2012).

Such effects of financial debt are not limited to developing countries. Working-class communities in affluent societies have experienced a gradual withdrawal of affordable financial services, including affordable credit (Williams 2004). In urban areas this spreading financial desert often precedes or occurs in parallel with gentrification, and aspiring middle-class citizens buy into weakly regulated debt products such as mortgages. While these products may stimulate real estate developments, they can turn into financial traps for those who sought to join the middle class but who find that their stagnant salaries cannot keep up with rising interest rates (Halawa 2015; Martin 2002; Palomera 2014; Stout 2016).

Beyond the financialisation of the everyday

Taken together, these two approaches show that contemporary debt is embedded in a series of moral relations that allow communities located at the top and the bottom of the global financial pyramid to negotiate their everyday encounters with finance. Indeed, as a group of scholars recently noted (Bear et al. 2015), these perspectives contain a portrait of financialisation as an open-ended domain imbued with social ferment. Despite their usefulness in portraying the relations that tie together communities and financial debt, however, analyses that focus on the everyday aspect of financialisation remain limited. All too often, ethnographic descriptions of the local usages and meanings of debt relations are unable to encompass the interconnectedness of financialised debt.

Partly, this reflects an inherent limitation of anthropological approaches. How can a discipline based on long-term participant observation encompass the scope and ramifications of financialised debt? It takes a long time to build relationships in the field, especially when money and debt are important topics. Equally, the places where anthropologists observe the dynamics of financialisation are embedded in cultural and historical trajectories that expand over considerable stretches of space and time. Even multi-sited field work cannot be expected to follow each step of financial debt circuits, so that researchers often are forced to interpolate many of the links that arise from financial transactions.

I think that we can mitigate the discipline's methodological limitations with a twofold strategy. Firstly, we can engage in collaborative, interdisciplinary projects, taking seriously the work of political economists, sociologists and others to situate and expand the representational value of the experiences that we collect and record. This requires engagement with different, quantitative methodologies and approaches, which can be best achieved by exploring these fields beginning in the early phases of graduate-level training, which is often difficult in anthropological programmes in the US and Western Europe. Secondly, I suggest that anthropologists can better capture the specific nature of financialised debt by focusing not on a single community, but on political spaces that shape the forms, effects and directions of debt relations. Specifically, I identify three articulations of the financial nexus of debt and politics: the connection of different layers of debt as a form of governance; the plurality of debts as new forms of dependency; the management of debt as a space for political struggle within state and super-state structures.

Layers of debt

Financial debt is protean and expansive, and very few spheres of life seem to be untouched by various forms of financial debt. As I noted already, individuals and households can utilise debt to purchase consumer goods, finance their education, start businesses or pay for their healthcare. Different debt products, such as credit cards, mortgages, consumer credit lines, car or business loans, pay-day loans and even investments in sovereign or private debt are common across developed and developing countries.

Much more than in other periods in history, financial debt is constitutive of our realities even when we are not directly involved in it. The things that we purchase are the result of financial investments, often financed by debt and transformed into financial assets. The states we rely on for social services finance their operations by contracting debt based on existing and future revenues (Ashton 2011). The companies that we rely on for our pay function thanks to rolling debt cycles. These different kinds of financial debt, however, are not independent of each other. Instead, they are tied together by financial infrastructures that tend to connect household, company and national debt.

What are the social implications of the increasing connections between different layers of debt? Some have taken up this challenge by understanding the expansion of financial debt as a process that integrates different domains of life into a single structure of governance. Following a Foucauldian approach particularly popular among scholars of finance (see Cooper 2011; Langley 2008), Melissa García-Lamarca and Maria Kaika (2016: 313) suggest that debt, and specifically the mortgage, is 'a biotechnology: a technology of power over life that forges an intimate relationship between global financial markets, everyday life and human labour'. In this perspective, the multiple scales of financial debt turn the social reproduction of social actors, together with their everyday and community life, into cogwheels in the machinery that can produce global financial bubbles.

Thinking about debt as a biotechnology highlights the disciplining power of finance, which stems from its capacity to connect very intimate spaces with very distant ones. In García-Lamarca and Kaika's example, Spanish citizens who signed mortgage contracts found themselves changing their personal behaviour, actively rooting for the success of real estate speculations because their livelihood was now dependent on the vagaries of financial markets. Biopower meant that mortgages could turn into a punitive technology that, once the bubble burst, affected not only people's finances but also their health and their relations within their community.

If it makes sense to think of financial debt as a disciplining, pathologising force (Núñez 2017), it should not be assumed that the resulting form of governance is necessarily a coherent one. The very fact of being enmeshed with multiple domains of social lives and actors that operate at different social levels means that a change in one layer of debt can produce unexpected consequences across the social system. In a later piece, García-Lamarca (2017) emphasises how, in the aftermath of the global financial crisis, a change in the global availability of credit generated a cascade of political protests and insurgent housing practices rather than simply docile, disciplined bodies.

This suggests that it might be worthwhile to develop a different approach to the expansive and sprawling characteristic of financial debt. That sprawl connects different domains of life and social institutions, which means increasing the number of intermediaries and the possibilities of friction and misunderstanding. This is demonstrated by Laura Bear (2015) in her book on austerity in India and its effects on activities on the Hooghly River. Trying to reduce public debt through austerity implied co-ordination between the central bank, government budget officials and local administrations, all forced to obey short-term fiscal imperatives even if they created increasingly dangerous and precarious working conditions. Precisely because they are increasingly embedded in layers of financial debt, however, those who work on the river find spaces to rework their masculine identities and their labour practices to reclaim a place in the financialised state.

Seen from this angle, the proliferation of debt across multiple social domains generates processes of dispossession but unleashes also other social forces that are worth considering ethnographically. In fact, these sites of struggle can allow ethnographers to understand the intrinsic motions of financialisation through the eyes of those who connect (or not) the various moving pieces that compose financial transactions. In other words, these approaches understand the complexity of financial debt as a site of contradictions rather than as an ineluctable logic that disciplines local communities or is negotiated by them.

Focusing on the contradictions of financial debt allows researchers to investigate what makes credit booms sustainable or fragile, an issue that animates Deborah James's (2015) work on financialisation in South Africa. Focused on indicators, fundamentals and other numeric measures, economists often are obsessed with trying to forecast the stability or sustainability of credit growth. But what are the social realities that make a process of credit expansion solid or fragile? As James illustrates, a fragile credit expansion can be supplemented by a surprising social density, which can help maintain a credit bubble. From its inception, South African credit expansion was seen as a means to develop a Black, post-apartheid middle class. However, that expansion quickly turned into an unlikely social glue that co-existed with the social divisions and inequalities of the country. Of course, the expansion of credit did not prevent conflicts between lenders and creditors. Instead, it proliferated the possibility of mutual exploitation, which, paradoxically, offset the immediate risk of economic collapse.

These are only some of the possible ways of understanding how different layers of debt are connected. By taking different approaches and focusing on different modes of articulation between social groups and economic strata, the work described here identifies potential sites for further research on the simultaneous actions of, and reactions to, debt at different levels of the social system.

Debt, financial pluralism and dependence

Among social scientists there is a tendency to analyse the proliferation of financial debt as a uniform, global process (see, e.g., Aalbers 2016). On a macroscopic level this sort of analysis is certainly reasonable. Financial debt trickles through various social institutions and embeds them in a web of financial limitations. There are, however, good reasons to doubt that these financial configurations follow homogeneous patterns or generate uniform social consequences.

A first opportunity to pay more attention to the plurality of financial debt is presented by the proliferation of debt products. Credit-card debt, loans, mortgages and sovereign debt present very different relations between creditors and debtors, often shaped by who owes the debt, where they are and how much they owe. For instance, as became clear in the aftermath of the global financial crisis, debt is more likely to be forgiven to banks than to individual debtors, at least in Western countries. Even more interestingly, financial debt often shifts form as it moves across different social domains, institutions and social layers. Contemporary finance operates across systems of payments that integrate formal and monetary transactions with informal, non-monetary ones. In other words, the heterogeneity of debt shows that the coherence of global finance cannot be taken for granted and should, instead, be approached as a research problem.

Excess liquidity is an excellent starting point to dissect ethnographically the construction of the global financial system, as critical theories of financialisation place excess liquidity at its heart. Liquidity is money or something that can be turned into money quickly, such as shares listed on stock exchanges, and all economies need liquidity if they are to operate. Excess liquidity occurs when those with wealth are not attracted by productive investments, but instead prefer to keep their wealth in liquid form. When unusually large amounts of wealth are held this way, that excess liquidity tends to lead to the proliferation of financial speculation (Aalbers 2016; Harvey 2007).

Accounts that focus on peripheral spaces, however, call this view into question. At the periphery, in fact, credit seems to expand even in the absence of cash and its equivalents, often through in-kind, non-monetary exchanges. In some cases barter exchanges supplement the volatility of monetary transactions (D'Avella 2014; Rogers 2005). In others, in-kind payments expand financial networks. For example, international loans contracted by the Macedonian government generated chains of in-kind payments as companies owned by oligarchs paid contractors with goods they did not want rather than with money, effectively forcing those contractors to provide monetary credit to the regime (Mattioli 2018). Regardless of their rationale, these very different economic, material and social debt relations suggest that a rising level of liquidity, rather than being a universal characteristic of financialisation, is in fact something that needs to be treated as problematic in terms of what it is, what brings it about and what its relationship with financialisation is (Pitluck 2013).

Ethnographers are well placed to explore the emergence and expansion of liquidity, as they can produce analyses of financial debt transactions that also reflect on the broader social relations that frame debt. For instance, ethnographic accounts such as Bear's study of the Hooghly River, described above, identify the proliferation of relations of dependency as a way in which financial pluralism is captured by an architecture of liquidity. Studies of microcredit in poorer countries confirm this intuition (see Kar 2017). Caroline Schuster (2015), for instance, suggests that international lending organisations target disempowered women rather than men precisely because of their presumed ability to draw on dependencies within local communities. Loans, in other words, in practice are issued against social collateral, turning what formally is a contract with an individual borrower into a collective obligation to repay. This financial design obliges women to turn their social networks into liquid resources from which they can extract money for their debt repayments. While for some women this conjuncture represents an opportunity to gain economic or social power (see Radhakrishnan 2018), most women experience the promise of microcredit schemes as a new form of dependency. Built on gender divisions, microcredit promotes liquidity by forcing women to transform personal favours into credit-card debt or cash-transfer allowances into collateral for gendered gifts (Badue and Ribeiro 2018).

The question of dependency and its relation to financial debt is attracting increasing interest among anthropologists. Partly this is because debt can easily reinforce pre-existing social divisions, including gender disparities (see also Cooper 2017). In domains such as the workplace, however, financial debt does not simply follow existing inequalities, but fills the gap between people's daily lives and emerging economic regimes. In fact, the development of new technologies and the constant relocation of production transform debt into a source of supplemental income for workers, or even a means of production to engage in the new precarious economy (Fleming 2017; Sandy 2009). But if work is increasingly generating dependency and debt rather than income and autonomy, it will likely shape new social dynamics and sensibilities not articulated around forms of individual autonomy. Addressing these questions will help unravel how financial inclusion shapes the identities and relations of target groups, and especially of those parts of society that are increasingly penalised by precarious work regimes. In addition, ethnographic research into new forms of debt dependency in the workplace has the potential to capture emerging social compounds where belonging might become conceived as more desirable than individual rights and self-affirmation (see Penfield 2017; see also Neumark this volume).

States, super-states and debt

The complexity of financial debt, which involves layers of institutions and multiple means of payments, cannot be adequately analysed without taking into account the political realm. Of course, political questions have been well represented in anthropological studies of debt since the work of Malinowski, especially with regards to social cohesion, stratification and inequality. The case of financial debt, however, shows a different engagement between politics and finance. The immateriality of financial debt, the speed of financial transactions and the proliferation of financial products rest upon myriad regulations and political decisions that build the infrastructure for the transmission and payment of debt. Because financial debt is an immaterial process that is deeply enmeshed in most of our lives, a few computer keystrokes can provide a small circle of people with an enormous power over countless lives. Unsurprisingly, financial debt generates a level of interdependence between politics and finance that was neither possible nor necessary with other, less abstract forms of debt, which could be dealt with directly through personal relationships.

This fact is often acknowledged politically, with calls to separate Wall Street and Main Street. However, as Pitluck et al. (2018) argue, there are few models that directly comprehend the interdependence of formal politics and financial debt. To address this lack, ethnographers should dedicate more attention to the different layers of formal politics, including geopolitics. National debt crises show that, if global finance is inundating the globe with cash, its waves are irregular and depend on specific political conjunctures. After all, at the height of the Greek debt crisis the negotiations and bailout packages were never just technical solutions. Rather, they came with political conditions that reaffirmed the dominance of German and French capital over that of other European states.

Some of the work done on the sociality of elites and their expertise describes the work of financial actors in central banks and in what can be called super-states, international organisations such as the International Monetary Fund and the

World Bank (Holmes 2013), but there are more actors that deal with debt at the geopolitical level. Diplomatic circles, divisions of finance ministries that deal with debt negotiations, banks, lobbyists, investment funds, rating agencies – all have played a role in dealing with the Greek debt crisis and similar situations. In fact, despite earlier portraits that understood them as dull and disciplining, bureaucracies host a variety of political struggles (Graeber 2015) that would be a gold mine of data for ethnographers interested in the social trajectory of important policies, including taxation, competition, healthcare and social security (Wigger 2012).

Focusing on the revolving door between banks and the public service (Kalaitzake 2017; Tsingou 2015) also offers a valuable perspective on the management of financial debt and its relation to neoliberalism. In fact, while neoliberalism and financialisation are often closely related, there is no theoretical necessity for this. Financial debt, for instance, was crucial to colonial and mercantilists forms of capitalism. Equally, recent work suggests that global financial debt can be mobilised to promote political goals that are not liberal or neoliberal. In my own work I observed how neoliberal EU interests colluded with a Macedonian autocratic regime around international loans (Mattioli 2018). Despite their neoliberal origin, these financial resources also were important for the rise of autocratic, centralised security states in other countries in Eastern Europe, including Hungary (Johnson and Barnes 2015), Russia (Dawisha 2015) and Georgia (Khalvashi 2015).

There are, however, other areas where researchers could explore the relationship between financialisation and neoliberalism. Lena Rethel (2018) argues that the creation of neoliberal capital markets in developing countries such as Malaysia can be part of efforts by national elites to use debt exchange in order to produce sovereignty. Equally, research that explores financial markets as sites of struggle could discover an empowering and progressive potential embedded in at least some financial debt relations. Geoff Mann (2017) and Hannah Appel (2014), for example, suggest that financial debt markets can be used to further autonomous and emancipatory aims, by funding independence movements in Quebec or by developing alternative banking systems in California. Ethnographic projects that move in this direction could provide a clearer picture of how progressive forces interact with the multiple scales and forms of financial debt.

A final domain where the relation between financial debt and politics is particularly important, and yet overlooked, is taxation. Scholars have generally discussed taxation as an instrument whereby states impose norms of valuation and control that call into question what it means to fulfil one's civic responsibilities (Björklund Larsen 2015, 2017; Boll 2014; Ries 1999; Roitman 2005). However, taxation can be analysed as well in terms of financialisation. As one of the few tools still available to states that seek to redistribute income, taxes are at the core of political struggles connected to the accumulation and management of debt. Typically, multinational corporations and their allies promote tax cuts with the promise of growth and the threat of relocating off-shore (Fernandez and Wigger 2016; Maurer 2005). As a result, states commonly compete with each other to attract international capital through policies or initiatives like low-tax special economic zones (Sampat 2010). These and other concessions to capital contribute to the loss of state revenue, obliging governments to transform anticipated future tax income into a capital asset by promising to use it to repay the new debt that states incur to meet their present expenses (Brash 2011; Weber 2010).

In this context, the most productive ethnography may well be that which analyses the fights that are waged to cut or implement specific taxation targets. Politicians seeking to maintain or increase tax revenue are often confronted with a mass of research that decries the perverse effect of taxation. In the face of this, those politicians often struggle to identify allies who will help them to formulate and implement tax systems that will fund important state activities and services. Anthropological studies of debt and taxation can be important here, not only by identifying who would be willing to pay taxes under what circumstances, but also by addressing the longer-term social implications that taxation generates for people's collective identity and solidarity.

Training and collaboration in the anthropology of debt

Identifying specific sites where financial debt interacts with formal politics can be important for increasing anthropological knowledge of contemporary economies and enhancing the role of anthropology in public debate. Yet nothing of that is likely to happen unless anthropologists embrace different methodological perspectives. Let me relate some of my own experiences to show what I mean by this.

In some of my most recent interviews with professionals who manage national debt in the Balkans, I found myself conversing about economic indicators, their comparative performance over time and the impact of various interest and tax rates on multiple forms of liquidity. The problem was that most of my graduate training was focused on rather classical approaches in anthropology and on major debates in the discipline and in the social sciences generally. This training allowed me to pursue a career as an academic anthropologist, but it did not prepare me to deal with the issues that those economists and professionals were talking about.

Likewise, when I was doing field work in Macedonia I observed odd in-kind exchanges, whereby people said that they had to accept payment in goods they did not want, rather than money. While this allowed me to grasp significant aspects of the dynamics of authoritarian politics in the country, later conversations with other experts in the field raised an important question: how representative were they of broader economic transformations taking place in the Balkans? To what extent was forced credit in Macedonia, produced by in-kind exchanges, an indicator of authoritarianism in neighbouring countries?

Trying to answer this question and trying to engage adequately with participants in my research required expertise in a discipline that I had seen from afar but never approached in depth. In other words, I had to proceed in the dark, learning the language and approach of political economy as I went. Because I did not have the support of peers who were engaged in cognate work in neighbouring countries, I was ill-equipped to argue the relevance of the Macedonian case. When I combed through quantitative data and reports produced by countless agencies, banks and international organisations I remained at the mercy of their methodology, which in such small countries is often piecemeal.

What this experience taught me is that ethnographers who want to understand the dynamics of financial debt beyond their moral impact on a local community need to be familiar with the tricks of political-economic analysis before heading to the field. While it is unlikely that post-graduate training would provide anthropologists with enough economic knowledge to understand the entire complexity of financial debt, they need to know enough to be able to contextualise what they observe in the field so that they can identify potential research partners and participants. The complexity of financial debt makes even the best single-authored monograph look like a lone leaf in a forest. Conversing in terms of quantitative political-economic data can help anthropologists to understand where each leaf is situated and so recognise the limitations of their case studies. Much better, however, would be combining ethnographic and quantitative analysis in interdisciplinary efforts.

The social impact of the anthropology of debt

In its immediate aftermath, the global financial crisis seemed to have unleashed progressive economic and political changes. The global financial system and its sprawling debt products appeared be on the verge of collapse. A powerful wave of protests in Europe, North America and North Africa appeared to usher in a new awakening for progressive politics. Unfortunately, these hopes were not realised. Ten years after the crisis, the global financial system has returned to its old functioning and continues to proliferate financial debt and inequality. Progressive movements have stalled or evolved into reactionary ones. Even the minimal social and individual rights achieved by liberal democracies are increasingly under siege.

How did such a hopeful momentum for change turn into our depressing post-crisis reality? This chapter suggests that studying the political logic of financial debt allows us to begin to make sense of many of the processes that have reconstituted the fabric of our societies since the onset of the financial crisis and even before. Specifically, I described the contributions of three emerging domains of enquiry that show how debt operates as an interconnected system of governance, as a multifaceted space for dependency and as a site of struggle inside national and super-state structures.

Taken together, these approaches use moments of political struggle to reconstruct the complexity of financialisation. Despite their different conceptual frameworks, the three emerging fields of enquiry that I have described recover long-standing intuitions that permeated anthropological studies of debt since the work of Malinowski, Mauss and Boas, for whom debt constituted a generative and relational process that intertwined disparate actors. Such political ramifications remained present in subsequent studies, although the analytical spotlight moved towards the sociality and ethics of financial debt and the vulnerability that it generated. Yet, the increasingly complex nature of financial systems encourages us to redirect our attention to the intrinsic relation between debt and politics. In this chapter I have argued that the analyses and materials produced by anthropologists will prove invaluable not only for theorists, but also for the policy-makers who have to navigate emerging economic challenges, often without a clear understanding of their impact on society.

To keep pace with financial innovations, which today range from mobile payment networks to crypto-currencies and carbon markets, anthropological projects are increasingly evolving towards large-scale, collaborative programmes that require anthropologists to be conversant with quantitative political-economic methodologies. I want to close by mentioning some of the research networks and groups that are analysing these new frontiers of financialised debt. These include the Grassroots Economics (GRECO) project at the University of Barcelona, the Unpayable Debt Working Group at Columbia University, the research group on financialisation at the Max Planck Institute for Social Anthropology, the Frontlines of Value research programme at the University of Bergen and the Western Bank in Eastern Europe project (GEOFIN) at Trinity College Dublin. Most of these groups have yet to publish their most relevant findings, but these collaborative projects have the potential to produce not only excellent theoretical scholarship but also accounts that will explain the relationship between politics and debt to a wider audience, which is a necessary step in restoring anthropology's relevance to the broader society in which is exists.

Acknowledgement

Many thanks to Aaron Z. Pitluck, Daniel Souleles and the participants of the 2017 conference of the Society for Economic Anthropology, whose lively engagement with issues of debt and credit inspired these thoughts.

References

Aalbers, Manuel B. 2016. *The Financialization of Housing: A Political Economy Approach.* London: Routledge.

Appel, Hannah 2014. Finance, figuration, and the alternative banking group of Occupy Wall Street. *Signs* 40 (1): 53–58.

Arrighi, Giovanni 1996. *The Long Twentieth Century: Money, Power and the Origins of Our Times.* London: Verso.

Ashton, Philip 2011. The financial exception and the reconfiguration of credit risk in US mortgage markets. *Environment and Planning A* 43 (8): 1796–1812.

Badue, Ana Flavia and Florbela Ribeiro 2018. Gendered redistribution and family debt: The ambiguities of a cash transfer program in Brazil. *Economic Anthropology* 5 (2): 261–73.

Bear, Laura 2015. *Navigating Austerity: Currents of Debt along a South Asian River*. Stanford: Stanford University Press.

Bear, Laura, Karen Ho, Anna Tsing and Sylvia Yanagisako 2015. Gens: A feminist manifesto for the study of capitalism. *Cultural Anthropology*. https://culanth.org/fieldsights/652-gens-a-feminist-mani festo-for-the-study-of-capitalism (accessed 16 October 2018)

Björklund Larsen, Lotta 2015. Common sense at the Swedish Tax Agency: Transactional boundaries that separate taxable and tax-free income. *Critical Perspectives on Accounting* 31: 75–89.

Björklund Larsen, Lotta 2017. Mind the (tax) gap: An ethnography of a number. *Journal of Cultural Economy* 10 (5): 419–33.

Boll, Karen 2014. Shady car dealings and taxing work practices: An ethnography of a tax audit process. *Accounting, Organizations and Society* 39 (1): 1–19.

Bonizzi, Bruno 2013. Financialization in developing and emerging countries. *International Journal of Political Economy* 42 (4): 83–107.

Brash, Julian 2011. *Bloomberg's New York: Class and Governance in the Luxury City*. Athens: University of Georgia Press.

Çalişkan, Koray and Michel Callon 2009. Economization, part 1: Shifting attention from the economy towards processes of economization. *Economy and Society* 38 (3): 369–98.

Callon, Michel 1998. Introduction: The embeddedness of economic markets in economics. In *The Laws of the Markets* (ed.) M. Callon, pp. 1–68. Oxford: Blackwell Publishers.

Chong, Kimberly and David Tuckett 2014. Constructing conviction through action and narrative: How money managers manage uncertainty and the consequence for financial market functioning. *Socio-Economic Review* 13 (2): 309–30.

Chu, Julie Y. 2010. *Cosmologies of Credit: Transnational Mobility and the Politics of Destination in China*. Durham, NC: Duke University Press.

Cooper, Melinda E. 2011. *Life as Surplus: Biotechnology and Capitalism in the Neoliberal Era*. Seattle: University of Washington Press.

Cooper, Melinda E. 2017. *Family Values: Between Neoliberalism and the New Social Conservatism*. Cambridge, MA: The MIT Press.

Cox, John 2014. Fast money schemes are risky business: Gamblers and investors in a Papua New Guinea Ponzi scheme. *Oceania* 84 (3): 289–305.

D'Avella, Nicholas 2014. Ecologies of investment: Crisis histories and brick futures in Argentina. *Cultural Anthropology* 29 (1): 173–99.

Dawisha, Karen 2015. *Putin's Kleptocracy: Who Owns Russia?* New York: Simon and Schuster.

Epstein, Gerald A. 2005. Introduction: Financialization and the world economy. In *Financialization and the World Economy* (ed.) G.A. Epstein, pp. 3–16. Cheltenham, UK and Northampton, MA, USA: Edward Elgar.

Erikson, Susan L. 2015. Secrets from whom? Following the money in global health finance. *Current Anthropology* 56 (S12): S306–16.

Ferguson, James 2015. *Give a Man a Fish: Reflections on the New Politics of Distribution*. Durham, NC: Duke University Press.

Fernandez, Rodrigo and Angela Wigger 2016. Lehman Brothers in the Dutch offshore financial center: The role of shadow banking in increasing leverage and facilitating debt. *Economy and Society* 45 (3–4): 407–30.

Fleming, Peter 2017. *The Death of Homo Economicus: Work, Debt and the Myth of Endless Accumulation*. London. Pluto Press.

García-Lamarca, Melissa 2017. From occupying plazas to recuperating housing: Insurgent practices in Spain. *International Journal of Urban and Regional Research* 41 (1): 37–53.

García-Lamarca, Melissa and Maria Kaika 2016. 'Mortgaged lives': The biopolitics of debt and housing financialisation. *Transactions of the Institute of British Geographers* 41 (3): 313–27.

Graeber, David 2011. *Debt: The First 5,000 Years*. Brooklyn: Melville House.

Graeber, David 2015. *The Utopia of Rules: On Technology, Stupidity, and the Secret Joys of Bureaucracy.* Brooklyn: Melville House.

Halawa, Mateusz 2015. In new Warsaw: Mortgage credit and the unfolding of space and time. *Cultural Studies* 29 (5–6): 707–32.

Han, Clara 2012. *Life in Debt: Times of Care and Violence in Neoliberal Chile*. Oakland: University of California Press.

Harvey, David 2003. *The New Imperialism*. Oxford: Oxford University Press.

Harvey, David 2007. *The Limits to Capital*. London: Verso.

Herzfeld, Michael 2009. *Evicted from Eternity: The Restructuring of Modern Rome*. Chicago: University of Chicago Press.

Ho, Karen 2009. *Liquidated: An Ethnography of Wall Street*. Durham, NC: Duke University Press.

Holmes, Douglas R. 2013. *Economy of Words: Communicative Imperatives in Central Banks*. Chicago: University of Chicago Press.

James, Deborah 2015. *Money from Nothing: Indebtedness and Aspiration in South Africa*. Stanford: Stanford University Press.

Johnson, Juliet and Andrew Barnes 2015. Financial nationalism and its international enablers: The Hungarian experience. *Review of International Political Economy* 22 (3): 535–69.

Kalaitzake, Manolas 2017. The political power of finance: The Institute of International Finance in the Greek debt crisis. *Politics and Society* 45 (3): 389–413.

Kar, Sohini 2017. Relative indemnity: Risk, insurance, and kinship in Indian microfinance. *Journal of the Royal Anthropological Institute* 23 (2): 302–19.

Kehr, Janina 2018. 'Exotic no more': Tuberculosis, public debt and global health in Berlin. *Global Public Health* 13 (3): 369–82.

Khalvashi, Tamta 2015. Peripheral affects: Shame, publics and performance on the margins of the Republic of Georgia. PhD Thesis, Department of Anthropology, University of Copenhagen.

Knorr Cetina, Karin and Alex Preda (eds) 2012. *The Oxford Handbook of the Sociology of Finance*. Oxford: Oxford University Press.

Krippner, Greta R. 2005. The financialization of the American economy. *Socioeconomic Review* 3 (2): 173–208.

Kwon, Hoenik 2007. The dollarization of Vietnamese ghost money. *Journal of the Royal Anthropological Institute* 13 (1): 73–90.

Langley, Paul 2008. Sub-prime mortgage lending: A cultural economy. *Economy and Society* 37 (4): 469–94.

Lapavitsas, Costas 2013. *Profiting Without Producing: How Finance Exploits Us All*. London: Verso Books.

MacKenzie, Donald 2008. *Material Markets: How Economic Agents are Constructed*. Oxford: Oxford University Press.

Malinowski, Bronislaw 1922. *Argonauts of the Western Pacific: An Account of Native Enterprise and Adventure in the Archipelagoes of Melanesian New Guinea*. London: Routledge.

Mann, Geoff 2017. Haute finance in the not-so-quiet revolution: Colonialisme Anglo-Saxonne and the bombing of la Bourse de Montréal. *Journal of Cultural Economy* 10 (4): 364–76.

Martin, Randy 2002. *Financialization of Daily Life*. Philadelphia: Temple University Press.

Mattioli, Fabio 2018. Financialization without liquidity: In-kind payments, forced credit, and authoritarianism at the periphery of Europe. *Journal of the Royal Anthropological Institute* 24 (3): 568–88.

Maurer, Bill 2005. Due diligence and 'reasonable man', offshore. *Cultural Anthropology* 20 (4): 474–505.

Maurer, Bill 2006. *Pious Property: Islamic Mortgages in the United States*. New York: Russell Sage Foundation.

Mauss, Marcel 1990 (1925). *The Gift: The Form and Reason for Exchange in Archaic Societies*. W.D. Halls, trans. London: Routledge.

Muniesa, Fabian 2014. *The Provoked Economy: Economic Reality and the Performative Turn*. Abingdon: Routledge.

Núñez, Jorge 2017. A clinical economy of speculation: Financial trading and gambling disorder in Spain. *Cultural Anthropology* 32 (2): 269–93.

O'Barr, William M. and John M. Conley 1992. *Fortune and Folly: The Wealth and Power of Institutional Investing*. Homewood: Business One Irwin.

Palomera, Jaime 2014. How did finance capital infiltrate the world of the urban poor? Homeownership and social fragmentation in a Spanish neighborhood. *International Journal of Urban and Regional Research* 38 (1): 218–35.

Peebles, Gustav 2010. The anthropology of credit and debt. *Annual Review of Anthropology* 39: 225–40.

Penfield, Amy 2017. Dodged debts and the submissive predator: Perspectives on Amazonian relations of dependence. *Journal of the Royal Anthropological Institute* 23 (2): 320–37.

Pitluck, Aaron Z. 2009. Moral behavior in stock markets: Islamic finance and socially responsible investment. In *Economics and Morality: Anthropological Approaches* (eds) Katherine E. Browne and B. Lynne Milgram, pp. 233–55. Lanham: AltaMira Press.

Pitluck, Aaron Z. 2013. Watching foreigners: How counterparties enable herds, crowds, and generate liquidity in financial markets. *Socio-Economic Review* 12 (1): 5–31.

Pitluck, Aaron Z., Fabio Mattioli and Daniel Souleles 2018. Finance beyond function: Three causal explanations for financialization. *Economic Anthropology* 5 (2): 157–71.

Pixley, Jocelyn 2004. *Emotions in Finance: Booms, Busts and Uncertainty*. Cambridge: Cambridge University Press.

Polillo, Simone 2018. Market efficiency as a revolution in data analysis. *Economic Anthropology* 5 (2): 197–208.

Radhakrishnan, Smitha 2018. Of loans and livelihoods: Gendered 'social work' in urban India. *Economic Anthropology* 5 (2): 234–45.

Rethel, Lena 2018. Capital market development in Southeast Asia: From speculative crisis to spectacles of financialization. *Economic Anthropology* 5 (2): 184–96.

Ries, Nancy 1999. Business, taxes, and corruption in Russia. *Anthropology of East Europe Review* 17 (1): 59–62.

Rogers, Douglas 2005. Moonshine, money, and the politics of liquidity in rural Russia. *American Ethnologist* 32 (1): 63–81.

Roitman, Janet 2005. *Fiscal Disobedience: An Anthropology of Economic Regulation in Central Africa*. Princeton, NJ: Princeton University Press.

Sahlins, Marshall D. 1972. *Stone Age Economics*. Chicago: Aldine.

Sampat, Preeti 2010. Special economic zones in India: Reconfiguring displacement in a neoliberal order? *City & Society* 22 (2): 166–82.

Sandy, Larissa 2009. 'Behind closed doors': Debt-bonded sex workers in Sihanoukville, Cambodia. *The Asia Pacific Journal of Anthropology* 10 (3): 216–30.

Schuster, Caroline E. 2015. *Social Collateral: Women and Microfinance in Paraguay's Smuggling Economy*. Oakland: University of California Press.

Schuster, Caroline E. 2016. Repaying the debts of the dead: Kinship, microfinance, and mortuary practice on the Paraguayan frontier. *Social Analysis* 60 (2): 65–81.

Shipton, Parker 2009. *Mortgaging the Ancestors: Ideologies of Attachment in Africa*. New Haven: Yale University Press.

Stout, Noelle 2016. Petitioning a giant: Debt, reciprocity, and mortgage modification in the Sacramento Valley. *American Ethnologist* 43 (1): 158–71.

Truitt, Allison 2018. Nationalizing gold: The Vietnamese SJC gold bar and the Indian gold coin. *Economic Anthropology* 5 (2): 223–33.

Tsingou, Eleni 2015. Club governance and the making of global financial rules. *Review of International Political Economy* 22 (2): 225–56.

Weber, Rachel 2010. Selling city futures: The financialization of urban redevelopment policy. *Economic Geography* 86 (3): 251–74.

Wennerlind, Carl 2003. Credit-money as the philosopher's stone: Alchemy and the coinage problem in seventeenth-century England. *History of Political Economy* 35 (ann. supp.): 234–61.

Wigger, Angela 2012. The political interface of financialisation and the regulation of mergers and acquisitions in the EU. *Journal of European Integration* 34 (6): 623–41.

Williams, Brett 2004. *Debt for Sale: A Social History of the Credit Trap*. Philadelphia: University of Pennsylvania Press.

Yudin, Greg and Ivan Pavlyutkin 2015. Recording the ambiguity: The moral economy of debt books in a Russian small town. *Cultural Studies* 29 (5–6): 807–26.

Zaloom, Caitlin 2006. *Out of the Pits: Traders and Technology from Chicago to London*. Chicago: University of Chicago Press.

5   Resources: Nature, value and time

Jaume Franquesa

In his essay 'Environment and economy', Eric Hirsch laments the lack of dialogue between economic and environmental anthropology. Environmental anthropologists, he suggests, tend to focus on the values associated with environment and ecology, often leaving unexplored how these values relate to capital's law of value. Economic anthropologists, for their part, tend to endorse a conception of the economy that is focused on 'the social relations of persons and things in the establishment of value' (Hirsch 2012: 328) and that hinders their ability to analyse the role that nature plays in articulating value relations.

The basis of this, Hirsch argues, lies in two doctrines that took shape in Western Europe early in the Modern period. One is the philosophy of property and political society derived from John Locke that legitimated a particular appropriation of nature, both in Europe and, especially, in the colonies (Whitehead 2010). The second is the doctrine of quantitative measurement, associated with objectivity, scientific discourse, technological prowess and trust in numbers (Mumford 1934). These two doctrines, together with the practices through which they took shape, form the basic framework that transforms nature into a collection of resources as the central relationship between economy and environment. It is this defining paradigm that constitutes the West and Modernity.

We can read Hirsch to be arguing that natural resources constitute the entity around which an economic anthropology sensitive to the particularities of environmental relations can be articulated. This is the point of departure of the present chapter, which is divided into two parts: approach and paths. The first explores the concept of resources and the key processes through which resources are made and argues that, beyond the specifics of case studies, research on natural resources finds its common ground in the dialectical analysis of value relations. In order to situate research on resources within a broader disciplinary framework, throughout my discussion I briefly engage with a series of issues that inform contemporary debates in anthropology: materiality, temporality, the nature–culture dualism. In the second part I offer a series of paths for future research. I identify a series of research areas, and within them I suggest potential research topics. Wherever possible, I illustrate these with specific examples and recent contributions. I conclude with a provocation to economic anthropologists to think big.

Approach: Resources as form and the dialectics of value

In its 2015 edition, *The Oxford English Dictionary* defines 'resources' thus: 'Stocks or reserves of money, materials, people, or some other asset, which can be drawn on when necessary.' A notable element of this definition is that it suggests that virtually anything (or at least anything that can be defined as a stock or an asset) is susceptible to inclusion: culture, natural parks, water and so forth. Indeed, Richard Handler (1985) argues that a key marker of capitalist Modernity is that an increasingly large range of things can be made into resources, and therefore be commodified and owned.

We should observe that the modular quality of the concept, evident in its capacity to be applied to an ever-growing domain of social reality, indicates that resources are a form, an abstract framework that can be applied to the universe of the concrete. In this respect, natural resources are not just one more kind of resource. Rather, as Elizabeth Ferry and Mandana Limbert (2008) argue, they are its classic historical exemplar, the object in relation to which this form was created. It is in relation to nature, what Karl Polanyi (1944) called land, that the logic of the resource was first systematically deployed. The two doctrines that Hirsch discusses are, no doubt, crucial in turning nature into an abstract stock, yet to understand the process fully we must connect these doctrines to a broad range of practices that create both dispossession and a whole new host of resource peripheries.

Finally, we must note the political dimension of resources. As Maurice Godelier (1986) has argued, there always exists an intimate relationship between the dominant social relations within a given society and that society's relationship with nature. So, we must assume that the resource form specifies not only a certain form of productive power (power over nature), but also a certain form of political power (power over people). Max Horkheimer and Theodore Adorno express this in blunt terms: 'What human beings seek from nature is how to use it [in order] to dominate wholly both it and human beings. Nothing else counts' (2002 [1947]: 2).

To better understand the resource form, I therefore suggest that we explore its materiality and the way power intervenes in its creation.

Materiality

Natural resources are eminently material, yet we also know that resources are not just blunt matter, things in themselves. Rather, as David Harvey (1974: 272) puts it, natural resources are 'materials "in nature" that are capable of being transformed into things of utility to man . . .. They are . . . technical and cultural appraisals of nature.' Thus, since resources are the cultural form through which capital and state relate with nature qua manageable matter, it is worth exploring how we can define their materiality. To answer this question, I will draw on Tim Ingold's (2012: 435) distinction between objects and materials:

> Anything we come across could, in principle, be regarded as either an object or a sample of material. To view it as an object is to take it for what it is: a complete and final form that confronts the viewer as a *fait accompli*. It is already made . . .. To view the same thing as a sample of material, by contrast, is to see it as a potential – for further making, growth, and transformation. Materials . . . are substances-in-becoming.

Given the growing interest in materiality across the social sciences, it seems clear that the way that we understand the materiality of resources will have theoretical implications. Indeed, Ingold's dichotomy aims to establish a distinction that is both epistemological, concerned with how we should approach the world of matter, and ontological, concerned with what the world of matter really is. On the one hand, 'objects' implies a positivist epistemology concerned with a world made of fixed forms. In contrast, 'materials' describes a world made of a multiplicity of agencies in flow demanding a posthumanist, ontological and, at least in Ingold's case, phenomenological approach.

I would suggest that resources occupy an intermediate status between Ingold's objects and materials. Unlike objects, resources are not complete or finished, they are generic and do not have stable boundaries; they do not exist for themselves but exist to allow for the production and reproduction of life. Similarly to Ingold's materials, resources are in process, for we cannot separate them from the process – mental and material, political and economic – through which they are made. However, they are not indeterminate: what they have to become has already been determined in that process. Indeed, Ferry and Limbert (2008: 4) suggest that resources are what fills the void between objects (or products) and materials (or sources): 'to define something as a resource is to suspend it between a past "source" and a future "product"'.

This intermediate status entails a distinct temporality. Whereas objects are anchored in the past and materials are open towards the future, the temporality of resources is teleological, only punctuated by spectacular discoveries and the permanent threat of scarcity. This teleology presents the existence of resources as self-evident, thus concealing not only the mental and material practices through which resources are produced, but also the power that permits the effacing of that process. To put it in Polanyi's (1944) terms, natural resources are fictitious commodities produced through a partial yet constant process that requires political intervention and extends beyond the production process proper.

This analysis of the materiality of resources has some methodological implications. Natural resources are not mere facts as a positivist approach would desire, but neither are they matter open to endless possibilities. Actually, they are, at once, neither and both of these. They thus demand a dialectical approach that attends to form and process, concept and matter, and that is focused on their production and hence situates history and power at the centre of the analysis.

The making of resources: Alienation, extraction, exhaustion

Anna Tsing argues that the key process in the conversion of nature into commodified resources is what she, obliquely drawing on Marx, calls alienation, separating people and things from their cultural, spatial and temporal context: 'Alienation obviates living-space entanglement. The dream of alienation inspires landscape modification in which only one stand-alone asset matters; everything else becomes weeds or waste' (Tsing 2015: 5–6). The result is the creation of 'abstract social nature' (Moore 2015: 193–217), abstracting a certain section of nature from its context.

James Scott opens *Seeing Like a State* with an historical example of this process, scientific forestry as it developed in Prussia during the eighteenth century. In this scheme, 'the actual tree with its vast number of possible uses was replaced by an abstract tree representing a volume of lumber or firewood' (Scott 1998: 12). If this example focuses on state schemes and quantitative measures (Hirsch's second doctrine), William Cronon describes something similar in a situation where the protagonists are capital's drive to accumulate and the appropriation of native land (Hirsch's first doctrine). He argues that the formation of the lumber industry in the American Midwest was anticipated by an alienating view of nature that he identifies in the narratives of certain travellers:

'The land', wrote one traveler in 1852 of the country around Manitowoc, Wisconsin, 'is heavily timbered, generally, with pine, oak, maple, and other varieties . . .'. To perceive the forest as this traveler did through the lens of that word 'timber' was already to shift into the domain of resources, commodities, and second nature. (Cronon 1991: 152)

Alienation paved the way for extraction, going hand in hand with it all along. Indeed, just a few years later the gaze that Cronon describes had been put to work through cutting, milling and timber-selling, turning the wealth of the northern pines into a second nature made of wooden houses and profits. Systematic extraction led to exhaustion and abandonment of the site of extraction while allowing accumulation to take place elsewhere. Scott's schemes yielded similar results: vulnerable, exhausted forests, eventually precipitating the movement of logging to other areas.

From guano to fracking, this classic formula of alienation–extraction–exhaustion has repeated for centuries all around the world, no matter how different the commodities and the technologies of their extraction (Clark and Foster 2012). The result is the division of the world into two kinds of places: peripheries of extraction and centres of accumulation (Bunker 1984). Rather, there are three kinds of places, for next to the usable extraction peripheries we find, in Ferguson's (2005) words and borrowing from the French colonial nomenclature for Africa, 'unusable' areas that are deemed valueless and are therefore of no consequence to capital.

Being aware of this general dynamic is of the utmost importance for the economic anthropologist doing research on resources. In the first place, it allows us to connect specific case studies with broader political-economic relationships, offering a framework for comparison. In the second place, it provides a basic understanding of the ecological dimension of the unequal exchanges that fuel capitalist accumulation and political domination, giving rise to ever-new forms of uneven development. The importance of this second consideration for future research in economic anthropology can hardly be over-emphasised. Not only does it allow for the analysis of the intricate relations between economic and ecological processes; more crucially, in so doing it enables much needed collaboration with other disciplines, from world-systems analysis to ecological economics.

Value relations

In its broadest sense, economic anthropology can be defined as the study of value, where value is not seen as a property of things but as a 'relational aspect of a structure of interdependent productive activities' (Turner 2008: 46; see also Collins 2017). Thus, the analysis of value is, always, the analysis of value relations. My argument is that increased attention to natural resources can help extend economic anthropology's understanding of value relations to include those that organise the social division of labour *and* nature.

Before examining the specific logic of the value dynamics relating environment and economy, it is necessary to clarify one point. As I suggested earlier, these dynamics possess an ecological dimension, made obvious in the unequal exchanges in terms of labour, materials and energy between centres and peripheries. However, as Alf Hornborg (2011: 102–17) argues, the value relations underpinning those unequal exchanges cannot be reduced to any single physical magnitude, be it energy, labour or tons of matter. Certainly, calculations of material flows are important for our understanding of society's metabolism and economic anthropologists would be well advised to take them seriously. Yet value is a sociocultural construct with political consequences mediated by the concrete abstractions of capital. Since economic anthropologists specialise in understanding the relationship between those constructs and concrete abstractions, I would argue that few are better equipped to understand the value relations that articulate the relationship between environment and economy.

At risk of oversimplifying, I suggest that the anthropological analysis of value relations in the study of natural resources and extractive activities should focus on two distinct dynamics: processes of (de)valorisation and value struggles. Taken together, their analysis constitutes a minimal programme for an economic anthropology of natural resources.

Processes of valorisation and devalorisation are central to the life of resources. From the perspective of the resource, the alienation–extraction–exhaustion cycle that I described earlier can be cast in value terms: the discovery of a hidden potential value leads to its exploitation, giving rise to the accumulation of congealed value (profits) and, ultimately, to an exhausted, devalued wasteland. The process through which a resource is construed as such, and therefore valued, is an important area of anthropological study. Analysing the value of a particular resource is, in large part, analysing how it is imbued with meaning, and also exploring the social projects and groups articulated around it (for a classic example, see Coronil 1997).

Devalorisation processes, although less studied, are at least as interesting. The making of resources involves, at a minimum, two such processes. Firstly, whereas the resource to be extracted is posited as valuable, all that exists alongside it is ignored in the productive process and devalued; in Tsing's terms, 'everything else becomes weeds or waste'. On the other hand, once it is inserted into the economic system, the resource itself must also be devalorised, made cheap, if accumulation is to proceed smoothly (Moore 2015). In other words, capital must appropriate nature without paying its full price, a fate that nature shares with large sections of the world population. Analysing this process of relative devalorisation can offer insights into the dynamics of crisis and accumulation in different corners of the world. Also, as I suggested earlier, this relative lack of value has a spatial correlate, for extraction activities tend to impose 'an at once profitable and pauperizing order' (Williams 1980: 79) on the areas where they take place.

The second value dynamic that I want to highlight is central to these processes of devalorisation. I am referring to the value struggles that often accompany extractive projects, constituting a central element of what Chris Ballard and Glenn Banks (2003) call 'resource wars'. Conflicts around specific extractive projects, usually involving corporations, states and local communities, are distribution conflicts with economic, ecological and cultural implications (Escobar 2006). Almost invariably, these conflicts are expressed as clashes between different languages of valuation, where opposition to extractive projects is framed, say, in religious or environmental terms (Martínez Alier 2003). Where the corporation values the alienated resource for its economic value, those who oppose the project challenge that singular metric by claiming a non-economic value that links the resource to that from which it has been alienated, be it the ecosystem, local livelihoods or a supernatural entity. Thus, if the making of resources is premised on a process of objectification that takes nature to be external to social relations, those opposing languages of valuation underpin what Hornborg (2011: 27–44) calls a 'struggle for relatedness'. Obviously, the ability to impose a certain value framework is a critical attribute of power (Gudeman 1986).

I am not arguing that all economic anthropologists working on resources should concede primacy to the study of value dynamics. Rather, my argument is both more modest and, perhaps, more daring. It is more modest because I claim only that the study of value relations allows for a connection between political-economic and sociocultural analysis, yielding a common ground that allows comparison and dialogue and that is wide enough to accommodate disparate research agendas. On the other hand, my position is more daring because, as suggested earlier, I contend that a focus on value relations can help bring the study of natural resources to the centre of economic anthropology in order to refine some of its central tenets and reinvigorate its agenda.

A final note: On the nature–culture dualism

According to Philippe Descola (2013), the division between nature and culture constitutes the ground zero of Modernity's ontology. In many ways, natural resources, as form, epitomise this division: an external nature to be dominated and expropriated.

In recent years a variety of attempts to rethink the relationship between nature and culture and to overcome that division have blossomed. Activist efforts to define nature as commons, legal initiatives to recognise nature as a holder of rights and Pope Francis's encyclical *Laudato si* are examples of this process. Even the calls of many environmental economists to internalise externalities could, with some qualification, be seen in this way. In the social sciences similar efforts criss-cross theoretical and disciplinary boundaries, from posthumanist STS (Haraway 2016) and Marxist political ecology (Moore 2015) to proponents of the ontological turn (de la Cadena 2015).

I believe that we, as economic anthropologists, need to engage with these debates, especially if, as I am proposing, we are to give greater analytical importance to environmental relations. Not doing so would likely lead to an unwelcome isolation. This work remains to be done, and I am not in the position to offer any kind of one-size-fits-all formula, which anyway probably does not exist. I will thus limit myself to suggesting two premises that I believe should guide this endeavour. Firstly, we should be careful to keep the analytical separation between native frameworks and our own theoretical approaches. Only in so doing can we be true to the anthropological tradition of building theoretical frameworks out of specific ethnographic engagements. Secondly, we should navigate between the Scylla of Modernist epistemologies defined in large part by the nature–culture dualism and the Charybdis of postmodern approaches that, in celebrating a flat world of incommensurable monads, tend to ignore the market. In sum, we should aim for an intermediate position between the radical difference of the ontologists and Modernist straitjackets that often beset political economy. The dialectical analysis of value relations can be a useful route to this goal.

Paths for future research

The research directions that I suggest here are connected to the general approach that I have delineated, but first a few caveats should be entered. Largely as a consequence of my own area of expertise, energy resources are over-represented. This is also the case geographically, with Europe and the Americas accounting for a good portion of the illustrative examples. In terms of the phases of the economic system, there is an emphasis on production (or extraction), although the importance of distribution and consumption is discussed and acknowledged. This emphasis stems from the importance of the dialectical analysis of the alienation–extraction–exhaustion cycle. Similarly, the stress I place on history reflects my conviction that historical analysis is crucial in order to expose the teleological temporality of natural resources and the power apparatus that such temporality both reflects and conceals.

Follow the resource

As I suggested earlier, one of economic anthropology's main strengths is the ability to analyse the dialectical relationship between capital's concrete abstractions and the local historical formation of anthropological subjects, 'real people doing real things' (Roseberry 1988: 163–64). More than three decades after it appeared, Sidney Mintz's *Sweetness and power* (1985) remains a hallmark of this approach, following sugar through time and space, examining local histories and global processes of production, exchange and consumption. Mintz's approach, following the sugar, can be usefully applied to research on resources, following the alienation–extraction–exhaustion cycle of particular resources. By following the resource, we should be able to connect the changing status of resources to the way their meaning is transformed, while examining the value dynamics and social strategies that get articulated around these transformations. This path allows for analysing the teleological temporality of the resource. To illustrate the virtues of this approach I will draw on the work of Ferry (2005, 2013) and Tsing (2015).[1]

Ferry's ethnography of a mining co-operative in Guanajuato, in Mexico, offers a detailed analysis of how the mining community conceptualises the silver they mine (Ferry 2005). Beyond the simple teleological temporality of a resource moving from ore to commodity in the global market, Ferry shows the local community's effort to treat silver as an inalienable possession that must always return to the community to contribute to its reproduction. This effort is manifest in a series of mechanisms: setting low and stable extractive quotas, tying jobs to kinship structures, and morally-sanctioned processes of reinvesting in the community the money obtained from silver. Describing how silver, under its different guises, leaves and returns to the area, Ferry shows how a local community strives to find an engagement with the global market that allows the reproduction of local livelihoods. Ferry's analysis also incorporates the state, showing how the existence of silver as a community resource is rooted in a complex history of national struggle for the control of natural resources, defined as patrimony, that reached its key moment during Lázaro Cárdenas's government in the 1930s. Treating silver as an inalienable commodity thus emerges as an ongoing effort to preserve and reproduce the political conditions that originally made communitarian control possible. In a later work, Ferry (2013) extends this approach by following the resource in new directions, exploring how silver mined in Mexico makes its way to markets and private collections across the Mexico–US border and how its value is managed and reformulated.

Tsing's (2015) ethnography follows matsutake, a kind of mushroom, from the Oregon forests where a diverse array of people pick them, to the restaurant tables and store windows of Japan. A lucrative commodity controlled by a small number of traders, matsutake is initially picked as a trophy and ends up being consumed as a gift. To understand how the market articulates with these processes of conversion, Tsing proposes the concept of salvage capitalism, which identifies the mechanisms through which capitalism appropriates forms of nature and labour that it neither values nor reproduces. Matsutake tends to grow in heavily disturbed forests, and much of Tsing's ethnography takes place in forests abandoned by the logging industry after decades of extraction. The author thus offers an ethnography of resource extraction taking place after previous extraction or, as she puts it, in a third nature brought about by the excesses of second nature, the capitalist transformation of the environment. This fragmented temporality informs the whole monograph, where matsutake underpins Tsing's effort to think towards a world where Modernity's progressive temporality has vanished. Matsutake pickers work in capitalist ruins, and Tsing shows how engaging with their activity can shed light upon a precarious condition that affects an increasingly large segment of the world's population.

The work of Ferry and Tsing teaches us an important lesson. When following the resource, its history becomes a series of processes of translation and articulation: how different forms of value and labour, as well as diverse social projects, are articulated within a specific resource value chain, and how they depend on a series of processes of (mis)translation connecting its diverse links. Ferry and Tsing thus show the social and cultural elements that underpin but are never fully contained in the alienation–extraction–exhaustion cycle. Moreover, these authors' work points towards a series of additional directions that I explore in the reminder of this chapter. Firstly, it shows that resources are intimately connected to changing regimes of accumulation, reflecting and articulating shifting value relations at multiple, overlapping scales. Secondly, it shows that understanding these value relations demands that we pay attention to labour regimes: the appropriation and expropriation of nature rests upon forms of labour exploitation and organisation that largely define value struggles over resources. Finally, they suggest the need to extend our analytical gaze beyond extraction; that is to say, to observe value relations beyond the alienation–extraction–exhaustion resource cycle.

Changing regimes of accumulation: Nature, debt and finance

Resources, especially energy resources, are rightly seen as playing a key role in bringing about new regimes of accumulation and in realigning world hegemony. Thus, if Dutch mercantile hegemony was built upon peat and Baltic wood, coal and steam signalled the emergence of British industrial hegemony, eventually yielding to a US economy built around oil (Podobnik 2006). Nonetheless, whereas the correlation between energy resources and regimes of accumulation is often presented as common sense, it is seldom explained. It is thus necessary to investigate the role that resources play in making these changes of regime possible. This should allow us to observe the ecological basis of accumulation and ultimately to show, in Jason Moore's (2015) terms, that every regime of accumulation is also an ecological regime. This effort seems especially important given our current historical context, in which growing anxieties around climate change and peak oil seem to indicate the inevitability of a new energy transition.

Andreas Malm (2016) and Tim Mitchell (2011) have recently contributed influential works illuminating, respectively, the role of coal in British industrialisation and the importance of Middle Eastern oil in the American century. Malm's book is a detailed attempt to solve a single riddle: why was coal the protagonist of the British Industrial Revolution if water power was widely available, cheaper and had a comparable productive capacity? Weaving together an historical enquiry with a sophisticated theoretical apparatus, Malm offers an answer that goes to the heart of the relationship between capital and labour. Coal, he argues, allowed manufacturers to be less constrained by the particularities of history and place and, in so doing, it gave them greater power over labour. In showing that control over coal became a basis of control over labour, Malm shows how power over nature and power over people interweave. Coal was better adjusted to capital's law of value, for it could more easily be alienated from its ecological bearings and thus be treated as inexhaustible.

Mitchell also pays attention to labour issues, particularly the different labour structures governing oil and coal extraction. However, his emphasis is on the economic calculations and regulatory mechanisms that were built around oil. He offers three principal insights. Firstly, cheap oil made possible the accounting mechanisms that we now associate with Keynesianism, such as GDP. Secondly, the hegemonic position that the US dollar achieved after the Second World War was inseparable from the fact that oil was denominated in this currency. Thirdly, the energy crisis of the 1970s provided the context for an increase in the price of oil that did away with the Bretton Woods agreements and paved the way for the neoliberalisation of the economy and the growing importance of finance.

Perhaps the main virtue of Malm's and Mitchell's analyses is that they offer non-deterministic accounts of the connection between energy shifts and societal transformations. They show that understanding those transformations requires us to pay attention to forms of labour reorganisation and geopolitical realignment that accompany these shifts, as well as the financial and accounting instruments that mediate the relation between resources and political-economic structures. Before returning to the issue of labour in the next section, I will now briefly expand on the connection between resources and financialisation.

Although anthropologists have paid a great deal of attention to finance, money and debt in recent years, they have largely ignored the role of resources. Consider, for instance, a book as influential as *Debt* (Graeber 2011), which says next to nothing about them. Tim Di Muzio and Richard Robbins acknowledge this gap in *Debt as Power* (2016), arguing that the expansion of the money supply that the world economy experienced in the eighteenth century could not have taken place without coal. They also concede, however, that the specific mechanisms linking these two processes are still largely unknown.

It thus seems clear that the study of the processes linking resources with debt and finance offers a major research avenue for economic anthropologists. Pursuing the role of debt seems to offer a particularly intriguing opportunity. For instance, although well known, the role that debt plays in forcing national governments to open resource frontiers in their territory deserves further scrutiny. As a second example, we have ample evidence that forms of debt linked to resources have been central in shaping structural adjustment programmes (Smith-Nonini 2016). In places as diverse as Spain, Greece and Puerto Rico, debt stemming from the electricity system has been instrumental in launching austerity programmes involving the transfer of wealth from citizens to corporations.

Finally, research is needed on the particular mechanisms through which nature is financialised. An obvious direction is research on the mechanisms linking popular national understandings of particular resources in resource-intensive economies like Qatar, Norway or Canada with the creation and activity of sovereign wealth funds. How resource markets are created and regulated, how they attempt to establish a univocal framework of value relations, is another topic that merits more attention. Aneil Tripathy's (2017) research on green bonds points towards another interesting direction, in this case more focused on the mechanisms of financial accounting. Green bonds are financial instruments intended to generate investment in low-carbon infrastructure such as clean energy and sustainable forest management. As Tripathy shows, these instruments involve the complex cultural task of accounting for nature, translating it into the language of finance. The complications that this translation involves promote the creation of novel intermediate financial instruments, further introducing nature into the logics of finance. Attention to natural resources, thus, can help shed light on the inner logic of financialisation.

Changing labour regimes

As suggested already, resources are deeply intertwined with labour issues. Although scholars have paid notable attention to this question, I believe that a lot more work needs to be done on this topic, especially with respect to linking it to value struggles. Here, I suggest two potential paths for further research.

The first is analysing how resource extraction is an arena of capitalist experimentation with new technologies and forms of labour organisation. Robert Vitalis (2009) argues that mineral extraction in the American Southwest involved the development of forms of race-based labour segmentation that later would be exported to the oil industry in the Middle East. If Vitalis analyses how a new labour regime is exported through the resource sector, Saulesh Yessenova (2012), Lesley Gill (2016) and Gabriela Valdivia and Marcela Benavides (2012) discuss how, in Kazakhstan, Colombia and Ecuador, labour transformations in the oil industry spill over onto other sectors of the national economy, promoting a neoliberal reorganisation of the labour regime that is contested through changing forms of labour struggle. As these authors show, the value relations linking labour and resources to the national economy depend on value struggles around the meaning of nature and national citizenship, or, in Coronil's (1997) expression, struggles to define the nation's double body, the natural and the political.

The intersection of labour and land-grabbing constitutes another area for future research. Land-grabbing is understood here as 'mainstream shorthand denoting the corporate scramble for land and water' (Hall et al. 2015: 474). Labour is central to understanding the causes and consequences of land grabs, as well as the dialectic interplay between processes of valorisation and devalorisation that stands at its heart. Tania Li (2010) shows that land grabs often occur in a context in which land is needed (and relatively valued) and labour is not (and relatively devalued), giving place to massive processes of dispossession and to labourless landscapes. On other occasions, however, capital needs both land and labour, thus giving rise to new dynamics that affect local economies and class formation. Analysing these labour dynamics is central to understanding different forms of resistance or acquiescence to land-grabbing. In her study of agricultural land grabs in the Ukraine, Natalia Mamonova (2015) argues that acquiescence is directly related to the fact that local farmers perceive large farms as a continuation of Soviet state farms. In this context, Ukrainian farmers adopt a series of strategies oriented towards their inclusion as labour within the newly formed large estates, generating complex processes of class differentiation.

Although I have limited myself here to the issue of labour, processes of land-grabbing can help illuminate a larger range of issues, from corporate reorganisation to changes in food regimes and understandings of national sovereignty. Therefore, land grabs deserve to be a major area for future research. Their importance for understanding the rise of extractivism and processes of enclosure and accumulation by dispossession, as well as resistance to them, can hardly be over-emphasised. In this respect, it seems important to shift emphasis from *ownership* and property dispossession towards a broader focus on the ways that capital and state actors achieve *control* of key resources (Ribot and Peluso 2003), analysing the myriad alignments of state, capital, labour and local community that make this control possible. Following the framework that I proposed in the first part of this chapter, I suggest that analysing the interplay of these mechanisms of control with value struggles and dynamics (i.e. with the conflicts generated by processes of valorisation and devalorisation) can offer key insights into land grabs and, by extension, into the various processes that fuel them.

Beyond extraction

A last research path points towards that which extends beyond the alienation–extraction–exhaustion cycle. Research on waste constitutes a major effort in this respect, and probably the one that has received the most interest (see, e.g.,

Alexander and Reno 2012; Gidwani and Reddy 2011). Exhausted landscapes suggest a second direction. Thus, in recent years there has been a burgeoning literature exploring the fears, anxieties and opportunities that accompany declining oil extraction in places as diverse as Mexico (Breglia 2013) and Oman (Limbert 2010). Whereas Lisa Breglia analyses how locals devoted to primary activities come to terms with a degraded environment, Limbert examines how Omanis grapple with a spectacular modernisation underpinned by oil that is vanishing as oil reserves decline, giving rise to a kaleidoscope of memories and forms of sociality that contravene the lineal temporality of Modernity and resources.

Renewable energy offers a third venue for research on resources beyond extraction. Conventional wisdom tends to understand renewables as the opposite of fossil fuels, thus promising a new form of economy and a new relationship with nature. By paying attention to the relations of production and power structures that govern its development, however, research on renewables often offers a different picture. In a landmark paper, Nicholas Argenti and Daniel M. Knight (2015) argue that renewable energy development in Greece works as a form of extractive economy and they show how the local population interprets these projects through the memory of past foreign military occupations. In my own work on wind farms in Spain (Franquesa 2018) I have found that these energy projects can further peripheralise the regions that are host to them, thus reinstating the rural–urban divide. In so doing, wind energy tends to reproduce, rather than challenge, the value relations articulating the social division of labour and nature in the country. Further, some scholars (e.g. Onorati and Pierfederici 2013) have suggested that wind and solar farms can work as a form of green-grabbing, land-grabbing in the name of the environment.

These findings can have important political implications. Indeed, such research fits within a wider literature exploring the political effects of green policies, and more specifically of the governance frameworks emerging in response to climate change. In reference to these frameworks, Joel Wainwright and Geoff Mann (2013) contend that the struggle between democratising and authoritarian forces will largely be played out in the seemingly technical (and therefore politically neutral) fields of climate change mitigation and natural resource management. The ethnography of renewables offers a good example of how anthropologists can participate in these debates, contributing key insights and showing the political character of the subject, thus dispelling the temptation to treat resources simply as inert things subject to smart management.

Yet, if we are to participate in these debates we must expand our analytical approach. Indeed, most of the existing anthropological studies devoted to renewables have focused narrowly on the local reaction to planned projects, rather than on their actual implementation (for an exception, see Powell 2018). Thus, we have little understanding of the broader regulatory frameworks, the organisational and economic connections with non-renewables and the larger patterns of accumulation within which the development of renewable energy occurs. Moreover, the focus on planned projects, coupled with a reliance on field work, means that our understanding of the effects of renewable energy development over the long term remains limited. Thus, I would argue that if we are to contribute to the understanding of the transition towards renewables, and perhaps even influence the outcome, more empirical, long-term research is needed that connects fine-grained analysis of particular efforts to the broader challenges and contradictions that pervade this form of energy production.

Conclusions: Thinking big

Natural resources have played a central role in important discussions like the population–resources debate as well as in some big concepts characterising political-economic phases like neoextractivism, the resource curse, Dutch disease and carbon democracy. Although as anthropologists we do not always feel comfortable with some of these labels or with the terms of those deliberations, we should admit that they have served to trigger both societal debate and innovative research areas. From my perspective, anthropologists have not participated enough in these debates in recent decades and this stems from our unwillingness to think big, to tackle big questions.

This is not an indictment of ethnographic work, which is a potent tool and anthropology's most distinctive feature. Rather, it is an invitation to combine case studies and attention to ethnographic detail with broader analysis of big questions about existing sociocultural systems and political-economic structures. The research directions that I have suggested here are aimed at this. Anthropologists could also take some cues from sociology and human geography and be a bit more daring. Not only should we ask big questions, we should also make informed predictions and build scenarios about forthcoming challenges. Such boldness will increase our visibility and clarify the value of our contributions.

NOTE
1 In recent years this approach has been successfully applied to infrastructures, often connected to natural resources (see, for instance, Hindery 2013).

References

Alexander, Catherine and Joshua Reno (eds) 2012. *Economies of Recycling: The Global Transformation of Materials, Values and Social Relations.* London: Zed Books.
Argenti, Nicolas and Daniel M. Knight 2015. Sun, wind, and the rebirth of extractive economies: Renewable energy investment and metanarratives of crisis in Greece. *Journal of the Royal Anthropological Institute* 21 (4): 781–802.
Ballard, Chris and Glenn Banks 2003. Resource wars: The anthropology of mining. *Annual Review of Anthropology* 32: 287–313.
Breglia, Lisa 2013. *Living with Oil: Promises, Peaks, and Declines on Mexico's Gulf Coast.* Austin: University of Texas Press.

Bunker, Stephen G. 1984. Modes of extraction, unequal exchange, and the progressive underdevelopment of an extreme periphery: The Brazilian Amazon, 1600–1980. *American Journal of Sociology* 89 (5): 1017–64.

Cadena, Marisol de la 2015. *Earth Beings: Ecologies of Practice across Andean Worlds.* Durham, NC: Duke University Press.

Clark, Brett and John B. Foster 2012. Guano: The global metabolic rift and the fertilizer trade. In *Ecology and Power: Struggles over Land and Material Resources in the Past, Present and Future* (eds) Alf Hornborg, Brett Clark and Kenneth Hermele, pp. 68–82. London: Routledge.

Collins, Jane 2017. *The Politics of Value: Three Movements to Change How We Think about the Economy.* Chicago: University of Chicago Press.

Coronil, Fernando 1997. *The Magical State: Nature, Money and Modernity in Venezuela.* Chicago: University of Chicago Press.

Cronon, William 1991. *Nature's Metropolis: Chicago and the Great West.* New York: W.W. Norton & Company.

Descola, Philippe 2013. *Beyond Nature and Culture.* Chicago: University of Chicago Press.

Di Muzio, Tim and Richard Robbins 2016. *Debt as Power.* Manchester: Manchester University Press.

Escobar, Arturo 2006. Difference and conflict in the struggle over natural resources: A political ecology framework. *Development* 49 (3): 6–13.

Ferguson, James 2005. Seeing like an oil company: Space, security, and global capital in neoliberal Africa. *American Anthropologist* 107 (3): 377–82.

Ferry, Elizabeth 2005. *Not Ours Alone: Patrimony, Value, and Collectivity in Contemporary Mexico.* New York: Columbia University Press.

Ferry, Elizabeth 2013. *Minerals, Collecting, and Value across the US–Mexico Border.* Bloomington: Indiana University Press.

Ferry, Elizabeth and Mandana Limbert 2008. Introduction. In *Timely Assets: The Politics of Resources and Their Temporalities* (eds) E. Ferry and M. Limbert, pp. 3–24. Santa Fe: SAR Press.

Franquesa, Jaume 2018. *Power Struggles: Dignity, Value, and the Renewable Energy Frontier in Spain.* Bloomington: Indiana University Press.

Gidwani, Vinay K. and Rajyashree N. Reddy 2011. The afterlives of 'waste': Notes for a minor history of capitalist surplus. *Antipode* 43 (5): 1625–58.

Gill, Lesley 2016. *A Century of Violence in a Red City: Popular Struggle, Counterinsurgency, and Human Rights in Colombia.* Durham, NC: Duke University Press.

Godelier, Maurice 1986. *The Mental and the Material.* London: Verso.

Graeber, David 2011. *Debt: The First 5000 Years.* Brooklyn: Melville House.

Gudeman, Stephen 1986. *Economics as Culture: Models and Metaphors of Livelihood.* London: Routledge and Kegan Paul.

Hall, Ruth, Marc Edelman, Saturnino M. Borras Jr, Ian Scoones, Ben White and Wendy Wolford 2015. Resistance, acquiescence or incorporation? An introduction to land grabbing and political reactions 'from below'. *The Journal of Peasant Studies* 42 (3): 467–88.

Handler, Richard 1985. On having a culture: Nationalism and the preservation of Quebec's *patrimoine.* In *Objects and Others: Essays on Museums and Material Culture* (ed.) George Stocking Jr, pp. 192–217. Madison: University of Wisconsin Press.

Haraway, Donna 2016. *Manifestly Haraway.* Minneapolis: University of Minnesota Press.

Harvey, David 1974. Population, resources, and the ideology of science. *Economic Geography* 50 (3): 256–77.

Hindery, Derrick 2013. *From Enron to Evo: Pipeline Politics, Global Environmentalism and Indigenous Rights in Bolivia.* Tucson: University of Arizona Press.

Hirsch, Eric 2012. Environment and economy. In *A Handbook of Economic Anthropology,* 2nd edition (ed.) James G. Carrier, pp. 325–43. Cheltenham, UK and Northampton, MA, USA: Edward Elgar.

Horkheimer, Max and Theodor W. Adorno 2002 (1947). *The Dialectic of Enlightenment: Philosophical Fragments*. Stanford: Stanford University Press.

Hornborg, Alf 2011. *Global Ecology and Unequal Exchange: Fetishism in a Zero-Sum World*. London: Routledge.

Ingold, Tim 2012. Toward an ecology of materials. *Annual Review of Anthropology* 41: 427–42.

Li, Tania 2010. To make live or let die? Rural dispossession and the protection of surplus populations. *Antipode* 41 (S1): 66–93.

Limbert, Mandana 2010. *In the Time of Oil: Piety, Memory and Social Life in an Omani Town*. Stanford: Stanford University Press.

Malm, Andreas 2016. *Fossil Capital: The Rise of Steam Power and the Roots of Global Warming*. London: Verso.

Mamonova, Natalia 2015. Resistance or adaptation? Ukrainian peasants' responses to large-scale land acquisitions. *Journal of Peasant Studies* 42 (3–4): 607–34.

Martínez Alier, Joan 2003. *The Environmentalism of the Poor: A Study of Ecological Conflicts and Valuation*. Cheltenham, UK and Northampton, MA, USA: Edward Elgar.

Mintz, Sidney W. 1985. *Sweetness and Power: The Place of Sugar in Modern History*. New York: Viking.

Mitchell, Timothy 2011. *Carbon Democracy: Political Power in the Age of Oil*. London: Verso.

Moore, Jason W. 2015. *Capitalism in the Web of Life*. London: Verso.

Mumford, Lewis 1934. *Technics and Civilization*. New York: Harcourt, Brace and Co.

Onorati, Antonio and Chiara Pierfederici 2013. Land concentration and green grabs in Italy: The case of Furtovoltaico in Sardinia. In *Land Concentration, Land Grabbing and People's Struggles in Europe* (eds) Jennifer Franco and Saturnino Borras Jr, pp. 70–90. The Hague: Transnational Institute.

Podobnik, Bruce 2006. *Global Energy Shifts: Fostering Sustainability in a Turbulent Age*. Philadelphia: Temple University Press.

Polanyi, Karl 1944. *The Great Transformation: The Political and Economic Origins of Our Time*. Boston: Beacon Press.

Powell, Dana E. 2018. *Landscapes of Power: Politics of Energy in the Navajo Nation*. Durham, NC: Duke University Press.

Ribot, Jesse and Nancy Peluso 2003. A theory of access. *Rural Sociology* 68 (2): 153–81.

Roseberry, William 1988. Political economy. *Annual Review of Anthropology* 17: 161–85.

Scott, James C. 1998. *Seeing Like a State: How Certain Schemes to Improve the Human Condition Have Failed*. New Haven: Yale University Press.

Smith-Nonini, Sandy 2016. The role of corporate oil and energy debt in creating the neoliberal era. *Economic Anthropology* 3 (1): 57–67.

Tripathy, Aneil 2017. Translating to risk: The legibility of climate change and nature in the green bond market. *Economic Anthropology* 4 (2): 239–50.

Tsing, Anna 2015. *The Mushroom at the End of the World: On the Possibility of Life in Capitalist Ruins*. Princeton, NJ: Princeton University Press.

Turner, Terence 2008. Marxian value theory: An anthropological perspective. *Anthropological Theory* 8 (1): 43–56.

Valdivia, Gabriela and Marcela Benavides 2012. Mobilizing for the petro-nation: Labor and petroleum in Ecuador. *Focaal* 63 (1): 69–82.

Vitalis, Robert 2009. *America's Kingdom: Mythmaking on the Saudi Oil Frontier*. London: Verso.

Wainwright, Joel and Geoff Mann 2013. Climate Leviathan. *Antipode* 45 (1): 1–22.

Whitehead, Judith 2010. *Development and Dispossession in the Narmada Valley*. Delhi: Pearson.

Williams, Raymond 1980. Ideas of nature. In *Problems in Materialism and Culture*, R. Williams, pp. 67–85. London: Verso.

Yessenova, Saulesh 2012. The Tengiz oil enclave: Labor, business, and the state. *PoLAR* 35 (1): 94–114.

6   Management

Stefan Leins

More than four decades after Laura Nader's (1972: 289) call to study 'colonizers rather than the colonized, the culture of power rather than the culture of the powerless, the culture of affluence rather than the culture of poverty', many anthropologists are still reluctant to study people in power. While one problem with studying them is the difficulty of getting access to their networks and institutions, a bigger problem is that, through the performance of authority and expertise, these people often succeed in framing what they do as particularly difficult to understand. Many anthropologists may thus be scared off because they think that they lack the knowledge necessary to understand these people and their worlds.

Still, when trying to understand current economic regimes, anthropologists cannot afford to treat powerful people such as managers, traders and investors as incomprehensible mysteries. These people influence economic processes in significant ways not only in global capital markets, but also in seemingly mundane economic transactions. Think, for example, of the everyday use of money, the setting of a commodity's price at a local market or the management of the supply chains that are the basis of the food that you eat and the clothes that you wear. All of these are influenced by the ideas and practices of those powerful people, the consequences of which trickle down to the everyday lives of individuals.

At the heart of such economic ideas and practices are often those who refer to themselves as managers. According to *The Oxford English Dictionary*, management is the 'process of dealing with or controlling things or people'. A manager can thus be someone who holds an intermediary position in an organisation or a person who exercises power, and often a manager does both. That dictionary definition indicates that what is to be managed can be either things or people, though commonly 'management' refers to control over the latter, especially employees in an organisation. You would not speak of managing people when describing the political authority of a king, chief, dictator or president. Further, management in this sense is not restricted to the private sector, for it exists as well in government agencies, NGOs and public institutions such as universities. It is, thus, not limited to the commercial realm in a narrow sense.

The fact that ideas and practices of management coming from the commercial realm have spread to public institutions is one aspect of the neoliberal turn that started in the 1970s and that has succeeded in turning all kinds of settings into quasi-commercial realms that should be guided by economic logic. Neoliberalism, according to David Harvey (2005: 2), is 'a theory of political economic practices that proposes that human well-being can best be advanced by liberating individual entrepreneurial freedoms and skills within an institutional framework character-ized by strong private property rights, free markets and free trade'.[1] Studying man-agement reveals how this ideology has colonised all areas of life and thus affects social lives and cultural realms that, at first sight, probably would not be considered as economic or commercial in a narrow sense. Accordingly, here I treat manage-ment as a mode of governing people or things in accordance with economic ideas and rationales. My use of 'governing' allows us to combine the notion of admin-istration and the notion of exercising control, and my approach to management encourages us to take into account the history and power of economic thinking that stands behind management. This is true for neoliberal thinking, as well as for the economic ideas and rationalities that preceded it.

A number of anthropologists have written about management practices, particu-larly in the field of financial markets (e.g. Hertz 1998; Ho 2009; Stein 2017), devel-opment aid (e.g. Escobar 1995; Mosse 2005; Rudnyckyj 2010) and the state (e.g. Ferguson 1990; Gupta 1998). Also, anthropologists working on corporate practices have discussed management, particularly the management of social and environ-mental risks (e.g. Rajak 2011; Welker 2014). Management is thus not completely absent from anthropological research. However, if we are to understand current economic regimes, we should make management a core field of research rather than treat it as a by-product of economic processes and the neoliberal turn. After all, management, a very practical field of doing economy and politics, is important for many anthropological questions about a globalised world and can be studied particularly well with ethnographic approaches.

In what follows I first give an overview of where we might locate management con-ceptually in the context of economic regimes. Then I discuss management practices in and beyond the economic realm. Here, I identify four areas in which manage-ment practices can play a decisive role and that deserve our attention: wealth and risk management; new public management and bureaucracy; management of the self; anthropological knowledge in management studies and practices. These areas illustrate how management is not simply something that is found in firms, but also is something that plays a critical role in public administration, the governance of the self and in science. In putting them forward, I hope to stimulate research in these areas.

Trapped between production and consumption

The classic way of studying economic fields and practices in anthropology is to identify them as part of either production (or labour) or consumption (or leisure). Even in the famous debates about gift exchange, the circulation of goods was studied in close relation to those who give and receive gifts. This might be justified in less complex forms of exchange, in which there are few, if any, intermediaries. In current capitalist exchange, however, there are a host of intermediaries involved in almost every transaction, and they are neither producers nor consumers. Their economic value derives from being involved in the management of the circulation of goods. They facilitate transactions by bringing together sellers and buyers, by collecting and distributing market information or by organising the movement of things between different parties. Traders are such market intermediaries, and their economic value derives from activities that are neither production nor consumption. Such intermediary roles historically attracted a certain degree of criticism from researchers and from ordinary people; as one mercantilist pamphleteer in the early nineteenth century put it, 'their meer *handing of Goods one to another*, no more increases any Wealth in the Province, then Persons *at a Fire* increase the *Water in a Pail*, by passing it thro' Twenty or Forty hands' (in Crowley 1974: 88; see Carrier 2012: 14). Like that pamphleteer, many of the critics draw a distinction between productive and unproductive work, or even between real economic processes and speculation (see Hertz and Leins 2012; Neiburg and Guyer 2017). In fact, however, the work of market intermediaries is just as real as the work of any other economic actor, for they establish real networks, link real producers to real consumers or manage real risk by either assuming it or transmitting it to other parties.

Management should be understood, like trading, as intermediary work. Managers play a critical role in the economy, but their work often is not directly linked to the production or consumption of a specific item. Rather, managers govern economic processes, try to make them more efficient and exercise control over circulating things as well as over people. Their fields of operation and influence are manifold. In almost every company and public agency we find managers. Of course, what they do can be linked to production and consumption, perhaps because they manage the supply rate of a producing firm or the purchasing strategies of a supermarket. Still, their work, like the work of many other intermediaries, remains generally invisible.

The invisibility of the work of managers normally turns into visibility only when there are scandals or crises. After the beginning of the financial crisis in 2007–08, for example, the role of wealth managers became subject to a broader public debate.[2] The question in that debate was the extent to which these wealth managers, who deal with the money of pension funds and public funds as well as individual investors, should be held accountable for recommending risky investments, such as collateralised debt obligations built on sub-prime loans. Similarly, in company scandals the role of managers has been questioned increasingly, mostly concerning their influence on the company's business strategy, and especially the ethical and legal foundations of those strategies. In addition, there are debates about the remuneration of managers, especially those referred to as 'top managers'. Are they worth the millions that they are paid? Do they deserve additional millions in bonuses? Is it justifiable that even the failure of their strategies results in golden parachutes when they leave, generous monetary and non-monetary benefits?

Apart from the debates that arise after scandals and in times of crisis, managers, as I said, usually remain invisible to a broader public. However, this does not mean that they are invisible within the economic realm. Management is taught in management and business schools and in many of the most prestigious universities, and an education in management often is key to a successful career in the private sector (Parker 2018). Unlike economics courses, management courses usually use case studies and aim to prepare people for everyday management practice. Also, students are taught how to become team leaders, which means how to manage people. Here again, it is clear that management is understood as a technique of governance, whether of people or things.

The power, the scandals and the high remuneration, combined with the common invisibility of management, has led to a negative image of management as a profession. Anthropologists studying management should not, however, be dissuaded by this negative framing. No matter how critical one might be about the work of managers, it has to be acknowledged that managers do real work. They are not unproductive middlemen who can easily be eliminated and, as I have suggested, their work and ideas influence the global economy in critical ways. To understand this influence, we need to look for areas in which management plays a defining role and use ethnographic methods to study how management practices are exercised on an everyday basis.

I have explained why I think that studying management is important if we want to think about how the economy is organised and how it works. Now I turn to those four areas in which, I said, management plays a key role.

Wealth and risk management

When thinking about management practices, one probably thinks about financial markets first. This is because phrases such as 'wealth management', 'asset management' and 'fund management' are prominent in advertisements, job descriptions and news reports that mention finance. All of these stand for the management of money in the widest sense. The manager, independently of whether he or she is called a wealth manager, asset manager or fund manager, is responsible for taking care of someone else's money and aims to increase, or at least protect, that person's wealth. Anthropologically, it is interesting that relationships between clients and managers usually are based on long relationships of trust that often also involve family affiliation, membership in similar social networks and the sharing of common pasts. Here, we might be reminded of kinship structures, which are similarly built upon networks of trust.

Not only do these relationships often deviate from the impersonal calculation that is part of economic rationality, the same is true of how these managers make investment decisions. Managers often base their decisions upon gut feeling and intuition. Contrary to what economists teach and would have us believe, then, such decision-making among managers is often affective, rather than being based on objective information and rational calculation. Also, managers often rely upon narratives about the future to help them make decisions in the present. Such narratives circulate widely among those concerned with the economy and create a notion of predictability and security, when in fact future economic developments remain largely uncertain (see Bear 2015a; Chong and Tuckett 2015; Leins 2013, 2018; Zaloom 2009).

One particularly interesting management practice that is found not only in finance but also in most other business sectors is risk management. Risk managers are responsible for evaluating the risk attached to a particular company, business sector or geographic region. They usually differentiate between different types of risk, such as operational risk, market risk and country risk. Operational risk is illustrated by the risk that, for example, a cargo to be delivered is damaged on its way to the recipient. Market risk is illustrated by the risk that the market price for a certain item rises or falls significantly while a commercial activity that involves it is being carried out. Country risk is illustrated by the risk of a change of legislation or government that changes the costs for parties involved in a transaction.

Risk managers usually lump risk into the categories of low, medium and high, so producing a degree of quantification of the level of risk. As with wealth management, however, risk management is by no means an exact science. This is due to the fact that, in order to assess risk, managers need to develop expectations about the future in order to assess what could happen. It thus involves some form of 'management of expectations' (Beckert 2016; see Appadurai 2013). Some of these expectations can be developed using probability calculations carried out on historical data. Other expectations, however, cannot be developed in that way, and economists call that Knightian uncertainty. The name refers to Frank Knight (1921), who distinguished between risk, something that can be expressed in terms of probabilities, and uncertainty, something that cannot be expressed that way.

While risk managers commonly present their conclusions with an air of confidence, generally they present only their conclusions rather than the steps by which they arrived at them. Anthropologists could offer important insights into the practical operations by means of which those managers distinguish between risk and uncertainty and how they produce their unitary conclusions about the future. Here, it is important to note that creating categories of risk is a mode of governing, as it creates the appearance that, through the assessment of risks, optimal decisions concerning the future can be made. Such discourse pervades the everyday work not only of wealth managers, but also of persons such as farmers or political authorities, who also create and use risk evaluations. They all do so because they all wish to have some confidence about the future and the challenges it may present, for these are important for helping them to decide how to structure their practices in the present and develop plans for the future. The practices linked to risk assessments are often practices of valuation and quantification, and anthropologists can benefit from the sociology of valuation and work by historians that investigates how economic actors produce cognitive frames and categories to define value, risk and opportunities (e.g. Callon et al. 2007; Chiapello 2015; Helgesson and Muniesa 2013; Poon 2009; Stark 2009; Vatin 2013).

In risk management, the question of power as part of management can be raised again: how do risk assessments circulate among different groups of actors and who benefits or suffers from them? In Switzerland, for example, migrants from the Balkans are charged higher rates for insurance when leasing a car, on the assumption that they drive faster than others and so are more likely to be involved in accidents. Similarly, Black people in the US often are charged higher interest when they take out a mortgage because they are considered to present a higher risk of default. On the other hand, those who do not smoke and those who exercise regularly get cheaper health insurance in some places. Under the appearance of neutral and technocratic evaluation, risk management can thus become a form of governance, as it distinguishes between those of higher and lower risk, often on the basis of ethnicity, class or gender.

Such risk assessments may be produced by a particular institution for its own purposes, but commonly they are sold to other interested parties, which can result in structural inequalities in access to goods and services that harm the groups considered to be of higher risk. Here, perhaps the most extreme example is the plan of the Chinese government to introduce a social credit system by 2020 (Chin and Wong 2016; Hatton 2015). The system is meant to collect data on social media use, online purchases and payment practices from all Chinese citizens to assess their trustworthiness. If the plan is carried out, it seems likely to have a critical influence on the stratification of Chinese society and the social mobility of particular groups, especially ethnic minorities and the poor. Here, anthropological research could examine how the introduction of such measurement of economic and other trustworthiness changes society, for whom it creates opportunities or disadvantages and how such a score plays out in the everyday lives of citizens. Also, it will be worth looking at the state apparatus behind the social credit system, including the practices of management linked to it and the new modes of governance that emerge from it.

New public management and bureaucracy

Another interesting field that calls for more research is the rise of new public management and its effects. New public management involves the application of management techniques developed in the private sector to the public sector. It became widespread in the 1980s, particularly due to its promotion by Ronald Reagan in the US and Margaret Thatcher in the UK. In the name of new public management, public institutions have been forced to behave as if they were actors in a competitive market seeking efficiency and profitability. Forcing public institutions to operate like private ones helped to spread neoliberal management practices, particularly through the movement of managers in the private sector to positions in the public sector and vice versa.

Today, new public management is at the centre of most public planning efforts and the governing of most public institutions, especially in Europe and North America. With its rise, economistic rationales and terminologies have taken over the public sector as government agencies have been obliged to show that they are efficient and competitive. This has happened in universities also. Today, professors and degree programmes are evaluated by student satisfaction, as if students were customers in a free market (see Miller 1998). And, as David Graeber (2018) observed, this has led to a boom in academic management, many times at the expense of the teaching and research staff who do the actual academic work. Graeber argues that academic management, then, does not necessarily facilitate academic work, but instead creates a new institutional environment in which academics have to write reports and prove to management that they are efficient and productive, a development that he calls 'managerial feudalism' or the 'bullshitization of academic life'.

Studying new public management, anthropologists can contribute to the analysis of neoliberalism through the exploration of particular management practices. How are categories of economic success socially constructed? How is competition embodied by private and public managers in everyday work practices? How is the ideology of the free market applied to public management, which is, by definition, not part of such a market? Research on such questions would be especially useful because current discussions of neoliberalism commonly take a macroscopic orientation or are concerned with historical causalities (e.g. Harvey 2005; Wacquant 2012). Anthropologists can temper these tendencies by studying the practices that lead to the integration of economistic ideologies into everyday work life, including in settings that had not previously been thought of in economistic terms.

The rise of new public management is also linked to questions of bureaucracy in general. In recent years, bureaucratic management practices have been addressed in work by Marilyn Strathern (2000), James Scott (2014) and David Graeber (2015). However, there are few full-scale ethnographic studies that focus on everyday bureaucratic management practices, whether in private corporations, NGOs, government agencies or elsewhere. To understand the relationship between the state, economy and society, anthropologists have to take on the study of everyday practices of bureaucracy. And, in doing so, we should not be deceived by the economists' narrative that bureaucracy is exclusively found in public institutions. As Graeber (2015) convincingly shows in his essay on bureaucracy, bureaucratic ideas and processes are equally present in the private sector and continue to play a critical role in how governments and firms make their plans in the current market economy.

One notable exception to my point that there are no ethnographies of the everyday practices of bureaucracy is Laura Bear's *Navigating austerity* (2015b).[3] Bear describes how management practices, influenced by austerity programmes and a state that sees itself as being in crisis, shape the lives of people living along the Hooghly River in India. The influence of bureaucratic practices introduced at the state level becomes apparent when looking at, for example, how people have switched from a long-term to a short-term perspective in personal economic planning, which has also affected their overall perception of time. Moreover, Bear shows how financialisation, in the sense of an overall effort in trying to find financial value in everything, has reframed not only economic activities, but also social relationships among the people living and working along the river. Bear's work teaches us that studying public and private management practices can be important for understanding the economic, political and social life of a community. Studying management is thus not important only for understanding businesses and state agencies; it is also important for understanding the nature of social lives in times of neoliberal economic thinking.

Anthropologists can extend such research by studying the influence of ideas and practices of management in different environments. Doing this, however, requires taking into account the transnational nature of management. Management practices link communities to the state and link everyday economic activities to global markets, and thus link the local to the global. Moreover, we need to be aware that the link goes both ways, as global management ideas and practices can be influenced by local ones. An example of this is emerging trends such as ethical consumption (Carrier and Luetchford 2012), corporate social responsibility (Dolan and Rajak 2016; Rajak 2011) and the variety of movements that address the ethics of transnational trade. They are all driven by local concerns about the fairness of economic activity and the ways that it can harm the environment. In so doing, those movements can change the terms of the production and circulation of things, the activities of transnational companies and the behaviour of producers and consumers. Anthropologists could, then, find out how the changes in values that are part of these local responses to globalisation are manifest in commodity chains, how forms of bureaucracy are linked to transnational trading and what forms of management are facilitated by it.

Management of the self

As we have learned from the work of Michel Foucault on neoliberal governmentality, management practices that are used to govern the economy and the state can also become embodied techniques that govern the self. Foucault used the notion of the entrepreneur of the self to describe how individuals can adapt and adopt governing tools and rationales coming from economic theory to optimise their own lives. Instead of seeing things as the result of social relations and interactions, the entrepreneur of the self understands social and economic merit as a result of 'being for himself his own capital, being for himself his own producer, being for himself the source of [his] earnings' (Foucault 2008: 226). The entrepreneur of the self is thus a new type of subject that uses particular management techniques to plan his or her life as if it were a fully economic project (see Bröckling 2016; Rose 1990).

The idea of the management of the self indicates that it can be productive for us to think about how ideas and practices of management can influence the way that people manage their daily personal lives. This would include things like studying people's self-optimisation strategies in their calculations to balance work and life, engaging in sports or cultivating healthy eating habits. It could also include attention to the increasing importance of career planning and yearly evaluations at work. Such influence of economic rationales on the management of the self can be studied very well by applying anthropology's methods of participant observation, interviewing and informal talk.

A good example of how to approach such neoliberal forms of self-governance ethnographically is Andrea Muehlebach's *The moral neoliberal* (2012). Muehlebach illustrates how neoliberal rationales have materialised in everyday lives due to people's ability to build upon moral orders, creating their own kind of neoliberal ethics. Interestingly, she shows that such neoliberal morality is not found only in the work and lives of people who value capitalism, but also can be found in the activities of socialist volunteers who offer people services to make up for the reduction of state welfare activities. Thus, she shows that the morality of neoliberalism can become powerful through the actions of supporters and critics alike.

While Muehlebach's study focuses on Italy, it would be interesting to explore how such moralities play out elsewhere, especially in the global South. While anthropology historically has dealt mainly with communities from the South, studies of neoliberal management practices tend to be focused on the global North, which is reasonable given that the academic institutions, think tanks, transnational corporations and international organisations that are the centres of neoliberal thinking are located mainly in the North. If we think of neoliberalism and its management practices as something that travels transnationally, however, we should also be able to identify them among people like African entrepreneurs, Arab bankers, South American state planners and the emerging East Asian educational elite. This suggests that we should investigate how the spread of ideas and practices of the management of the self has influenced perceptions of the self in different cultural contexts, which would allow us to understand both the adaptability of the ideas and practices of neoliberal management and the emerging forms of resistance to them.

Moreover, technological change plays an important role in managing the self through devices such as online calendars, smartphone pedometers and social media platforms. These devices are, however, more than simple tools of application. That is because they carry with them the ideas that their developers have about how to organise life. This has been investigated in the science and technology studies (STS) and the social studies of finance, under the name of 'performation' (Callon 2007; MacKenzie 2006). Building upon speech–act theory, scholars have argued that the inscription of ideas into devices encourages the materialisation of those ideas in the everyday lives of the people who use the devices. While the idea of performation points to the ways that ideas embedded in devices shape the lives and acts of those who use the devices, anthropologists can empirically test that. Investigating people's use and understandings of such devices for the management of the self, anthropologists can thus help to study management in the context of culture and technology.

Anthropological knowledge in management studies and practices

Another way to think about the relationship between anthropology and management would be to investigate the way that current anthropology has influenced management studies and practices. In 1997, Stephen Linstead's 'The social anthropology of management' was published. In it, Linstead said that anthropology could inspire future management scholars conceptually as well as methodologically. Conceptually, he claimed, management studies could benefit from anthropology's focus on culture, critique and change. Methodologically, Linstead argued, ethnographic approaches could help management scholars to understand everyday management practices more thoroughly.

Linstead's arguments seem to have found a receptive readership in the field of management and organisation studies, where the influence of anthropology is now hard to miss. Journals such as *Academy of Management Review, Journal of Management Studies* and *Organization Studies* increasingly publish articles that raise issues of culture, formulate cultural critique and often use anthropological literature to support their claims. Further, the ethnographic study of everyday practice has become popular in the field. In 2011, for example, the editors of the *Journal of Management Studies* called for more ethnography and invited Tony J. Watson (2011) and John Van Maanen (2011) to discuss the topic. Borrowing from anthropology, management scholars increasingly study cultural codes and attitudes, everyday interactions and social dynamics in management. Even though their ethnographies are often rather short-term case studies and less focused on a holistic understanding of the settings that they describe, there is real interest in understanding anthropology's ideas and approaches and in applying them to the study of management and organisation.

Alongside this development, and probably linked to it, anthropological knowledge also has gained popularity in the practical realm of management. Consider this example. In 2017 a project manager, Olivia Jardine, published a blog '5 ways studying anthropology can make you a better project manager'. In it, Jardine, an anthropology graduate from Sussex and Berkeley, explains how anthropology can enhance management skills. She summarises her key points as follows:

> Try your hand at ethnographic research when working out how to best influence and garner support from stakeholders.

> Use enhanced listening techniques to gain a deeper understanding of your end user.

> Practice empathy and compassion in your leadership to improve your relationship with your team members and team output.

Develop the cultural know-how to deliver projects globally, even with distributed teams.

Improve creativity and innovation on projects, ask unique questions and be curious.

Jardine also mentions companies that are hiring anthropologists for project management or are engaging in ethnographic research to find out about consumer demand, including Microsoft and the jeans producer Levi Strauss. Similar developments are reported by David Burrows (2014), who urges marketing professionals to use ethnography as a way to study consumption. Burrows mentions two other companies, household-goods producer Miele and mobile-phone manufacturer HTC, as examples of corporations that use ethnographic methods to study consumer demand (a fairly early advocate of this is Sunderland and Denny 2007).

In contrast to the perception of many anthropologists, these cases show that anthropological ideas circulate outside of academia and even make their way into management studies and practices. That circulation, however, has not been the subject of anthropological research. We might want to investigate how anthropological knowledge is applied in management and how this contributes to changing the concepts of management and of consumer research. Such investigation would be interesting not only because it throws a different light on anthropology, usually considered to be a discipline without much value to the private economy. In addition, it could help to conceptualise anthropology not simply as a closed academic discipline, but as something that has an influence on the larger world. This in turn could challenge the discipline's rejection of neoliberalism as alien and anathema, for it would show how anthropological ideas and practices have become part of neoliberal management.

Conclusion

I have argued that management practices and their underlying ideas deserve more attention in anthropological research, and I suggested that this lack of attention arises in part from the fact that management is located in neither the realm of production nor the realm of consumption, instead occupying an intermediary place in governing global economic regimes, acting with almost invisible hands. These hands of the managers should be made visible through the work of anthropologists who want to understand the ideas, rationales, narratives and practices that structure transnational economic processes and planning. To stimulate such research, I identified four areas in which management takes on a decisive role.

Firstly, I argued that wealth and risk management is an area where anthropologists can explore how risk is perceived and categories of risk are constructed in order to cope with the uncertain future. Here, I pointed out that the assessment of risk is not only an economic process but is also a political one, as it contains ideas about how society should be governed and affects the processes by which different people and groups are included or excluded from social benefits. Secondly, I highlighted the realm of new public management and bureaucracy, illustrating how ideas about management, and particularly neoliberal management, have been implemented in public institutions and are now to be found in many fields outside of the private sector. I referred to the work of a number of anthropologists who have been working on bureaucracy and I sketched ways to advance this field of research. Thirdly, I showed that ideas of management can also be applied to the ways that people plan their lives and govern themselves – Foucault's neoliberal governmentality. Drawing upon studies of the management of the self, I said that anthropologists can expand their research by looking at the role of morality and technology to gain a broader sense of how such government plays out in everyday life. Fourthly, I identified the influence of anthropology on the emerging area of management and organisation studies as another field worth exploring. Without the knowledge of many academic anthropologists, anthropological ideas and methods are gaining recognition among management scholars and are applied in consumer studies. Here, anthropologists could turn their attention to how the discipline's ideas circulate beyond its borders and how these ideas are transformed and materialised in management practices.

Based on the elaboration of these four fields, I conclude by stating that management should be understood as a technique of governing persons and things that is based on an economistic perspective on life and labour. While management practices originated in the economic realm, they have colonised various fields, including the organisation of everyday life and the governing of society at large. Because of this, studying the ideas and practices of management is critical not just to economic anthropology but to the discipline as a whole. Researchers taking management as an emerging topic of study will thus contribute not only to debates in economic anthropology, but also to the more general question of how society is organised and structured through ideas and everyday practices and what role economic thinking has in this process.

NOTES

1 There are many ways to define neoliberalism and make it a productive concept. Nuanced discussions of it in anthropology are in Birch (2017), Hilgers (2011), Ortner (2011) and Wacquant (2012).

2 In anthropology similar topics became the subject of broader interest due to the financial crisis (e.g. Applebaum 2009; Carrier 2018; Gudeman 2008; Hart and Ortiz 2008).

3 Another ethnography of bureaucracy, albeit in the context of migration rather than the more purely economic realm, is Tuckett (2018).

References

Appadurai, Arjun 2013. *The Future as Cultural Fact: Essays on the Global Condition*. London: Verso.

Applebaum, Kalman 2009. Free markets and the unfettered imagination of value: A response to Hart/Ortiz and Gudeman. *Anthropology Today* 24 (6): 26–27.

Bear, Laura 2015a. Capitalist divination: Populist-speculators and technologies of imagination on the Hooghly River. *Comparative Studies in South Asia, Africa and the Middle East* 35 (3): 408–23.

Bear, Laura 2015b. *Navigating Austerity: Currents of Debt Along a South Asian River*. Stanford: Stanford University Press.

Beckert, Jens 2016. *Imagined Futures: Fictional Expectations and Capitalist Dynamics*. Cambridge, MA: Harvard University Press.

Birch, Kean 2017. *A Research Agenda for Neoliberalism*. Cheltenham, UK and Northampton, MA, USA: Edward Elgar.

Bröckling, Ulrich 2016. *The Entrepreneurial Self: Fabricating a New Type of Subject*. Thousand Oaks: Sage.

Burrows, David 2014. How to use ethnography for in-depth consumer insight. *Marketing Week* (9 May). www.marketingweek.com/2014/05/09/how-to-use-ethnography-for-in-depth-consumer-insight/ (accessed 17 October 2018)

Callon, Michel 2007. What does it mean to say that economics is performative? In *Do Economists Make Markets? On the Performativity of Economics* (eds) Donald MacKenzie, Fabian Muniesa and Lucia Siu, pp. 311–57. Princeton, NJ: Princeton University Press.

Callon, Michel, Yuval Millo and Fabian Muniesa (eds) 2007. *Market Devices*. Oxford: Blackwell Publishing.

Carrier, James G. 2012. Introduction. In *Ethical Consumption: Social Value and Economic Practice* (eds) J.G. Carrier and Peter Luetchford, pp. 1–36. Oxford: Berghahn Books.

Carrier, James G. (ed.) 2018. *Economy, Crime and Wrong in a Neoliberal Era*. Oxford: Berghahn Books.

Carrier, James G. and Peter Luetchford (eds) 2012. *Ethical Consumption: Social Value and Economic Practice*. Oxford: Berghahn Books.

Chiapello, Eve 2015. Financialisation of valuation. *Human Studies* 38 (1): 13–35.

Chin, Josh and Gillian Wong 2016. China's new tool for social control: A credit rating for everything. *The Wall Street Journal* (28 November). www.wsj.com/articles/chinas-new-tool-for-social-control-a-credit-rating-for-everything-1480351590 (accessed 16 October 2018)

Chong, Kimberley and David Tuckett 2015. Constructing conviction through action and narrative: How money managers manage uncertainty and the consequence for financial market functioning. *Socio-Economic Review* 13 (2): 309–30.

Crowley, J.E. 1974. *This Sheba, Self: The Conceptualization of Economic Life in Eighteenth-Century America*. Baltimore: Johns Hopkins University Press.

Dolan, Catherine and Dinah Rajak (eds) 2016. *The Anthropology of Corporate Social Responsibility*. Oxford: Berghahn Books.

Escobar, Arturo 1995. *Encountering Development: The Making and Unmaking of the Third World*. Princeton, NJ: Princeton University Press.

Ferguson, James 1990. *The Anti-Politics Machine: Development, Depoliticization, and Bureaucratic Power in Lesotho*. Cambridge: Cambridge University Press.

Foucault, Michel 2008. *The Birth of Biopolitics: Lectures at the Collège de France, 1978–1979*. Houndmills: Palgrave Macmillan.

Graeber, David 2015. *The Utopia of Rules: On Technology, Stupidity, and the Secret Joys of Bureaucracy*. Brooklyn: Melville House.

Graeber, David 2018. Are you in a BS job? In academe, you're hardly alone. *The Chronicle of Higher Education* (6 May). www.chronicle.com/article/Are-You-in-a-BS-Job-In/243318 (accessed 1 August 2018)

Gudeman, Stephen 2008. Watching Wall Street: A global earthquake. *Anthropology Today* 24 (6): 20–24.

Gupta, Akhil 1998. *Postcolonial Developments: Agriculture in the Making of Modern India*. Durham, NC: Duke University Press.

Hart, Keith and Horacio Ortiz 2008. Anthropology in the financial crisis. *Anthropology Today* 24 (6): 1–3.

Harvey, David 2005. *A Brief History of Neoliberalism*. Oxford: Oxford University Press.

Hatton, Celia 2015. China 'social credit': Beijing sets up huge system. BBC News (26 October). www.bbc.com/news/world-asia-china-34592186 (accessed 16 October 2018)

Helgesson, Claes-Fredrik and Fabian Muniesa 2013. For what it's worth: An introduction to valuation studies. *Valuation Studies* 1 (1): 1–10.

Hertz, Ellen 1998. *The Trading Crowd: An Ethnography of the Shanghai Stock Market*. Cambridge: Cambridge University Press.

Hertz, Ellen and Stefan Leins 2012. The 'real economy' and its pariahs: Questioning moral dichotomies in contemporary capitalism. *Cultural Anthropology* (15 May). https://culanth.org/fieldsights/339-the-real-economy-and-its-pariahs-questioning-moral-dichotomies-in-contemporary-capitalism (accessed 1 August 2018)

Hilgers, Mathieu 2011. The three anthropological approaches to neoliberalism. *International Social Science Journal* 61 (202): 351–64.

Ho, Karen 2009. *Liquidated: An Ethnography of Wall Street*. Durham, NC: Duke University Press.

Jardine, Olivia 2017. 5 ways studying anthropology can make you a better project manager. Capterra Project Management Blog (24 April). https://blog.capterra.com/project-management-anthropology/ (accessed 1 August 2018)

Knight, Frank 1921. *Risk, Uncertainty, and Profit*. Boston: Houghton Mifflin.

Leins, Stefan 2013. Playing the market? The role of risk, uncertainty and authority in the construction of stock market forecasts. In *Qualitative Research in Gambling: Exploring the Production and Consumption of Risk* (eds) Rebecca Cassidy, Andrea Pisac and Claire Loussouarn, pp. 218–32. London: Routledge.

Leins, Stefan 2018. *Stories of Capitalism: Inside the Role of Financial Analysts*. Chicago: University of Chicago Press.

Linstead, Stephen 1997. The social anthropology of management. *British Journal of Management* 8 (1): 85–98.

MacKenzie, Donald 2006. *An Engine, Not a Camera: How Financial Models Shape Markets*. Cambridge, MA: The MIT Press.

Miller, Daniel 1998. A theory of virtualism. In *Virtualism: A New Political Economy* (eds) James G. Carrier and D. Miller, pp. 187–215. Oxford: Berg.

Mosse, David 2005. *Cultivating Development: An Ethnography of Aid Policy and Practice*. London: Pluto Press.

Muehlebach, Andrea 2012. *The Moral Neoliberal: Welfare and Citizenship in Italy*. Chicago: University of Chicago Press.

Nader, Laura 1972. Up the anthropologist: Perspectives gained from studying up. In *Reinventing Anthropology* (ed.) Dell Hymes, pp. 284–311. New York: Pantheon Books.

Neiburg, Federico and Jane Guyer 2017. The real in the real economy. *Hau* 7 (3): 261–79.

Ortner, Sherry B. 2011. On neoliberalism. *Anthropology of this Century* 1. aotcpress.com/articles/neoliberalism/ (accessed 1 August 2018)

Parker, Martin 2018. *Shut Down the Business School: What's Wrong with Management Education*. London: Pluto Press.

Poon, Martha 2009. From New Deal institutions to capital markets: Commercial consumer risk scores and the making of subprime mortgage finance. *Accounting, Organizations and Society* 34 (5): 654–74.

Rajak, Dinah 2011. *In Good Company: An Anatomy of Corporate Social Responsibility*. Stanford: Stanford University Press.

Rose, Nikolas 1990. *Governing the Soul: Shaping of the Private Self*. London: Routledge.

Rudnyckyj, Daromir 2010. *Spiritual Economies: Islam, Globalization, and the Afterlife of Development*. Ithaca: Cornell University Press.

Scott, James C. 2014. *Two Cheers for Anarchism: Six Easy Pieces on Autonomy, Dignity, and Meaningful Work and Play*. Princeton, NJ: Princeton University Press.

Stark, David 2009. *The Sense of Dissonance: Accounts of Worth in Economic Life*. Princeton, NJ: Princeton University Press.

Stein, Felix 2017. *Work, Sleep, Repeat: The Abstract Labour of German Management Consultants*. London: Bloomsbury.

Strathern, Marilyn (ed.) 2000. *Audit Cultures: Anthropological Studies in Accountability, Ethics and the Academy*. London: Routledge.

Sunderland, Patricia L. and Rita M. Denny 2007. *Doing Anthropology in Consumer Research*. Walnut Creek, CA: Left Coast Press.

Tuckett, Anna 2018. *Rules, Paper, Status: Migrants and Precarious Bureaucracy in Contemporary Italy*. Stanford: Stanford University Press.

Van Maanen, John 2011. Ethnography as work: Some rules of engagement. *Journal of Management Studies* 48 (1): 218–34.

Vatin, François 2013. Valuation as evaluating and valorizing. *Valuation Studies* 1 (1): 31–50.

Wacquant, Löic 2012. Three steps to a historical anthropology of actually existing neoliberalism. *Social Anthropology* 20 (1): 66–79.

Watson, Tony J. 2011. Ethnography, reality, and truth: The vital need for studies of 'how things work' in organizations and management. *Journal of Management Studies* 48 (1): 202–17.

Welker, Marina 2014. *Enacting the Corporation: An American Mining Firm in Post-Authoritarian Indonesia*. Berkeley: University of California Press.

Zaloom, Caitlin 2009. How to read the future: The yield curve, affect, and financial prediction. *Public Culture* 21 (2): 245–68.

7 Mobilisation, activism and economic alternatives

Valeria Siniscalchi

The people who camp for weeks in the public squares of Montreal, others marching in the streets of Barcelona or forcing their way into a bank in protest against a housing mortgage system, employees assembled at a factory in Southern France where work was stopped when the company moved production off-shore, the dozens of activists manning strategic spots at an enormous open-air cheese exhibition in a small city in Northwest Italy – what do these people have in common? Not much at first glance, yet there are common elements, even if they take different specific forms in different specific circumstances. In all of these cases, people have mobilised against a market system or some aspect of it.

'Why do people mobilise?' asks Daniel Cefaï in his analysis of 'theories of collective action'. According to him, collective action 'refers to any attempt to establish a more or less formalised or institutionalised collective by individuals seeking to reach a shared goal' (Cefaï 2007: 8). In his reflections on what political movements have in common, Jeff Pratt (2003) emphasises their dynamics of identity. Marc Edelman surveyed studies of social movements and underlines that they reveal 'an intensifying transnational activism, a disenchantment on the part of diverse activists with identity politics, and a resurgence of varied kinds of struggles against inequality' (Edelman 2001: 286). Reflecting on mobilisations for the protection of land, cultural identities and autonomy, June Nash notes that a 'notion of human rights, environmental conservation, and pluricultural autonomy developed along with and in response to the changes brought about by global integration' (Nash 2005: 3).

Such mobilisations are diverse and evolve. In some cases they assume the form of open protest or emerge in situations of conflict where they acquire national or international visibility. In other cases they are less visible and more diffused while expressing disagreement with the dominant system or one of its forms. Still other cases seem to escape the definition of activism. The challenge of this chapter is to analyse these phenomena, so distant from one another both geographically and in terms of their immediate goals, using the tools of economic anthropology and trying to identify lines of thought for future research.

Contemporary economic change

The initiatives and mobilisations that I mentioned make it possible to see the interweaving of economic and political forces that is often neglected in the work of anthropologists, but analysing forms of mobilisation is also an excellent way to interpret contemporary economic and political transformations. These changes are not an annex to anthropological field work, but rather are a key to understanding social realities. That is because one of the central issues of the present is the reconfiguration of economic spaces: places of production, work spaces, networks of exchange and distribution. Further, and more than they have in the past, economic questions permeate society and define people's way of life and the power relations in which they act or to which they are subjected. Internationalised markets, new monetary and financing systems and the systematic weakening of labour have modified the scale of regulation, forms of negotiation and the structuring of economic activities. Jean Comaroff and John Comaroff (2000: 363–64) summarise the new state of affairs thus: 'as the market has become the dominant organizing principle of economic life it has imposed its rationality on society, naturalizing economic activity and turning commodities into narrowly "economic" things, stripped of their symbolic and political significance'.

Comaroff and Comaroff (2000: 370) observe, moreover, that this increasing economisation of life can generate criticism that could 'expand the spaces where alternative visions of humanity are imagined, whether in "pockets of resistance" to capital, in places still free from its hegemony, or within its own contradictory locations'. Indeed, today there seem to be numerous expressions of new social imaginations in the form of resistance or alternative economies that seek to modify the paradigm of the market system and its associated social configurations, imaginations and values (see also Streinzer this volume). However, we need to heed Susana Narotzky's warning. If we contrast the dominant political economy to those new imaginations, to the advocacy of 'a social economy, solidarity economy, care economy, or postcapitalist economy' (Narotzky 2012: 239), we run the risk of creating dichotomies that can make it hard to understand that those movements and imaginations that social actors and researchers conceive as alternative are in reality an integral part of the capitalist system (2012: 248).

This observation is my starting point for an analysis of experiments that have taken place within the confines of the dominant political and economic system; experiments attempting to resist, oppose or modify that system, sometimes obscurely in its interstices and sometimes in more visible places. That analysis is concerned with the reasons why individuals and groups mobilise and how those mobilisations can help us to understand current economic reconfigurations. However, it is also important to attend to the evolution of activism, to the new configurations that it can produce and to its interaction with market logics. That activism encourages people to question the relationships of production and power, and the neoliberal economic system in general, and to rethink forms of production, distribution, exchange and consumption. It also is important to recognise that experiments in new economic and political relationships are not pursued without conflict, and an important concern of this chapter is the ways that tension and conflict are constitutive elements in the processes of economic reconfiguration not only in the arenas where the mobilisations are active, but also within the mobilisations themselves. For anthropologists, these conflicts offer fertile ground for analysis.

Themes and domains of mobilisation

At the heart of many present-day alternative economic projects we find classic themes and concepts of economic anthropology. Mary Douglas and Baron Isherwood's *The world of goods* (1979) was an early anthropological study of consumption and the place of goods in the process of social and cultural reproduction, including the possibilities of using consumption to reject existing cultural frameworks and produce change. The practice of consumption as 'engaged' or 'ethical' that is part of some contemporary mobilisations echoes some of what Douglas and Isherwood had to say, for it encourages people to rethink the relationship between the acquisition of goods and the ways that this can allow individuals and groups to challenge aspects of the dominant political and economic system (Carrier and Luetchford 2012; Dubuisson-Quellier 2009; Streinzer this volume). Further, in movements that encourage alternative economic practices that stress social exchange and reciprocity we observe criticisms of the market system that echo the ideas of Karl Polanyi (1957) and classic work in economic anthropology (e.g. Bohannan and Bohannan 1968; Sahlins 1972). Insights from this classic work are incorporated into the idea of a human economy (Hart et al. 2010), aimed at reinserting the social and human at the centre of the economy.

Recently, debates about public resources and mobilisations for the common good have raised the long-standing question of the appropriation and collective management of resources. This continues to be a point of tension between farmers and pastoralists in various parts of the world (Nonini 2007) and is a question that environmentalist movements confront in their protests for the sharing and preservation of resources and 'nature'. The question of common goods can appear also in urban contexts concerning the appropriation of spaces and places (Low and Lawrence-Zúñiga 2003). These debates encourage people to address once again the distinction of and interactions between the public and the private and, much as historians of rights do, examine the elements that the notions of public and private alone do not fully address (Quarta and Spanò 2016).

In her work on agricultural development strategies, Marian Stuiver uses 'retro-innovation' to refer to new practices that are based on old models: 'Retro-innovation is about developing knowledge and expertise that combines elements and practices from the past (from before modernisation) and the present and configures these elements for new and future purposes' (Stuiver 2006: 163). Proposed practices relating to things like exchange, production and property often are presented as innovations, while at the same time they maintain links with past, often idealised practices.

Notions like 'reciprocity' and 'gift' were previously used in different research contexts to describe specific forms of transaction (Mauss 1923–24; see also Gregory 1982), but now often are used outside of those contexts. They have come to denote 'good economies' that are opposed to the capitalist market system. Unfortunately, such use contributes to the consolidation of an artificial dichotomy between capitalism and 'other forms' of economy that are considered radically different from capitalism (Narotzky 2012: 247).

Although it is important not to succumb to such dichotomisation, I think that the ideas emerging from mobilisations about economic alternatives can help us to understand the internal dynamics of the neoliberal system. After all, the imaginations of the economy that are part of those mobilisations arise in the context of the market system that they criticise. Taking them seriously requires that we take account of the social and political values that support or arise from these alternatives and their practical achievements and variations as well as their co-existence with the logics of the market system.

A useful area for pursuing this point is that of food, which is both a concrete reality of great social significance that is intimately linked to daily life and vital necessity, and a catalyst of mobilisations in domains that range from the environment to social justice and workers' rights. Recent studies have used a comparative approach to examine the forms of activism in food production and consumption (e.g. Counihan and Siniscalchi 2014; Pratt and Luetchford 2014; Siniscalchi and Harper 2019). The notion of food activism has provided an analytical framework that can be applied to phenomena and actions at different scales, such as movements with a structured organisation, associations or co-operatives that link the different poles of the food chain and less structured actions aimed at establishing alternative modes of production or consumption.

One consequence of the economic crisis and the Great Recession and the government austerity that followed is that food mobilisations developed rapidly, and did so in a way that made the boundaries between distinct forms of activism increasingly permeable. Making sense of these mobilisations and their interactions requires flexible analytical instruments and a willingness to forego the sort of typologies often used in the literature on food movements, which can lead to unfortunate distinctions such as that between peasant movements and consumer movements or local food movements and food justice movements. As an example of this, the literature on food movements distinguishes between producer movements and consumer movements, forgetting what happens in between production and consumption, even though there are numerous associations and co-operatives that define themselves as organisations of both producers and consumers. An apt description of this link between production and consumption is the notion of co-producer, introduced by scholars such as Jan Douwe Van der Pleog (2006) to refer to interaction between individuals and living nature, which spread widely with its integration into the terminology of the Slow Food movement to indicate consumers who put themselves in the shoes of producers and get closer to the problems of production.

The forms of mobilisation

Mobilisations and instances of activism assume a variety of configurations, ranging from structured organisations to informal networks and forms of collective engagements. While these configurations often are matters of conscious decisions to innovate, the notion of retro-innovation can be applied to the structure of these mobilisations, suggesting that often they are not really new. After all, co-operatives and leaderless groups have been around for a long time. Also, such movements operate in a number of spheres at the same time, so that an economic alternative that a movement may advocate also is likely to be a political and social alternative and democratic forms are reassessed through their associated economic relationships and vice versa.

Many things shape the functioning of associations and movements, such as ways of recruiting volunteers or paid staff, how work is organised, how decisions are made and how governance is carried on. Moreover, these can change over the course of time, as can relationships among organisation members and their orientation towards the organisation and its goals. This is apparent in the occupation of the Unilever factory in Gémenos, near Marseille, by a worker collective in 2011 (Berlioux 2018). In the meetings and exchanges that occurred during 1,336 days of protest and occupation, workers engaged in the definition of their project of taking over the factory, but they also redefined relationships among working men and women, union activists, long-term employees, newer employees and temporary workers, all of whom had different relationships with the factory and the work. Mobilisations like this one may be collective phenomena, but the modalities, duration and reasons for engagement are not the same for everyone: individuals can have specific and sometimes divergent visions while remaining part of the group. At the end of the mobilisation there were a lot fewer workers engaged in the occupation than there were at the beginning. This suggests that we should pay attention to relations within such mobilisations and how they change over time at the individual level.

Equally, the internal organisation of a movement can generate inequalities in spite of its democratic ideals or the declared absence of formal leaders. The articulation between a movement's values and its organisation and practices can produce friction, dissonance and conflict. This is especially likely when the reproduction of the group and its goals are at issue, for instance when there are institutional or political changes or the group's leaders change. More than focusing only on the conflicts that can occur at such times or the contradictions that can exist between the declared values and practices, we have to analyse how the participants compromise or cope with dissonance and conflict. The result can be that the movement and its goals take on a different form, one that can diverge from what they were originally. Contradictions are part of these phenomena and attending to the ways that participants adjust to them can be useful for revealing the social dynamics of the movement.

It is also important to look at the relationship between groups and the individuals who are members of them. This has been addressed in terms of the dynamics of inclusion and exclusion in movements (Pratt 2003; Siniscalchi 2018), but we should look as well at how people's orientation can change over the course of time, perhaps becoming more involved with the group, less involved with it or even leaving it. The members of the AMAP (Association pour le Maintien d'une Agriculture Paysanne, a French association supporting peasant agriculture) and the members of the Slow Food movement provide fruitful examples: individuals become members for very different reasons, sometimes idealistic, sometimes quite instrumental, but membership itself produces effects on those individuals and mobilisations affect the individuals' involvement; they can produce activists in a performative way. In this process, those who may join a movement because it is stylish or out of curiosity or for economic reasons can become more involved with other aspects of the movement and so change the depth and strength of their involvement: the casual volunteer can turn into a professional volunteer (Gros 2014).

Slow Food illustrates this transformation of individuals and roles that gradually takes place at the core of mobilisations. What started as an association created by friends grew over time, to the point that it included a foundation for biodiversity, a commercial structure, a publisher, a private university, an international structure and several associated national structures. At the beginning, volunteers in Italy did a large part of the work at the core of the association and the first employees, largely recruited from volunteers, circulated among various tasks. Over time, the increasing size and complexity of the association led to a greater internal division of labour, so that the initial 'band of friends' became in large part a body of specialists, many of them former volunteers, who were in different departments carrying out different projects, attached to which was a body of volunteer activists at work in a number of locations in Italy and elsewhere (Siniscalchi 2019).

In mobilisations, employees can change their roles and statuses, and hence their view of their situation: workers in an occupied factory can become works managers and assume the functions of those who previously were the opposition. After a conflict that lasted more than three years at the Unilever factory in Gémenos, the 70 or so workers who remained and became part of a workers' co-operative project no longer had the same perspective on and relationship with the work, with the internal hierarchy, with the means of production or with production itself. Not only had the mobilisation changed them, but the project in which they engaged at the end of the conflict continued to modify those perspectives and require adjustments and compromises in those people's daily routines and in their economic and political aims (Berlioux 2018). One widespread observation is that factories that have been taken over by workers often are confronted with the realities of the market, realities that ultimately dilute the initial project. But how is this alternative project renegotiated, and how does this dilution operate at the scale of individuals?

These changes should alert us to the dangers of typologies that we may be tempted to create to classify diverse forms of mobilisation, especially their tendency to treat as fixed what in reality evolves over time. In the case of the Slow Food movement, the earliest members could generally be classed as gourmets – although their motivations, histories and aspirations were not the same – while today they are so heterogeneous that any such label would hinder our understanding of the movement rather than enhance it. Classification in terms of a gourmet elite would in effect obscure the changes that happened at the core of the association over the last 20 years, and remain attached to journalistic images in spite of the structure's internal dynamics (Siniscalchi 2013). Because mobilisations and the people who are part of them change over the course of time, studying them requires an approach that takes account of the processes and connections that are part of that change and that places them and the mobilisation at issue in their social, political and cultural context.

Scales of action and networks

The scale of actions in mobilisations varies. In some cases, associations and movements are distinctly local and actions are limited to regional or even more restricted levels. Other groups operate at a national or international scale or serve to connect transnational networks of diverse movements, as does La Via Campesina (Borras et al. 2008; Thivet 2014). We must bear in mind, however, that even when the scale of action is limited, even to a space as small as a site of production or a group of consumers, the objectives of the mobilisation need not be, but can include goals that are much more extensive.

For instance, when the workers at Unilever in Gémenos were contemplating their project for a workers' co-operative and resuming the production of herbal teas, they met with workers from the VIO.MA factory in Greece that had been taken over by workers. Also, because they wanted to increase the use of natural flavours, they established links with the producers of *tilleul* (lime tree or linden) in Provence and encouraged them to increase their output. Environmental motivations were thus mixed with those of preserving the factory and jobs, and with the goal of revitalising neighbouring local economies (Berlioux 2018). In this way, themes and struggles can grow and migrate from one place to another. Opposition to genetically modified organisms (Fitting 2010; Müller 2008) or a protest like Occupy (Mitchell et al. 2013), starting in one place, can be reinforced when extended or transferred to other places and integrated in other movements. As a part of this, key phrases circulate, and they can be transformed in the process, as happened with 'food sovereignty', developed by La Via Campesina (see, e.g., Heller 2013), and 'slow', introduced by the Slow Food movement.

As ideas can circulate and be appropriated, so can forms of mobilisation. The point that there is strength in numbers for individuals applies equally at the level of the organisations in which those individuals are involved. The networks and connections between the sites of various mobilisations become platforms of political and other exchanges for various lengths of time. These can lead to alliances, sometimes temporary or situational and other times more structured and stable, and the networks that result can function as autonomous organisms. Sometimes they are task forces established for precise goals such as the fight against the privatisation of water in Italy in 2011, which produced novel alliances between particularly heterogeneous institutions and associations. These inter-actions and connections, and the changes that they generate, would surely be an avenue for interesting research.

Attention to the way that mobilisations change over the course of time is useful also because it can help us to see the changing relationships that movements may establish with other institutions. Opposition, conflict and intransigence may co-exist with political and economic negotiations or produce collaborations with other institutions that formerly were considered the movement's enemy. For instance, as the French organisation AMAP, mentioned previously, became larger it began to pay staff. In order to find financing to help pay for these employees, it sought to establish relations with local elected officials, including those on the other side of the political fence. Similarly, leaders of the Slow Food movement occasionally establish ambivalent links with government ministers, regional officials and com-mercial firms in order to help finance large events like Slow Food product exhibi-tions. These forays into establishment quarters can, of course, leave the association exposed to criticism from both inside and outside.

These examples also point to the potential usefulness of studying something that anthropologists generally have ignored. That is, the ways in which mobilisations and alternative economic projects get the money that they need to operate, which may take conventional forms integrated with market logics but may also reflect efforts to find and secure alternative funding. Conventional or alternative move-ments have to get money if they are to survive and continue their activities, and in their efforts to get it they confront the pervasiveness of the capitalist system. Getting and spending money, effectively movements' budgets, are parts of alterna-tive experiments that are likely to affect the nature and orientation of movements, which makes them an important subject of analysis.

Resistance, resilience, alternative

Many of the mobilisations and experiments aimed at changing the economic system are concerned with food. Some are responses to material changes in food production such as the appearance of genetically modified organisms, the reduc-tion in farmland, changes in agricultural prices and food sovereignty. Others reflect concerns with quality and traceability, the conditions of production – defending quality and small-scale agricultural production – and the valorisation of local production (Pratt 2007). How are these objectives realised in practice? Some of these mobilisations seek to replace conventional commercial farming with methods identified as biodynamic, permacultural, organic and sustainable (Pratt and Luetchford 2014). Others emphasise the organisation and economics of production and distribution by questioning classical power hierarchies and through the collective ownership of means of production and worker co-operatives. In some cases, a more direct exchange between producers and consumers is emphasised: the social dimension of the exchange becomes a value to preserve or to reintroduce when it seems to have disappeared.

What kind of paradoxes are produced by these objectives when they face the practical realities? Mobilisation seeking a more democratic food system may decide to eliminate commercial intermediaries in distribution and instead have direct transactions between producers and consumers. Doing away with intermediaries, however, does not mean doing away with all of the work that they do. Volunteers may be willing to compensate for the absence of distribution professionals. In these cases, producers' work is valued in the same way as the volunteers' work, as is described in different case studies (Rakopoulos 2019). As this example indicates, if we are to understand these mobilisations, we must also analyse the tensions and contradictions that these experiments produce, and the ways that people deal with them.

Replacing an intermediary earning a living with an unpaid volunteer is explained by the attempt to have control over the food system. The individual is thought of as being able, through his or her daily efforts and by virtue of his or her engagement, to change the economic system. As Narotzky (2012: 245) observes, the 'hegemonic ideology of individual freedom of choice and decision making capacity [is] the "moral" realm of mainstream economy (i.e. liberal individualism)'. The potential for changes through individual actions should be situated in its cultural context, which gives a predominant place to the individual. At the same time, involvement assumes a political aspect, and the individual's action takes on a collective sense as well. Direct relationships, voluntary work and bartering are all cases where social relationships are valued and seem to develop in opposition to market relationships. The commercial dimension becomes secondary, sometimes even hidden, when compared to the ensemble of other values that intervene in the construction of the economic value of goods produced and exchanged. Nevertheless, the market relationships reappear, or are never completely eliminated.

This is illustrated by the movements in Spain that emerged after the onset of the financial crisis and that sought to protect people from the ill effects of the financial system, especially concerning mortgages on people's homes. Those movements directed attention to mortgages and the ways that they were advertised and sold, but also highlighted the undesirable effects of financial and property speculation and of the logic of financial practices, and the effect of mortgage debt on the life of people in general (Palomera 2014; Ravelli 2017). Organisations in that broad movement engaged in concrete action aimed at intervening in foreclosure, at cancelling the debts of those who had lost their homes and at trying to find new ways to house people. In overturning the power relation and moving the responsibility for dispossession from borrowers to banks, their speculations and their financial and commercial practices, the movement cast itself as a form of practical opposition to the effects of financialisation (Ravelli 2013). However, those organisations did not question the concept of private property in housing, the modality of access to home ownership, nor did they question the type of economy that real estate speculation had fostered. The alternatives that they proposed, then, appeared as something internal to the system that accepted the basic way that housing is allocated in Spain, and sought only to make the economy of housing somewhat more moral.

There is another fairly cultural factor that affects both anthropologists and ordinary people in the West, especially those who object to the current economic system. That is the idea that money has the power to subvert the moral order of societies (but see Parry and Bloch 1989: 1). This demonisation of money may account for the fact that analysts often ignore it even though, as I noted, it is an important element in mobilisations. In some economic alternatives, money seems to disappear or is reinvented as an object and a special means of exchange (see Streinzer this volume). In other cases, money is the focus of attention, perhaps in the form of a product's fair price and the fair remuneration of producers. These attitudes are the two sides of the same coin, in which money is either obscured or placed openly in the centre of the political arena.

When mobilisations are concerned with the price of products or the remuneration of producers, money becomes a vehicle for expressing other concerns and values. An example is the Sardinian Movimento Pastori Sardi (Pitzalis and Zerilli 2013; Zerilli and Pitzalis 2019), which uses the price of milk to urge recognition by regional and national officials of the social and economic role played by shepherds. In the case of AMAP, mentioned previously, money does not appear to circulate during the weekly distribution of vegetables because the association's members negotiate quarterly or annual contracts with farmers who are paid in separate transactions (Lamine 2008; Siniscalchi 2015). Money does become apparent during meetings between farmers and voluntary advisors or when contracts are renegotiated. At these times, group members settle on a price with farmers that assures that they will have enough income to support a reasonable livelihood, so that the system will operate fairly (Siniscalchi and Harper 2019).

Money acquires a particular value in alternative systems that seek to place solidarity at the centre of interactions in the economic realm. The spirit of solidarity is promoted in various mobilisations, often in situations of economic crisis but not only then, and it can take on different forms and significations. Seen as being in opposition to the competitive capitalist market system and to the power relationships that are part of that system, solidarity bring us an ideal equilibrium and is supposed to introduce an affective dimension to economic relations. But it is important that we investigate how it is put into practice, for solidarity not only calls on participants to do things differently, it also is likely to be a source of friction.

We can ask ourselves about the degree to which an economic alternative is diffused, which I have mentioned already, but also it is important to study the ability of a movement to generate new, or imaged as new, practices, sensibilities and models of economic action. And in doing so, we should consider both those movements that look like successes as vehicles of change and also those that look like failures. Further, once a movement ends, whether as a success or failure, we need to ask what happens afterwards. Once the fight is over, how is the existence of the alternative negotiated, normalised or rejected?

Conclusion

In this chapter I have invoked a variety of movements, like protests against mortgage foreclosures, factory workers fighting for their jobs and Slow Food advocates urging a food system oriented towards quality and respect for workers and the environment. These are diverse movements whose members engage in collective action of different sorts. But all of them seek to have some level of control over the economic system and influence the way in which it permeates their lives, and to do this they have engaged collectively.

This collective action and the emergence of groups associated with it has consequences: the group's form affects its own evolution and that of the individuals who are part of the movement. I think that it is important that we analyse the processes involved and the point of view of the people who are part of it. We must ask not only how mobilisations themselves are modified and evolve over time, how they reproduce themselves or fail to do so, we must also ask how these processes affect the individuals involved. These processes and questions form the lines of research that should be the basis of the analysis of mobilisations that emerge in the interstices of the neoliberal system. That is, we should not look only at the overt goals of such movements but need also to attend to the conflicts and frictions that are part of their emergence and internal evolution.

The spaces of experimentation in forms of resistance or alternative economics, such as those that I have sketched in this chapter, are also spaces that produce new social, political and economic imaginations, and new social configurations. Property rights, work relationships, profit, exchange, representation and democracy all are tested and re-examined. We need, however, to do more than catalogue those imaginations and configurations. We need also to study the place of alternatives at the core of the dominant economic system and their effects. How is the market system modified under pressure from these experiments? How does it absorb alternatives or even produce new ones? How do new economic forms emerge? How are they renegotiated? What are the various articulations between ideals and practices? Sometimes external factors require making a change; sometimes there is a desire to return to an imagined past that is thought to offer better social and economic relationships. Then again, sometimes there is a will to preserve the status quo, the existing social, legal or economic situation in the face of a breakdown or an imposed change.

Mobilisations are both responses to change and ways to implement change, and, as I have stressed, they themselves change over time for a variety of reasons. Thus, to consider what people conceive of as alternative or experimental and how they might seek to bring it about, whether among themselves or more broadly, we need to avoid the temptation of thinking in terms of types of movements. Instead, we should think in terms of connections, evolutions, tensions and instabilities. Doing this is not easy, for it requires that we attend to entities and processes at very different scales, and that we do so with an ethnographic eye.

References

Berlioux, Florent 2018. *Salariés et Salariées de Fralib à Gémenos: Une Anthropologie des Subjectivités Ouvrières (vers 1980–2014)*. PhD Thesis, École des Hautes Études en Sciences Sociales.

Bohannan, Paul and Laura Bohannan 1968. *Tiv Economy*. Evanston: Northwestern University Press.

Borras, Jr, Saturnino M., Marc Edelman and Cristóbal Kay (eds) 2008. *Transnational Agrarian Movements confronting globalization*. Chichester: Wiley Blackwell.

Carrier, James G. and Peter G. Luetchford (eds) 2012. *Ethical Consumption: Social Value and Economic practice*. Oxford: Berghahn Books.

Cefaï, Daniel 2007. *Pourquoi se mobilise-t-on? Les théories de l'action collective*. Paris: La Découverte.

Comaroff, Jean and John L. Comaroff 2000. Millennial capitalism: First thoughts on a second coming. *Public Culture* 12 (2): 291–343.

Counihan, Carole and Valeria Siniscalchi (eds) 2014. *Food Activism: Agency, Democracy and Economy*. London: Bloomsbury.

Douglas, Mary and Baron Isherwood 1979. *The World of goods: Towards an Anthropology of Consumption*. New York: Basic Books.

Dubuisson-Quellier, Sophie 2009. *La consommation engagée*. Paris: Les Presses de Sciences Po.

Edelman, Marc 2001. Social movements: Changing paradigms and forms of politics. *Annual Review of Anthropology* 30: 285–317.

Fitting, Elisabeth 2010. *The Struggle for Maize: Campesinos, Workers, and Transgenic Corn in the Mexican Countryside*. Durham, NC: Duke University Press.

Gregory, C.A. 1982. *Gifts and Commodities*. London: Academic Press.

Gros, Joan E. 2014. Food activism in Western Oregon. In *Food Activism: Agency, Democracy and Economy* (eds) Carole Counihan and Valeria Siniscalchi, pp. 15–30. London: Bloomsbury.

Harper, Krista and Valeria Siniscalchi (eds) 2019. Value and values in food projects in Europe. In *Food values in Europe* (eds) Valeria Siniscalchi and Krista Harper, pp. 1–14. London: Bloomsbury (forthcoming).

Hart, Keith, Jean-Louis Laville and Antonio David Cattani 2010. *The Human Economy*. Cambridge: Polity Press.

Heller, Chaia 2013. *Food, Farms and Solidarity: French Farmers Challenge Industrial Agriculture and Genetically Modified Crops*. Durham, NC: Duke University Press.

Lamine, Claire 2008. *Les AMAP: Un Nouveau Pacte entre Producteurs et Consommateurs?* Gap: Éditions Yves Michel.

Low, Setha M. and Denise Lawrence-Zúñiga 2003. Locating culture. In *The Anthropology of Space and Place* (eds) S.M. Low and D. Lawrence-Zúñiga, pp. 1–47. Oxford: Blackwell.

Mauss, Marcel 1923–24. Essai sur le don: Forme et raison de l'échange dans les sociétés archaïques. *Année Sociologique* (nouvelle série) 1: 30–186.

Mitchell, W.C.T., Bernard E. Harcourt and Michel Taussig 2013. *Occupy: Three Enquires in Disobedience.* Chicago: Chicago University Press.

Müller, Birgit 2008. *La Bataille des OGM: Combat Vital ou d'Arrière-Garde?* Paris: Editions Ellipses.

Narotzky, Susana 2012. Alternatives to expanded accumulation and the anthropological imagination: Turning necessity into a challenge to capitalism. In *Confronting Capital: Critique and Engagement in Anthropology* (eds) Pauline Gardiner Barber, Belinda Leach and Winnie Lem, pp. 239–52. New York: Routledge.

Nash, June (ed.) 2005. *Social Movements: An Anthropological Reader.* Oxford: Blackwell.

Nonini, Donald (ed.) 2007. *The Global Idea of 'The Commons'.* Oxford: Berghahn Books.

Palomera, Jaime 2014. How did finance capital infiltrate the world of the urban poor? Homeownership and social fragmentation in a Spanish neighborhood. *International Journal of Urban and Regional Research* 38 (1): 218–35.

Parry, Jonathan and Maurice Bloch 1989. Introduction: Money and the morality of exchange. In *Money and the Morality of Exchange* (eds) J. Parry and M. Bloch, pp. 1–32. Cambridge: Cambridge University Press.

Pitzalis, Marco and Filippo Zerilli 2013. Pastore Sardu non t'arrendas como! Il movimento pastori Sardi: Alterità, resistenza, complicità. *Rassegna Italiana di Sociologia* 54 (3): 379–400.

Polanyi, Karl 1957. The economy as instituted process. In *Trade and Market in the Early Empires: Economies in History and Theory* (eds) K. Polanyi, Conrad M. Arensberg and Harry W. Pearson, pp. 243–69. New York: The Free Press.

Pratt, Jeff 2003. *Class, Nation and Identity: The Anthropology of Political Movements.* London: Pluto Press.

Pratt, Jeff 2007. Food values: The local and the authentic. *Critique of Anthropology* 27 (3): 285–300.

Pratt, Jeff and Peter Luetchford 2014. *Food for Change: The Politics and Values of Social Movements.* London: Pluto Press.

Quarta, Alessandra and Michele Spanò (eds) 2016. *Beni Comuni 2.0: Contro-Egemonia e Nuove Istituzioni.* Milan-Udine: Mimesis.

Rakopoulos, Theodoros 2019. 70% Zapatista? Solidarity 'ecosystems' and the troubles of valuing labor in food cooperatives. In *Food Values in Europe* (eds) Valeria Siniscalchi and Krista Harper, pp. 147–62. London: Bloomsbury (forthcoming).

Ravelli, Quentin 2013. Le charme du ladrillo: Une histoire de briques au cœur de la crise espagnole. *Vacarme* 63 (2): 142–61.

Ravelli, Quentin 2017. *Les Briques Rouges: Dettes, Logement et Luttes Sociales en Espagne.* Paris: Editions Amsterdam.

Sahlins, Marshall 1972. *Stone Age Economics.* Chicago: Aldine-Atherthon.

Siniscalchi, Valeria 2013. Slow versus fast: Economie et écologie dans le mouvement Slow Food. *Terrain* 60: 132–47.

Siniscalchi, Valeria 2015. Food activism en Europe: Changer de pratiques, changer de paradigms. *Anthropology of Food*, S11. http://aof.revues.org/7920 (accessed 30 November 2018)

Siniscalchi, Valeria 2018. Political taste: Inclusion and exclusion in the Slow Food movement. In *Making Taste Public* (eds) Carole Counihan and Susan Højlund, pp. 185–97. London: Bloomsbury.

Siniscalchi, Valeria 2019. *Slow Food: The Economy and Politics of a Global Movement.* London: Bloomsbury (forthcoming).

Siniscalchi, Valeria and Krista Harper (eds) 2019. *Food Values in Europe.* London: Bloomsbury (forthcoming).

Stuiver, Marion 2006. Highlighting the retro side of innovation and its potential for regime change in agriculture. In *Between the Local and the Global* (eds) Terry Marsden and Jonathan Murdoch, pp. 147–73. Bingley: Emerald Group Publishing.

Thivet, Delphine 2014. Peasants' transnational mobilization for food sovereignty. In *Food Activism: Agency, Democracy and Economy* (eds) Carole Counihan and Valeria Siniscalchi, pp. 193–209. London: Bloomsbury.

Van der Pleog, Jan Douwe 2006. *Oltre la Modernizzazione: Processi di Sviluppo Rurale in Europa.* Soveria Mannelli: Rubbettino.

Zerilli, Filippo and Marco Pitzalis 2019. From milk price to milk value: Sardinian sheep herders facing neoliberal restructuring. In *Food Values in Europe* (eds) Valeria Siniscalchi and Krista Harper, pp. 79–94. London: Bloomsbury (forthcoming).

8 Ethical economic practice

Andreas Streinzer

The financial crisis of 2007–08 prompted many economic anthropologists to take stock of the sub-discipline. Scholars raised big issues: the need to return to interest in systems instead of individuals (Carrier 2012a), to reassess the relationship between political and moral economy (Narotzky and Besnier 2014), to see distribution as a central concern (Gregory 2009), to rethink the history of capitalism between 1970 and 2008 (Hart and Ortiz 2008).

In addition, in the world at large big questions about capitalism were on the agenda yet again. Governments and central bankers discussed systemic hazards of capitalism. In Southern Europe protests against austerity and bank bailouts brought millions of people onto the streets. New political movements, alternative economic networks and consumer groups mounted criticisms of economic structures by referring to social values such as equality, solidarity, fairness and dignity. They raised questions about the relationship between the preconditions for social reproduction and environmental sustainability on the one hand, and the orientation towards profit and gain on the other.

Those mobilisations that challenged economic structures led to hopeful enthusiasm among economic anthropologists, who took them as expressions of an increasing politicisation of economic systems and their outcomes, an increasing awareness that the economy is a product of cultural ideas, social construction and political negotiation. Influential authors such as J.K. Gibson-Graham (2008: 613) called for explicit engagement with such movements, asking: 'how might academic practices contribute to the exciting proliferation of economic experiments occurring worldwide in the current moment?' and urging us 'to bring marginalized, hidden and alternative economic activities to light in order to make them more real and more credible as objects of policy and activism'. It is not surprising, then, that social values and ethical action became one of the major topics in economic anthropology. This chapter is about how to maintain that enthusiasm while adjusting our analytical tools, our perspectives and our optimism.

The implicit hope was that the repoliticisation of things economic would be progressive. However, ten years after the crisis the world has become increasingly populated by regressive forms (Nachtwey 2016). In the US, Donald Trump was elected president on promises of a redistribution of jobs to people who are predominantly White and male. These economic promises were accompanied by a series of attacks on minorities, migrants, women and people of colour by groups on the radical Right. In Europe, governments in Hungary, Austria and Poland include Right or far-Right groups, backed by an intensifying mobilisation of citizens around nationalist, fascist, racist and sexist values and moral panics about refugees, gender equality and race. That shift to the Right in Europe has been going on since the early 1990s and is addressed in various sub-fields of anthropology (Gingrich and Banks 2006), but by only a few economic anthropologists (Kalb 2014). These phenomena raise issues of identity and recognition, but they are also explicitly about distribution, about channelling funding and social transfers away from marginalised groups, buying according to nationalist criteria and questioning the right of minority groups to economic and social inclusion.

Economic anthropologists had hoped for a widespread questioning of the apolitical and asocial idea of the economy that was dominant before the crisis, but probably not the growing politicisation from the Right. The simultaneous appearance of polarised Left and Right movements claiming to promote the general good should concern a comparative discipline. It raises questions about the specific contexts in which values are mobilised and about the more general question of how we ought to analyse them. Economic anthropology is in a privileged position to take up these questions, the study of which presently seems scattered across several sub-fields.

A useful way to consider such a wide range of value mobilisations might be to ask how people advocate and engage in ethical economic activities of all sorts, rather than just the more progressive activities that have attracted the most scholarly attention. Such an approach might help us achieve a comparative analysis of how people act upon, question and negotiate material relations, and thus reinvigorate the study of how political economies become politicised again.

To argue for a renewed focus on such forms of practice, I will proceed in a series of steps. Firstly, I aim to define the issue at stake as an abstract idea of values and what Stephen Gudeman (1986) calls 'things economic'. Secondly, I turn to the empirical fields in which anthropologists detect such practices. I argue that there is a bias towards conflating 'values' with what analysts think is good, which makes it hard to see the range of ways in which people align social values and economic practice and hard to recognise the scale of mobilisations. Thirdly, I formulate a renewed research agenda for economic anthropology that is historical and comparative.

The aim of this chapter is to maintain the enthusiasm about studying values and economic relations, but to do so in a fairly analytical way that builds on anthropology's tradition of comparison and generalisation. Such an analytical approach allows us to question the kinds of processes by which people draw attention to the evaluations of economic systems and principles of distribution, and thus to those bigger questions that economic anthropologists began to ask after the crisis. Such an approach can help us to ask what these forms of addressing economic relations have to do with the larger political-economic structures that shape and constrain what becomes politicised, by whom and how, and thus equip us for an analysis of the broader shifts in political and moral economies since 2007–08.

Anthropologies of ethical economic practice

The idea of ethical economic practice is peculiar, in the sense that it is a rather eccentric combination that exists only in specific historical moments and social conditions. More specifically, the phrase presupposes a distinction between the ethical and the economic. Such differentiation between social values and the economy began emerging in Europe and North America in the eighteenth century (Carrier 2012b: 7 ff.). Since then, the economy increasingly came to be seen as a realm in which short-term exchange and monetary profit reigned, while the social realm was said to exhibit values associated with kinship, religion or even society itself. This emergent understanding of a separation of spheres was further solidified by social scientists like Max Weber, who distinguished *Wirtschaft und Gesellschaft* (published in English as *Economy and society*, Weber 1978 [c. 1914]), and Karl Polanyi (1944), who wrote about *The great transformation*. While this differentiation is situated in the historical transformation from feudal and mercantile societies to industrial capitalism in the West, it resembles a pattern found in a wide range of societies that distinguish different 'transactional orders' (Parry and Bloch 1989: 23). Often, these orders exhibit 'a strikingly similar concern with the relationship between a cycle of short-term exchange which is the legitimate domain of individual – often acquisitive – activity, and a cycle of long-term exchanges concerned with the reproduction of the social and cosmic order' (Parry and Bloch 1989: 2).

For the capitalist societies that are my main focus here, the idea of distinct spheres might serve as a 'pragmatic device' (Gudeman 1986: 29) to ask how and why people relate those seemingly distinct spheres with each other. There are at least three ways in which such relationships are framed. The first is a reaffirmation of the distinction, a concern to keep them separate and in some kind of balance, illustrated by David Schneider's (1980 [1968]: 45 ff.) statement that in the US people understand spheres of work and spheres of domestic life as opposed to one another. A second is the conviction that the realm of the economy embodies ideal forms of behaviour and should therefore be used as a model to shape the social sphere to bring it into line with the principles taken to characterise the economic sphere, described by James Carrier and Daniel Miller (1998) as virtualism. This idealisation of the values associated with the economic sphere is an important mode of thought in the world and in scholarship: Gary Becker received a Nobel prize in economics for a theoretical model implying such a proposition. A third way to distinguish and relate the spheres is what we usually understand as ethical economic practice, which commonly rests on the claim that the sphere of the economy is too little infused with social values. People who hold this view can attempt to make the economy more ethical through ethical economic practice.

Such practice is a key idea in four bodies of recent scholarship in economic anthropology. The first is concerned with ethical consumption (Carrier and Luetchford 2012; de Neve et al. 2008), exemplified by fair trade. Its means are consumers' purchasing decisions which are 'shaped by their assessment of the moral nature' (Carrier 2012b: 1) of the context of commodities. In other words, ethical consumers buy commodities whose production tends to support social values, including protecting the environment. Today, ethical consumption is a billion-dollar market in which large multinational corporations have an increasing stake. For instance, one can buy orangutan-friendly copy paper, offset CO_2 emissions from airplanes by donating to environmental projects and hear music on a charity iPod to support needy populations.

A second body of work is concerned with corporate social responsibility (CSR). It investigates how corporations urge a more humane capitalism (Dolan and Rajak 2016: 1) by reducing corporate harm to the environment and the people involved in production. Related to this, what are called social enterprises merge profit-seeking with a claim to solve social or environmental problems (Mauksch et al. 2017). One famous example is the Grameen Bank, founded by Muhammad Yunus. The bank and Yunus shared the Nobel Peace Prize in 2006 for extending microcredits to poor people, a practice which has come under mounting criticism from anthropologists (e.g. Rahman 1999; Schuster 2015).

A third strand in the literature is focused on solidarity economies that emerged during the economic crisis in Southern Europe, where organisations stressing solidarity have been spreading. Some of them seek to fill the gaps left by state austerity and falling incomes (Dalakoglou 2016), such as soup kitchens, social pharmacies and refugee support groups. Others attempt to build alternative economic structures to secure relative autonomy from state or capitalist market arrangements, such as groups in the No Middleman Movement (Rakopoulos 2016) and local exchange and trading systems (LETS). Unlike fair trade and CSR, these groups seek alternatives to capitalist market relations rather than using them to bring about social change.

The fourth body of work is concerned with moral economies, and it addresses disjunctures in what is considered as legitimate economic practice. While there is debate about the concept (e.g. Carrier 2018; Hann 2018; Palomera and Vetta 2016), it often refers to how economic arrangements are contested on moral grounds in situations of crisis.

These bodies of work indicate the thriving state of research into value mobilisations in economic practice after the crisis. Anthropologists take up issues of exploitation, environmental destruction, inequality, crises of social reproduction and ethical activities aimed at human flourishing. Such work gives hope that the dark (Ortner 2016) sides of our world are questioned and criticised instead of legitimated. Yet stepping back from the empirical phenomena discussed in this work, we might ask whether such optimism speaks to our own hopes more than it reflects a careful assessment of efforts to inject social values into economic relations.

Alternative values, giving voice and pragmatic devices

Research in economic anthropology on ethical consumption, CSR, solidarity economies and moral economies has made the increasing importance of ethical economic practices visible in the sub-discipline. However, a comparative economic anthropology needs to ask if these are the only ways in which groups seek to shape their economic practices in order to bring about what they consider to be good. If they are not, what are the fields and the groups? What are their claims and values? These questions are important if we want a comprehensive view of how people understand the relation between economy and society.

In 2018, the answers to these questions are more complicated and less comfortable than they seem to have been in 2008. That is because anthropologists generally have addressed the question of ethical economic practice in terms of the liberal, progressive or neo-communitarian values that many of them hold, while the world seems to be moving in another direction.

An example is the Chick-fil-A same-sex marriage controversy (Severson 2012). In June 2012 the head of Chick-fil-A, a fast-food chain in the US that is owned by a Baptist family, made several public comments opposing same-sex marriage, and it turned out that the company supported anti-LGBT groups. What followed started like many other consumer activist campaigns, with liberal groups calling for a boycott of the company and mayors announcing that they did not want the chain in their cities. However, things began to change. Conservative groups started urging people to buy from Chick-fil-A in order to show their support for its anti-LGBT and anti-same-sex marriage stance. A conservative state governor initiated a 'Chick-fil-A appreciation day movement' and, in the end, the chain increased their sales by 12 per cent (Couret 2013). Buying a sandwich to protest against LGBT rights clearly falls under a reasonable definition of ethical economic practice, for it involves the use of economic actions to express values relating to the social realm. However, identifying it this way is unusual in the sub-discipline, sufficiently so that it raises the question of how seriously anthropologists are taking the Natives. Following Eduardo Dullo, the groups boycotting Chick-fil-A would be those that anthropologists try to 'give voice to', while those supporting the chain's opposition to LGBT rights would be 'repugnant others' who deserve not voice but 'denunciation and suspicion' (Dullo 2016: 134). One particularly unfortunate outcome of that orientation is that we, as anthropologists, know little about the strategies of these Others and why their claims appear attractive to growing numbers of people.

Our analytical instruments may be getting better, but it seems that we deploy them in a way that does not detect major shifts in the kinds of values that lead people to seek change in the world. Anthropologists' surprise and puzzlement arising from Donald Trump's appeal, the Brexit vote in Britain and the emergence of far-Right parties in Europe speak of these blind spots (see also Moberg this volume). Considering the increasing dominance of such values, we need to try to figure out what keeps us from seeing them or taking them seriously. When I say that we should take them seriously I do not mean that we should validate their claims or give voice to their ideologies, but I do mean that we ought to separate endorsement and critical scholarship (as proposed by Pasieka 2016).

Those blind spots arise from the relationship between the ethnographic, analytical and normative dimensions of anthropological practice. An important tendency in this regard is to collapse the 'cultural construction of the good' (Robbins 2013: 457) into a normative understanding of a phenomenon as good, which complicates our attempts to understand how values relate to economic practice. The interlocking of ethnographic and normative levels is evident in the idea that anthropology should be primarily about the giving voice that Dullo mentioned, which would, again in Gibson-Graham's (2008: 613) words, 'bring marginalized, hidden and alternative economic activities to light in order to make them more real and more credible as objects of policy and activism'. Such an approach has value, but conceiving of our practice as a way to give legitimacy to those we study in order to make them more real and credible can keep us from understanding how diverse people and their motivations and practices really are. In extreme cases, this can lead to an 'ethnographic refusal' (Ortner 1995) that deliberately masks disagreements about 'the good' (on the ethical dilemmas of 'solidarity', see Papataxiarchis 2016).

One way around this problem is to treat what people consider as good as an open question. Human flourishing, well-being and the good life are abstract concepts that need to be studied in their constructions and enactments, as the 'production of morality' (Lashaw 2013) or 'ethicality' (Carrier 2012b), and in terms of the circumstances of that production. Such disentanglement of ethnographic and normative levels avoids the practical and ethical problems of studying mostly movements that accord with the sensibilities of many anthropologists.

I want to summarise what I have said thus far in terms of two basic points. One is that we need to cultivate a vigilant eye on the variety of value mobilisations in the world. It is understandable that researchers who expect to spend a long time with their interlocutors would want to study people with whom they are broadly sympathetic. That, however, keeps us from seeing other values in the world, along with the actions and institutions associated with them. I do not suggest that we become sympathetic to them or that we ought to validate their claims simply because they are in the world. Rather, I think that it is important for us to gain knowledge about groups and values that envision radically different worlds and that seek to put them to practice. Doing so would help us to consider a broad range of values and actions and institutions, and so address questions about who raises which values concerning what economic relations, when and how, and how those values and the actions associated with them are shaped by economic relations, models of thought and arrangements of power.

My other basic point concerns the distinction between economy and society. That may, as Gudeman said, be a good pragmatic device, but we need to be careful that we do not end up ignoring what we know about the economy as an instituted process and instead see it as the constitutive Other of society, the one oppressive and the other progressive. This tendency is apparent in the confusing literature (Hann 2018: 3) on the distinction between society and economy, much of which implies that embedded forms of economy are somehow free of domination (Fraser 2014). The reality is more complicated. When Polanyi described the double movement of efforts to constrain expanding markets and their effects, he pointed out that those efforts were not led by emancipators but by aristocrats and elites who feared that the emerging industrial capitalists would threaten their own positions of power and authority.

These basic points suggest how I think that we might reorient our research in the future. I turn to that now.

An agenda for research on ethical economic practice

The core of my suggestion is that we move our focus away from narrow attention to 'the good', for such a focus can make it harder to see the variety of values that are mobilised when people actually engage in ethical economic activities. Also, it makes it even harder to understand the attraction of values that are radically different from the progressive values that usually attract anthropologists' attention. Focusing on that engagement, on practical economic activity and the values and factors that shape it, should make it easier to take seriously a greater variety of ethical economic activities. It may also make it easier to incorporate arguments about what shapes economic activities that are produced by feminists and those working on migration or race, which are more pertinent to economic anthropology than their current influence on the sub-discipline suggests.

The purpose of this proposed reorientation is not simply to extend our knowledge of human diversity. Rather, I see a focus on ethical economic practice as a way to ask about the larger transformation of social reproduction and how it is politicised. The promise, then, is not only to help us to understand present social realities, but also to encourage economic anthropology to be a comparative and generalising discipline.

Despite the recovery of neoliberalism as thought and practice (Mirowski 2014), the financial crisis of 2007–08 and the Great Recession that followed have led to heightened criticism of market fundamentalism as a basis for how societies ought to organise their reproduction. If what unfolds before us is an era after the Washington Consensus and the crisis of 2007–08, how might that era look?

From promise and possibility to ambivalence and everyday politics

Many recent anthropologies of value and morality convey an air of hope, promise and potentiality, as considerations of the 'differing ways in which people live for the good' (Robbins 2013: 459). This orientation towards life-projects as driven by what appears to be positive social values is reflected in recent literature such as the anthropology of hope. Arjun Appadurai (2013), for instance, has called for a shift away from what he calls an 'ethics of probability', one that sees idealist change in the world as unlikely, and towards an 'ethics of possibility', one that stresses future potentiality and that employs a strategic ignorance of what Gramsci called the pessimism of the intellect.

To some extent, an ethics of possibility is necessary when mass movements seek to change an economic world seen as devoid of social values. Such movements often invoke utopian goals to be approached through logics of promise and possibility. Insightful work can be done on how such movements articulate different temporalities in their evaluation of their own practice and of their redoing 'the ethical' in relation to 'the economical', illustrated by Davina Cooper's (2013a) work on 'everyday utopias'. However, this can be misleading if used as an ethnographic guide for mapping ethical economic practice. The potentialities identified in that work are primarily located in low-level initiatives, face-to-face networks and social movements of a particular kind of horizontalist and pre-figurative politics. For a renewed agenda, investigating the appeal of Right-leaning social movements (Gledhill 2000: 184) might be an important direction to take. Broadening the empirical scope of where potentiality of social values and economic relations are identified might also detect state actions. That would be useful because in the scholarly literature the possibility that has attracted attention is anti-state and anti-market, while 'hope for the state' (Jansen 2015: 104) is generally ignored.

The focus on potentiality and possibility also can lead to a disregard for the challenges, failures and ambivalences experienced in projects that seek to realise social values in economic life. An example of this is literature on LETS, literature and systems that mushroomed in the 1990s in the US and the UK. LETS are alternative trade systems that create money that is valid among their members and so allow for a relatively sovereign mechanism of exchange. Monetary pluralism is a feature of most societies using money and complementary currencies can be traced back to regional experiments like that in Wörgl, in Austria, in the 1930s. LETS are the IT-age version of such social technology and, in the present, mostly used by alternative and often horizontalist groups to achieve more equitable and solidary local economic structures. The hope and optimism of the 1980s' and 1990s' literature on LETS was contagious and inspired many LETS initiatives around the world, including where I was doing field work in Greece between 2014 and 2017.

The problem is that this literature dried up when the promise of LETS presented in it did not translate into successful practice. Hopeful initiatives faltered and failed to generate the 'virtuous cycle promised' by advocates: members saw neither their economic nor their political expectations met (Cooper 2013b: 50). LETS scholars, it turned out, were better at explaining schemes' potential and participants' optimism than they were at analysing the limitations and challenges of LETS (Cooper 2013b: 32). Not only did the optimism of the early LETS years disappear, academics also failed to produce a consideration of the constraints and conditions that hindered

LETS projects, and so made it harder for people to learn from their mistakes (an exception is North 2007). More broadly, they ignored the opportunity to consider kinds of ecology of hope,[1] to suggest particular imaginations of ethical economic practice and to make sense of when those imaginations fade and those practices fail.

This intellectual failure can lead to what I saw among the people where I was doing field work in Greece. They had turned to anthropological literature to understand social life in action and were distressed to find no mention of key aspects of their own experiences with failure, difficulty and ambivalence. They were, that is, more interested in having critical friends than in reading enthusiastic studies of people seeking to do good. This failure also is a sign of a larger problem, that alternative practice appears to be interesting to analysts only so long as it has promise. To avoid that failure in the future, we should attend not only to the hopeful, idealistic and good, but attend also to the contradictions and challenges that people experience and to which they accommodate in ethical economic practice. Several scholars have in fact been working towards an approach that seems suitable for framing ethical economic practice as inherently contradictory, a matter of uncertainty and serious negotiation and not necessarily successful.

One such approach looks at how communities pursuing alternative economic goals wrestle with the reproduction of hegemonic norms. For instance, Nazima Kadir studied squatter communities seeking to create horizontalist livelihoods. She (Kadir 2016: 12) found that in several ways they were failing to meet that goal and instead exhibited considerable hierarchy and the adoption of hegemonic norms. Andrea Muehlebach's ethnography of volunteers in Italy makes the same point in a somewhat different way. She shows how volunteers were uneasy about being implicated in an 'exploitation of their free labor' by Right-leaning governments (Muehlebach 2012: 170). Such work can tell us about the way that the ethical is produced and negotiated by describing how activists and volunteers organising around values of community and solidarity run into contradictions and how they deal with, accommodate to or ignore them.

There are analytical tools that allow for serious ethnographic consideration of the contradictions and dilemmas faced by people who seek to follow particular ethics and that encourage anthropologists to think clearly about the ethical challenges that can arise when seeking to publish such consideration. Those tools avoid a heroic understanding of resistance and a simple binary understanding of power. Instead, they treat power and its play as being located in all social relations (Ortner 1995). Such a move refocuses attention on the negotiations and tensions that occur when people interact with hegemonic norms and try to manipulate or alter them. Don Kalb captures this process by using the notion of 'everyday politics', which he developed in order to understand how people navigate class in Brabant, in the Netherlands. The concept captures 'negotiation from below, not only with one's superiors but also with one's self or with significant others' (Kalb 1997: 22). Further, treating resistance in less exotic and more dispassionate terms (e.g. Theodossopoulos 2014, 2017) can be useful for going beyond what, I noted previously, Dullo describes as the two main anthropological stances, giving voice to those of whom we approve and denouncing those whom we do not. Such a dispassionate approach would help us to understand ethical economic practice not as a sphere of purified exceptionality, but as a practice that has to accommodate itself to and combine contradictory realms of social life as it seeks to achieve its goals.

Comparing and contrasting; or, how ethical economic practice actually plays out

Attending to the everyday politics of ethical economic practice rather than ignoring it would allow us to consider the complexities of the actual doing of values. Several authors have suggested this sort of processual and relational approach. Amanda Lashaw (2013: 518) proposes focusing on 'morality-making' as the object of study to circumvent the ethical difficulties of what she understands as criticising those whom she studied. Carrier (2012b) writes of 'ethicality' to analyse how abstract ideas such as fairness are made concrete, recognisable and attractive to people who buy 'fair' commodities. One of the advantages of the idea of ethicality and the concern with the way that the features of an object are made into a recognisable representation of value is the way that it helps to distinguish the idea of a good from that which is produced as something that ought to be good. These tools allow us to frame ethical economic practices as the translation back and forth between abstract values on the one hand, and features of actual practices, objects and relations on the other. The literature on fair trade has produced such studies, whose analytical tools might be useful for taking the research on ethicality further, and I want to mention some of them.

Mark Moberg and Sarah Lyon (2010: 12 ff.) provide an example of how such translation became controversial in the debate between the International Fairtrade Foundation and Fairtrade US, about whether plantations should be eligible for certification or if Fairtrade should support only smallholders. For Fairtrade US, such expansion would allow the organisation to achieve better working conditions and wages for plantation workers. Most other Fairtrade organisations were against including plantation-grown goods in their certification practices, for they saw it as a dilution of ethical standards and feared that it would allow plantation produce to compete more directly with what smallholders grow, which usually was more expensive. Both organisations claimed the same abstract goal, fairness for workers, but their means were different and actually opposed to each another. In the end, Fairtrade US left the international foundation, showing the practical consequences of differences in understandings of how the ethical ought to be made concrete.

In another study, Moberg showed how Fairtrade proponents and Caribbean banana farmers operate with different notions of the ethicality of fair trade. He traces how the difference between their moral frameworks became apparent when market prices for Fairtrade bananas were sinking while certification requirements were rising, resulting in lower profit margins for producers who felt pressured by

Fairtrade instead of supported by it. Such disagreements about the meaning of the 'ethical' in 'ethical economic practice' have motivated some of the studies of CSR and ethical practice in commodity chains (Dolan and Rajak 2016: 2).

Such a view of the tensions and negotiations surrounding specific attempts to realise ethical economic practice challenges bland representations of doing good. Efforts to ameliorate domination and inequality in production and circulation through market means can in fact be highly contested terrain in which various actors have stakes in defining and negotiating what social values are important and how they are to be realised in practice. As the Chick-fil-A incident described above shows, this can be the case even when different groups use similar means to achieve their goals.

In that case, both pro- and anti-LGBT activists used market signals to put pressure on the company, by encouraging others to either buy or not buy the firm's products. Although the two sides in the dispute were working towards opposing goals, both were claiming that the income of a private firm is, in effect, a matter of public interest, action and dispute. Indeed, if it were treated as an extended case study, the Chick-fil-A case could show how the ethicality of chicken sandwiches is shaped by American politics, conservative lobbying and consumer groups, all concerned in different ways with the nature of gender and kinship in American society. What I am suggesting is an enquiry into the kinds of 'cosmopolitics' (Blaser 2016: 584) that can fetishise chicken sandwiches as de-socialised, de-politicised commodities or that can make them contentious embodiments of conflicting ways of understanding the world.

The Chick-fil-A case also encourages us to attend to the increasing number of organisations, networks and political groups that take up techniques that we know only from their progressive use. In the US, for example, there is a growing advocacy of boycotts by conservative Christian groups that see the heteronormative patriarchal family as ideal and that object to companies that have advertisements featuring homosexual couples or trans people. Equally, the organisation Blue Lives Matter (2016), formed in support of the police and in opposition to Black Lives Matter, called for the boycott of an ice cream company that supported Black Lives Matter. In Europe, groups such as Die Identitären (The Identitarians), a radical-Right youth organisation, advocate nationalist commerce under the slogan 'our money for our people' and host on their website crowd-funding pages that sell goods and services whose purchase is said to support everything from anti-immigration lobbying to attacking liberal cultural productions. Their aims are clear: divest from Others, deny them social transfers, reclaim the nation-state as a defence against free-market fundamentalism and cosmopolitanism. And it turns out that we are strangely unprepared for a consideration of what they want, how we should deal with their various ethicalities and their appeal to what seems like a growing base of support.

Presentism, genealogies and historical comparison

As mentioned earlier, in the West the idea that the economic realm is separate from the social arose in the eighteenth century. However, the presentism in our accounts of ethical economic practice suggests that those practices are creatures of the last third of the twentieth century. Our historical blinkers also hinder a broad consideration of such forms of practice and make it more difficult to engage with a variety of other disciplines.

As against other social sciences focused on things economic, economic anthropology reserves for itself the status of being comparative, for it does not build its understanding primarily from research on the West or from social arrangements in which market exchange is dominant. I have described some of the variety of means and moralities at play in present-day ethical economic practice, but we need to do more than attend to the here and now: few studies engage in historical comparison. We can turn to economic historians like Frank Trentmann in order to learn of the historical contextualisation of things like fair trade. Trentmann traces the 'historical genealogies' (Trentmann 2008: 253) of the idea of fair trade back to imperial Britain and finds women in the Conservative Party rallying for 'Empire Fair Trade' (2008: 254) as predecessors of contemporary anti-globalisation activists.

Such 'alternative or ambivalent moralities' (Trentmann 2008: 254) in the history of consumption practices are useful for understanding how purchasing for political reasons has changed. Those historical genealogies also can be used to see how the means and ends of organisations such as those that came out of the co-operative movement in the nineteenth century have changed. At that time, workers and peasants started to organise co-operative financial organisations such as saving clubs, insurance companies and banks. Friedrich Wilhelm Raiffeisen was an early advocate of co-operatives and his ideas about co-operative ownership and mutual support spread across Europe and developing countries. Today, 330,000 organisations espouse his ideas, one of the most significant among them being Raiffeisen Zentralbank. It is one of the largest banks in Central and Eastern Europe, and recently was involved in several corruption and money-laundering scandals (Höller 2011) and associated with fraudulent lending practices (Mikuš 2018). Histories such as that of Raiffeisen Zentralbank can complicate our understanding of what ethical practice is and how it might change over time. Another promising way to approach such questions is to look at value projects that did not make it. Mariya Ivancheva does so by using Walter Benjamin's ideas in her work on Venezuela, Bulgaria and South Africa, work that she describes as that of 'a historian of lost projects of radical social change' (Thorkelson 2017). Studying historical changes allows us to ask how historical precedents resemble and differ from contemporary ethical economic practices and can serve to question the 'progressive mode' in which the history of such practices usually is written (Trentmann 2008: 254).

While Trentmann refers to historical genealogies, I think it is important to stress the history rather than just the genealogy. That is because the genealogical approach is oriented towards understanding other times, but it considers them primarily in their relation to the present, to see how the contemporary state of affairs came about (on CSR see, e.g., Dolan and Rajak 2016: 6). As I have argued already, the view of ethical economic practice today tends to focus on progressive forms, so that restricting ourselves to genealogy can make it hard for us to see values at play in the past that may have been important then but that find no descendants among progressive movements in the present.

This means that a truly comparative anthropology must go beyond the genealogical if the past is to become a resource for understanding how people at different times in different places have sought to conjoin their values and their economic practices. Why is that important? As we aim to understand our concerns as political subjects and the world that we see around us, we should not be looking only at the familiar. We should be looking as well at practices that challenge our perspective on the phenomena at issue. Such an approach employs a 'distant comparison' (Fillitz 2002: 217; Kapferer 1989: 166) and would help us to rethink what we have come to understand as ethical economic practice and to approach it in a more analytical way. Instead of finding cases that resemble what is going on now, we would see the different ways in which ethical economic practice was and is being done. In his discussion of ethical consumption, Carrier does something like this. He (Carrier 2012b: 1) starts with a fairly general definition of ethical consumption as consumption that takes into account the circumstances of the product that is to be consumed. He then violates our unspoken assumptions by saying that this definition includes American Whites who, in the 1940s and 1950s, refused to drink from a glass that a person of colour had previously used and Germans in the 1930s who refused to buy things sold by Jewish people.

For a comparative economic anthropology, neglecting such examples of consumption that people understand as ethical is a serious shortcoming, for it ignores the range of things that people value and that shape their social relations and economic activities. That ignorance makes it difficult to see and understand the groups, with their distributional claims and exclusionary mechanisms, that seek hegemony, and thus the ways in which the economy is brought into relation with society.

A comparative approach to ethical economic practice

I have suggested a number of ways in which we might build on existing work in order to make economic anthropology more clearly a generalising and historical discipline grounded in ethnography and comparative anthropology. I think that we should start from an understanding of ethical economic practice as rooted in the idea that society and economy are two distinct spheres of value and human action that operate on different premises. As I noted, this distinction is not universal but reflects specific cultural and historical circumstances. I also think that we need to take seriously the difference between the cases that have attracted attention in the sub-discipline and the cases that have not. We would benefit if we use the analytical tools developed in the study of progressive social movements to investigate the practices that we have ignored and that seem to have caught us unprepared.

I have made three suggestions about how we might approach such investigation and the comparisons that it allows. Firstly, we should study ambivalence and everyday politics in social movements seeking to change economic practice, rather than thinking of them in terms of their promise and possibility (see Siniscalchi this volume). I have mentioned work on LETS schemes, which suggests that such a move is necessary for understanding how forms of economic circulation are shaped and constrained or enabled by political-economic contexts, the aims and means of those involved and the complex negotiation of values, interests and needs that occurs in those movements. Secondly, we should attend to ethicality as the process by which economic practice is evaluated, contested and made meaningful according to social values. The production of ethical economic practice thus needs to be studied through observations of how and when things economic become contentious and how their legitimacy is negotiated and challenged. Finally, we should take advantage of the historical depth of ethical economic practice, either with a genealogical approach that seeks the antecedents of present forms of that practice or with a more purely historical approach that is open to movements urging ethical economic practices of all sorts. Such comparative work could allow us to think carefully about what we mean by the ethical as well as what we mean by the economic.

Combined with the larger questions following from the economic crisis that I mentioned at the beginning of this chapter, such thought can strengthen our sub-discipline's contribution to anthropological understandings of the world. Especially, it can help us to address issues that are pertinent for an understanding of power and distribution and that are usually raised in other sub-disciplines. I want to mention two briefly. Firstly, Black Lives Matter published a dossier on economic justice in 2016 (Rudiger et al. 2016). It addresses how Black communities are affected by divestment and lack of redistribution, it protests tax codes and their unequal effects, it defends the right to unionise and comments on commons, co-operatives and the social economy. Secondly, some of the impulse to renew economic anthropology arises from feminist work. Laura Bear, Karen Ho, Anna Tsing and Sylvia Yanagisako (2015) put forward a feminist manifesto for studying capitalism, in which they 'challenge the boundedness of the domain of "the economic"' and propose a definition of class that recognises the shifting dynamics of race, gender, sexuality and kinship. The approach of Bear and her fellows, like the concerns of Black Lives Matter, seem especially helpful for renewing economic anthropology as a sub-discipline integrating key insights about the intersections of class with race and gender.

Conclusion

The increased importance of economic anthropology since the onset of the Great Recession rests in significant part on the repoliticisation of things economic, as social movements opposed to economic injustice and inequality have become more active and more visible. That repoliticisation, like work on ethical consumption, CSR and solidarity economies, reflects and questions the distinction between what is understood as society, a realm of social values, and economy, a realm of rational calculation and maximisation. Those who are my main concern in this chapter, people who engage in ethical economic practice, claim in one way or another that they bring social values and economic practice together through things like buying fair-trade products, offsetting CO_2 emissions and organising LETS. Studying such practices has become one entry point for studying the large questions of capitalism, distribution and justice. In this chapter, I have asked what a renewed agenda for studying such practices could look like, how it could build on the existing literature and how the study of divergent forms of such practices in the past and the present might help generate novel insights.

In 2018, things look different than they did in 2007–08. What seemed at the time to be a wave of progressive social movements aiming to repoliticise the economy has been made more complex with the increased visibility of movements that seem clearly racist and nationalist. Many economic anthropologists seem to have seen 'values' as a synonym for 'good', and the newer movements caught them off guard. I have proposed that we get around this problem by taking a more dispassionate approach and treat as good, at least for analytical purposes, the activities that people engage in when they are doing what they deem good and right. This would allow us to take a fresh look at the variation in how people actually do ethics. This broader view is, I think, necessary if we are to ask important questions about ethical economic practice in general: When does it occur? Who argues that economic practice needs to be shaped by social values? What negotiations and struggles occur around the means and ends of such practices? Which practices and relations are thought of as lacking values?

Such questions need to be asked if we are to make sense of how social reproduction is understood and organised, and of the practices that people and organisations engage in, negotiate about and fight over as they seek to infuse economic practice with social values; which is to say, how they do ethics. Understanding how people do ethics is important in its own right but it also can be the basis of a comparative anthropology intended to understand the circumstances that enable or constrain such behaviour and how they do so. It would, in John Gledhill's (2000: 9) words, help us to understand 'possibilities and limitations . . . within particular historical contexts and larger fields of power relations'.

This expansive understanding of where the ethical is helps to sharpen the analytical tools that help us detect and explain it. The comparative and generalising mode of economic anthropology that I have urged here can help us to build an anthropology of ethical economic practice that would enable us to use the small acts of economic life to address the larger questions about economic systems, forms of distribution and social reproduction.

NOTE

1 Thanks to Martin Fotta for the wording and for conversations on the topic.

References

Appadurai, Arjun 2013. *The Future as Cultural Fact: Essays on the Global Condition*. London: Verso.

Bear, Laura, Karen Ho, Anna Tsing and Sylvia Yanagisako 2015. Gens: A feminist manifesto for the study of capitalism. *Cultural Anthropology*. https://culanth.org/fieldsights/652-gens-a-feminist-mani festo-for-the-study-of-capitalism (accessed 29 March 2018)

Blaser, Mario 2016. Is another cosmopolitics possible? *Cultural Anthropology* 31 (4): 545–70.

Blue Lives Matter 2016. Blue Lives Matter is asking all Americans to boycott Ben & Jerry's Ice Cream. *Blue Lives Matter* (11 October). www.themaven.net/bluelivesmatter/news/L-Yc7_BLykai3 IAb39tRZw (accessed 21 September 2018)

Carrier, James G. 2012a. Anthropology after the crisis. *Focaal* 64: 115–28.

Carrier, James G. 2012b. Introduction. In *Ethical Consumption: Social Value and Economic Practice* (eds) J.G. Carrier and Peter L. Luetchford, pp. 1–35. Oxford: Berghahn Books.

Carrier, James G. 2018. Moral economy: What's in a name. *Anthropological Theory* 18 (1): 18–35.

Carrier, James G. and Peter L. Luetchford (eds) 2012. *Ethical Consumption: Social Value and Economic Practice*. Oxford: Berghahn Books.

Carrier, James G. and Daniel Miller (eds) 1998. *Virtualism: A New Political Economy*. Oxford: Berg Publishers.

Cooper, Davina 2013a. *Everyday Utopias: The Conceptual Life of Promising Spaces*. Durham, NC: Duke University Press.

Cooper, Davina 2013b. Time against time: Normative temporalities and the failure of community labour in local exchange trading schemes. *Time & Society* 22 (1): 31–54.

Couret, Jaques 2013. Chick-fil-A sales jump 12% in 2012. *Atlanta Business Chronicle* (30 January). www. bizjournals.com/atlanta/news/2013/01/30/chick-fil-a-sales-jump-12-in-2012.html   (accessed   24 September 2018)

Dalakoglou, Dimitris 2016. Infrastructural gap: Commons, state and anthropology. *City* 20 (6): 822–31.

de Neve, Geert, Peter Luetchford and Jeff Pratt (eds) 2008. *Hidden Hands in the Market: Ethnographies of Fair Trade, Ethical Consumption, and Corporate Social Responsibility*. Bingley: Emerald Publishing.

Dolan, Catherine and Dinah Rajak 2016. Toward the anthropology of corporate social responsibility. In *The Anthropology of Corporate Social Responsibility* (eds) C. Dolan and D. Rajak, pp. 1–28. Oxford: Berghahn Books.

Dullo, Eduardo 2016. Seriously enough? Describing or analysing the Native(s)'s point of view. In *After the Crisis: Anthropological Thought, Neoliberalism and the Aftermath* (ed.) James G. Carrier, pp. 133–53. London: Routledge.

Fillitz, Thomas 2002. The notion of art: From regional to distant comparison. In *Anthropology, by Comparison* (eds) Richard G. Fox and Andre Gingrich, pp. 204–24. London: Routledge.

Fraser, Nancy 2014. Can society be commodities all the way down? Post-Polanyian reflections on captalist crisis. *Economy and Society* 43 (4): 541–58.

Gibson-Graham, J.K. 2008. Diverse economies: Performative practices for 'other worlds'. *Progress in Human Geography* 32 (5): 613–32.

Gingrich, Andre and Marcus Banks (eds) 2006. *Neo-Nationalism in Europe and Beyond*. Oxford: Berghahn Books.

Gledhill, John 2000. *Power and Its Disguises*. London: Pluto.

Gregory, Chris 2009. Whatever happened to economic anthropology? *The Australian Journal of Anthropology* 20 (3): 285–300.

Gudeman, Stephen 1986. *Economics as Culture: Models and Metaphors of Livelihood*. London: Routledge and Kegan Paul.

Hann, Chris 2018. Moral(ity and) economy: Work, workfare, and fairness in provincial Hungary. *European Journal of Sociology* 59 (2): 225–54.

Hart, Keith and Horacio Ortiz 2008. Anthropology in the financial crisis. *Anthropology Today* 24 (6): 1–3.

Höller, Herwig 2011. Giebelkreuz und Russendisko. *Die Zeit* (8 December). www.zeit.de/2011/50/A-RZB (accessed 21 September 2018)

Jansen, Stef 2015. *Yearnings in the Meantime: 'Normal Lives' and the State in a Sarajevo Apartment Complex*. Oxford: Berghahn Books.

Kadir, Nazima 2016. *The Autonomous Life? Paradoxes of Hierarchy and Authority in the Squatters' Movement in Amsterdam*. Manchester: Manchester University Press.

Kalb, Don 1997. *Expanding Class: Power and Everyday Politics in Industrial Communities, the Netherlands, 1850–1950*. Durham, NC: Duke University Press.

Kalb, Don 2014. 'History repeats itself' – Subversive insights of a Polish populist. In *Does East Go West? Anthropological Pathways Through Postsocialism* (eds) Christian Giordano, Francois Ruegg and Andrea Boscoboinik, pp. 109–30. Berlin: Lit Verlag.

Kapferer, Bruce 1989. Nationalist ideology and a comparative anthropology. *Ethnos* 54 (3–4): 161–99.

Lashaw, Amanda 2013. How progressive culture resists critique: The impasse of NGO Studies. *Ethnography* 14 (4): 501–22.

Mauksch, Stefanie, Pascal Dey, Mike Rowe and Simon Teasdale 2017. Ethnographies of social enterprise. *Social Enterprise Journal* 13 (2): 114–27.

Mikuš, Marek 2018. Contesting household debt in Croatia: Money, expropriation and the double movement of financialization in Eastern European peripheries. MS.

Mirowski, Philip 2014. *Never Let a Serious Crisis Go to Waste: How Neoliberalism Survived the Financial Meltdown*. London: Verso.

Moberg, Mark and Sarah Lyon 2010. What's fair? The paradox of seeking justice through markets. In *Fair Trade and Social Justice: Global Ethnographies* (eds) M. Moberg and S. Lyon, pp. 1–23. New York: New York University Press.

Muehlebach, Andrea 2012. *The Moral Neoliberal: Welfare and Citizenship in Italy*. Chicago: University of Chicago Press.

Nachtwey, Oliver 2016. *Die Abstiegsgesellschaft: Über das Aufbegehren in der regressiven Moderne*. Berlin: Suhrkamp.

Narotzky, Susana and Nico Besnier 2014. Crisis, value, and hope: Rethinking the economy. *Current Anthropology* 55 (S9): 4–16.

North, Peter 2007. *Money and Liberation: The Micropolitics of Alterative Currency Movements*. Minneapolis: University of Minnesota Press.

Ortner, Sherry B. 1995. Resistance and the problem of ethnographic refusal. *Comparative Studies in Society and History* 37 (1): 173–93.

Ortner, Sherry B. 2016. Dark anthropology and its others. *Hau* 6 (1): 47–73.

Palomera, Jaime and Theodora Vetta 2016. Moral economy: Rethinking a radical concept. *Anthropological Theory* 16 (4): 413–32.

Papataxiarchis, Evthymios 2016. Unwrapping solidarity? Society reborn in austerity. *Social Anthropology* 24 (2): 205–10.

Parry, Jonathan and Maurice Bloch 1989. Introduction: Money and the morality of exchange. In *Money and the Morality of Exchange* (eds) J. Parry and M. Bloch, pp. 1–32. Cambridge: Cambridge University Press.

Pasieka, Agnieszka 2016. Taking far-right claims seriously and literally: Anthropology and the study of right-wing radicalism. *Slavic Review* 76 (S1): 19–29.

Polanyi, Karl 1944. *The Great Transformation: The Political and Economic Origins of Our Time*. Boston: Beacon Press.

Rahman, Aminur 1999. *Women and Microcredit in Rural Bangladesh: An Anthropological Study of Grameen Bank Lending*. Boulder, CO: Westview Press.

Rakopoulos, Theodoros 2016. Solidarity: The egalitarian tensions of a bridge-concept. In *The Other Side of Crisis: Solidarity Networks in Greece* (eds) Heath Cabot and T. Rakopoulos. *Social Anthropology* 24 (2, special issue): 142–51.

Robbins, Joel 2013. Beyond the suffering subject: Toward an anthropology of the good. *Journal of the Royal Anthropological Institute* 19 (3): 447–62.

Rudiger, Anja, Cathy Albisa and Karl Kumodzi 2016. Economic justice. *The Movement for Black Lives*. https://policy.m4bl.org/economic-justice/ (accessed 21 September 2018)

Schneider, David 1980 (1968). *American Kinship: A Cultural Account*, 2nd edition. Chicago: University of Chicago Press.

Schuster, Caroline 2015. Your family and friends are collateral: Microfinance and the social. *Cultural Anthropology*. https://culanth.org/fieldsights/660-your-family-and-friends-are-collateral-microfinance-and-the-social (accessed 29 March 2018)

Severson, Kim 2012. Chick-fil-A thrust back into spotlight on gay rights. *The New York Times* (25 July). www.nytimes.com/2012/07/26/us/gay-rights-uproar-over-chick-fil-a-widens.html?mtrref=duckduckgo.com&gwh=0C25CB1726F0B74158FE7CB43353B1B4&gwt=pay (accessed 18 October 2018)

Theodossopoulos, Dimitrios 2014. The ambivalence of anti-austerity indignation in Greece: Resistance, hegemony and complicity. *History and Anthropology* 25 (4): 488–506.

Theodossopoulos, Dimitrios (ed.) 2017. *De-Pathologizing Resistance: Anthropological Interventions*. London: Routledge.

Thorkelson, Eli 2017. Interview with Mariya Ivancheva (University of Leeds). *Academography* (7 April). https://academography.org/2017/04/07/interview-with-mariya-ivancheva-university-of-leeds/ (accessed 21 September 2018)

Trentmann, Frank 2008. Before fair trade: Empire, free trade and the moral economies of food in the modern world. In *Food and Globalization: Consumption, Markets and Politics in the Modern World* (eds) Alexander Nützenadel and F. Trentmann, pp. 253–76. Oxford: Berg Publishing.

Weber, Max 1978 (c. 1914). *Economy and Society*. Guenther Roth and Claus Wittich, trans and eds. Berkeley: University of California Press.

Weiss, Hadas 2015. Capitalist normativitiy: Value and values. *Anthropological Theory* 15 (2): 239–53.

9   An anthropology of the Deplorable

Mark Moberg

No work better defined the emergence of a critical, politically-engaged anthropology in the last third of the twentieth century than Dell Hymes's 1972 edited collection *Reinventing anthropology*. Responding to revolutionary movements throughout the newly post-colonial world, efforts to contain them by the capitalist West and rising demands at home in the US for racial and social justice, the volume outlined a vision of anthropology unreservedly committed to human liberation. *Reinventing anthropology* inaugurated many of the themes that have since defined the discipline's research agendas and pedagogy, including acknowledging anthropology's past collaborations with colonialism, rejecting the notion of bounded, static communities and a willingness to challenge oppression and to identify with its victims.

After dominating anthropology's rhetorical centre stage for more than four decades, it is difficult to appreciate just how revolutionary these arguments once were. They signalled the discipline's reinvention from an explanatory social science to a politically-committed endeavour, what Roy D'Andrade (1995) called a shift from an 'objective' to a 'moral' understanding of the social world. The purpose of this chapter is not to champion one such understanding over another. As intellectuals from Marx to Boas to Eric Wolf have maintained, social analysis need not exclude political engagement. But valuable as the insights of a moral model have been, it may also have blinded anthropologists to key social and political processes at work in what they once euphemistically termed 'late capitalism'. Much more so than earlier anthropologists, researchers in recent decades have identified with and projected their own values on the people they study, assuming, for example, that poor people reflexively resist neoliberalism and that they do so with class-based loyalties, effectively ignoring attitudes among the poor that advance Right-wing agendas. Similarly, anthropologists' tendency to focus on those who are seen as deserving sympathy, such as working people who practice class and racial inclusiveness rather than those who do not (e.g. White nationalists), have hindered enquiry into the ways in which political action occurs under neoliberalism (see Streinzer this volume).

In sum, *Reinventing anthropology* may have prepared us not for the world as it is, but for the one that we wish it to be. In this chapter I examine some of the ways in which anthropological research programmes in recent decades have left us unprepared for key social processes at work in the contemporary world. Rectifying this requires us to consider seriously people whose values we not only do not share, but may find repugnant, an endeavour that I call 'anthropology of the Deplorable'. It also requires anthropologists to penetrate sites of power too often ignored in our tendency to identify with the oppressed. And it will certainly require us, after decades of deferring to the voice of Others, to attend equally to the pervasive economic and political structures through which their voices are generated and heard.

For economic anthropologists who came of age since the 1970s, the topical and methodological cues from *Reinventing anthropology* seemed clear enough. Writing in the late 1960s, Richard Salisbury (1968: 481) identified the primary question in economic anthropology as whether 'primitives' were economically rational, a question that they had debated since the time of Malinowski. In the wake of *Reinventing anthropology* such concerns seemed impossibly naïve, or even complicit with Cold War objectives. Gone were unproductive debates on the suitability of formal microeconomic theory for non-market contexts and sterile efforts to formally model decision-making in tribal societies. In their place came an engagement with Marxism and its variants, such as world-systems theory, and an understanding that local economies everywhere articulated with national and global processes of surplus extraction. If the rediscovery of Chayanov's work in the 1960s defined that decade's preoccupation with peasant households and their decision-making, economic anthropologists in subsequent decades increasingly turned to Lenin, even if not by name, to reveal the inevitability of processes that transform peasants into proletarians.

During the 1970s and 1980s many came to see that a politically-engaged research programme required solidarity with the victims of capitalist (and other) oppression. Hence, the anthropological subject became not the rational actor of formal economics but a politically-conscious, even heroic, small farmer or wage labourer. As academic and broader fixations on identity grew during the 1990s, that agent may have been seen as gendered, racially or ethnically marginalised or queer, but for most anthropologists the agent's subaltern and oppressed status remained a given. So too did resistance to oppression, even if anthropologists' focus shifted from collective, class-based action to individual, surreptitious defiance of the everyday variety (Scott 1985). For many researchers, the focus on resistance reflected a conscious decision to accompany the victims of social suffering through their own testimony, an argument that Nancy Scheper-Hughes (1995) laid out in her 'proposition for a militant anthropology'.[1] Key to all this was a realignment of anthropology's core mission from that of analytical explanation of the social world to that of an overt identification with our informants.

The value of testimony

The emergence of anthropology's moral voice on behalf of the oppressed is traceable to multiple sources of the 1960s and 1970s, all redefining how researchers conduct their work and conceive of their subjects.[2] By then, anthropologists were free to confront their predecessors' collaborations with the British Colonial Office, the US Bureau of Indian Affairs or military and intelligence establishments because, on the whole, they had grown less reliant on such institutions for research support. Concerns about the field's earlier colonial associations converged with an emerging crisis of representation. Well before the postmodern turn of the late twentieth century, the question of representation had simmered quietly on the discipline's backburners, but it became more urgent when Malinowski's Trobriand diaries were published in 1967.

The ensuing scandal did more than damage the reputation of the discipline's consummate field worker; it provoked close scrutiny of all claims, following Malinowski's own, to produce authoritative accounts of other ways of life. Critics questioned how it was possible that Malinowski could compartmentalise the intense inner emotions revealed in his diary, including the racist vitriol he directed at his hosts, while maintaining the objectivity of science that he professed in his published work. And if the authority of the discipline's most revered field worker was called into question, what did that imply for all the ensuing accounts from the legions of anthropologists who could only aspire to his level of depth and thoroughness?

Perhaps because of such developments – a widely-felt shame at past colonial collaborations and recognition that behind ethnographic claims to objectivity are highly subjective observers – by the 1980s the field gravitated inexorably towards poststructuralism. While similar pressures have grown over the last generation in many disciplines, anthropology is unique in its embrace of postmodern and poststructural thought originating in philosophy and linguistics. Among these ideas, the most influential has been Foucault's assertion that all claims to knowledge are also claims to power, and that the discourses of science have historically disadvantaged those lacking institutional or credentialled access to such knowledge. By the end of the century, such claims became a dominant assumption within Anglo-American sociocultural anthropology, although they never moved beyond the margins in sociology and are virtually unknown in political science or psychology. They have also had an enduring impact on how anthropologists conduct their work and value their own perspectives relative to those of their informants. As revealed in the extended debate between Marshall Sahlins and Gananath Obeyesekere (see Carrier 2012: 122), in the final years of the twentieth century few anthropologists openly affirmed their own voices, much less their analytical categories, over those of the people they studied. By the discipline's poststructural conventions, researchers were to become the conduits for the long-suppressed voices of the Other, as the imposition of any structure-based meta-narrative was thought to disempower the people that they sought to understand.

Despite the demands for increased public relevance in *Reinventing anthropology*, the audience for anthropological writing has changed little. We still write largely for other anthropologists, most of whom are active or aspiring professionals. Whether our readers are undergraduates, doctoral students, academics or practising professionals, they remain overwhelmingly well-educated, middle-class Europeans or North Americans for whom the specific social fields that we describe are unfamiliar. The value of research as cultural translation is inestimable, especially for those of us who see teaching as important for instilling empathy among students whose backgrounds would incline them to a stereotypical understanding of the people we describe. Through the ethnographic work of Scheper-Hughes, Philippe Bourgois and Paul Farmer, all of whom convey harrowing social circumstances through informant narratives, my students report that their outlooks on the world have been radically changed. Yet there is an unavoidable paradox in anthropologists' embrace of a moral voice challenging oppression and their claim to privilege the voice of the Other.

What if the Other is not a victim of oppression, but its perpetrator or enabler? Does empathic understanding cease when we seek to understand not the poor who negotiate structures of oppression, but those responsible for such structures in the first place? These questions are key to understanding a neoliberal order that has created legions of downwardly mobile people whose anger finds its most convenient target in the traditional subjects of anthropology: immigrants, those in racial, ethnic and sexual minorities, the poor. As Sindre Bangstad (2017) observed, recent political trends present a challenge to anthropologists who have studied 'those people who in some way or other can be said to "suffer." When we speak of "suffering," images of white male populist right-wing sympathisers are perhaps not the first images that cross our anthropological minds, though some of them both *feel* and *are* marginalised and suffering.' Indeed, the resentments fuelled by such suffering have become a driving political force in the contemporary world. Anthropologists who ignore such sentiments and those who express them do so at their peril.

Towards an anthropology of the Deplorable

At the beginning of the twenty-first century, anthropologists took generalised resistance to global neoliberalism as a given. Two decades on, we are grappling with the fact that such resistance often does not assume the forms that we expected or wished. Among ostensibly well-informed observers, anthropologists have not been alone in expressing dismay at the triumph of Right-wing populism, reflected in the UK's Brexit vote, the rise of xenophobic political forces on the European continent and the election of Donald Trump in the US. Given our participant observation and professed solidarity with the victims of neoliberal policy, we should have been less surprised at these political outcomes.

At the 2016 annual conference of the American Anthropological Association, held one week after the US election, visibly traumatised attendees registered anger and shock at the prospect of a Trump presidency. A round-table session on the election, subtitled 'Anthropologists reflect on what happened',[3] had to be relocated to a larger venue to accommodate an audience of over 800, far more than first expected. Planned when a different outcome was anticipated, the panel instead dwelt on Trump's mobilisation of racist voters and promotion of violence at his campaign rallies. Clearly, many anthropologists, almost all of whom see themselves as politically Left or liberal, had failed to appreciate the depth of nativist, racist and misogynist sentiments in the electorate. Nor did they anticipate that those sentiments were held strongly by many of the (White) victims of the very neoliberal policies that anthropologists had long criticised. Although the political Right has long been said to screen out evidence not consonant with its worldview, the Left's shocked astonishment underscored a similarly blinkered view of the world.

Several months earlier, during the election campaign, Hillary Clinton was widely rebuked for her statement that 'half' of Trump's supporters could 'be put in a basket of deplorables', those she described as 'racist, sexist, homophobic, xeno- phobic, Islamaphobic – you name it' (Reilly 2016). Remarkably, in the weeks that followed many adopted Deplorable as a badge of honour, apparently revelling in the label Clinton had given them. Bumper stickers appeared proclaiming 'Another Deplorable for Trump' and 'Proud to be Deplorable'. Such sentiments were par- ticularly prevalent in my deeply conservative state of Alabama, and some chalked up Trump's victory to long-standing racial animus in the Deep South. But the electoral map of the US revealed a much more complex pattern. Trump had easily won over broad swaths of the White working class, including those who had reli- ably voted for liberal Democrats in the past.

This was especially true in regions that had experienced the brunt of de-industri- alisation and the loss of what had long been considered stable middle-class jobs. Surveys reveal that between 10 and 13 per cent of Trump's voters had cast ballots for Obama in previous elections, many saying that they had grown disheartened as the recovery from the Great Recession benefited mostly the already very wealthy. In formerly Democratic-leaning states of the Midwestern Rust Belt, these defec- tions tipped the election, and the presidency, to Trump. With his refrain that the system was rigged against White working people, pledges to 'drain the swamp' by eliminating the influence of wealthy lobbyists and promises to return manufactur- ing jobs to suffering communities, Trump tapped into the grievances of those who felt that their lives had been unmoored by recent economic policies. He was, in sum, the embodiment of resistance to neoliberalism, even if his voters would never have described their support in such terms. That he channelled such resistance into racial resentment mattered less than the fact that he defied the status quo and appeared to champion their interests.

What, then, are anthropologists to make of the Deplorables? Were we blind-sided by Right-wing populist challenges to neoliberalism because our sympathies also blinded us to those who harbour conservative beliefs? Do we limit our insights to those victims of neoliberalism whom we view sympathetically because of our political preferences? If so, how do we regard millions of people who we considered politically intelligible when they voted for Obama in 2012, but not when they voted for Trump four years later? These questions point to an existential dilemma for the discipline as it has emerged over the last several decades. In tandem with the disciplinary changes mentioned in this chapter, James Carrier observes that within anthropology attention to representation and local knowledge has grown, while economic and social structures have been banished to the sidelines of research. This new-found attention has been deployed in the service of liberation and more broadly an appreciation of cultural diversity. However laudable these goals in the abstract, we now confront the practical dilemma that 'not all diversity is good, especially (and paradoxically) if it hinders diversity' (Carrier 2012: 126).

From the outset of the postmodern turn, and even earlier, critics warned that if anthropologists were to adopt as their mission attention to the voice of the Other, that necessarily included Others whose ideas we regard as repugnant (Deplorable). As long as racists, misogynists and xenophobes remained on the political margins, we seemed content to ignore this warning. But now such voices are actively engaged in policy-making and have begun to shape the world in which we live. And by virtue of the fact that our sympathies dictate which Others we attend to and which we ignore (Dullo 2016), we find ourselves disarmed in understanding where they come from.

Long ago the marginalised Other – the immigrant, the refugee, the racial or ethnic minority, the transgender or queer person – became the dominant subject of anthropological research and writing, notwithstanding their often-hidden status within society as a whole. Given their exposure to persecution in today's perilous circumstances, this is no time to abandon solidarity with those who will experience the brunt of Right-wing populism or for the activists within our disciplinary ranks to stop speaking out in their research and teaching. Anthropologists need to document what happens to immigrant children suffering the loss of their parents due to deportation, the travails of people fleeing war-torn places for hostile destinations and those who face everyday persecution for their racial or gender identity. There is no end to a potential anthropology of witness in a world shaped by Right-wing populism. But it is equally imperative to understand the origins of these forces, and to do so anthropologists must attend to those whom they neither understand well nor closely sympathise with.

Recent research in North American anthropology, bringing concern with economic and social structure back from the sidelines, has looked at how neoliberal restructuring devastated working-class families caught between precarious job prospects and a disappearing social safety net. The studies assembled by Jane Collins, Micaela di Leonardo and Brett Williams (2008) examined how de-industrialisation and privatisation have exacerbated class disparities, creating new 'landscapes of inequality' in working-class communities. Marianne Cooper's collection of narratives from Silicon Valley, *Cut adrift* (2014), depicts the anxiety and desperate measures with which working-class families have weathered the Great Recession.[4] Such work deserves our attention. However, the implication of most anthropological research in the US is that the deepening precarity of working-class life finds expression in class-based resistance to corporations and their clients in government, which leaves us poorly equipped to think about working people whose politics are more closely aligned with xenophobic appeals. Journalists, sociologists and political scientists have been less averse than anthropologists to studying working-class people who have gravitated to American Right-wing populism. One such volume, *Hillbilly elegy* by J.D. Vance (2016), offered a personal account of growing up in Appalachia, whose poor Whites have been ravaged by a collapsing labour market and opioid epidemic. Criticised on the Left for his 'blame the victim' analysis of poverty, Vance does suggest why Appalachia's poor Whites found Trump's volatile mix of nostalgia and cultural resentment so compelling.

Whether informed by neo-Marxism or conservative cultural critique, however, most approaches to American working-class communities under neoliberalism circumvent race as an analytical category and racism as a feature of working-class populism. A notable exception is the ethnographic work of a sociologist, Arlie Hochschild (2016), among downwardly mobile working-class Whites in southern Louisiana who describe themselves as 'strangers in their own land'. A common narrative among her informants is the analogy of standing in a long line to the American Dream. While they waited patiently for their turn, they believed that immigrant newcomers and less deserving non-Whites were ushered ahead of them by the country's first non-White president, Barack Obama. These beliefs, together with sharply deteriorating life and employment prospects for White working-class men, created a receptive audience for Trump's persistent attacks on Obama's legitimacy and the racially-tinged conspiracy theories that fuel Right-wing media and internet outlets.

Given American anthropology's poststructuralist sensibilities and attention to social suffering, it is little surprise that most ethnographic field work among Right-wing sympathisers has originated from elsewhere. Douglas Holmes's wide-ranging volume *Integral Europe* (2001) related the expansion of regional governance throughout the European Union to the growth of Right-wing sympathies in White working-class neighbourhoods of France and England. The cultural resentments found in such places were manifested a decade later in the UK's Brexit vote and electoral support for Marine Le Pen's National Front. Andre Gingrich and Marcus Banks (2006) assembled ethnographic studies of Right-wing nationalists across Europe, whose political identities developed in response to the continent's rising tide of immigration and multiculturalism. Don Kalb (2009) has conducted field work among Eastern European far-Right activists for whom the collapse of socialism created a political void and sense of displacement, giving rise to some of the continent's most virulent anti-immigrant ideologies. In her ethnographic work in German schools, Cynthia Miller-Idriss (2009) examined how post-war anti-nationalist taboos are increasingly challenged by working-class students facing uncertain futures and fewer of the social-welfare guarantees enjoyed by their parents and teachers.

All of this research was compiled before the emergence of Right-wing populism as an active legislative presence on the continent but has proven remarkably prescient given the recent electoral gains of parties such as Alternative for Germany, France's National Front (now National Rally), Poland's Law and Justice party and Austria's Freedom Party. What this may imply for the continent's political future was recently outlined by Nitzan Shoshan (2016), whose ethnographic work centres on the nexus between a liberal German state seeking to maintain an anti-nationalist ideology with disenfranchised youth looking back to a far more ominous German past as a source of identity. A common theme expressed in the narratives of Right-wing supporters across the continent is one of nostalgia for an imagined past of culturally and racially homogeneous societies with secure borders, beliefs similar to those expressed by Louisiana's White working class.

Extending from participant observation in single locales to wide-ranging interviews across national boundaries, these ethnographies suggest what an anthropology of the Deplorable can accomplish: reveal how neoliberal policies and structural-economic changes foster cultural and racial resentment. Right-wing discourses may be gleaned from listservs and Facebook pages, but anthropology's greatest strength has always been fine-grained ethnographic description achieved through interviews and participant observation. However, ethnographers of the Deplorable must attend not only to voice, but also to structure, culture and economy to reveal the paradoxical outcomes of populist politics. This does not mean that researchers divest themselves of empathy when working among those with whom they disagree; Hochschild's compassionate account never loses sight of the humanity of her informants even while she herself does not embrace their view of the world. Acting on grievances of identity and displacement, many of those newly cut adrift under neoliberalism have ushered in political forces that will worsen their own plight. Such already is the case in the Trump presidency, whose policies have undercut incomes and social services for most of the working-class and rural voters who supported his rise to power. To understand such paradoxical outcomes, anthropologists should restore to their analytical tool-kit Marxist elements that have been long ignored, those of hegemony and false consciousness. Also required is that anthropologists study up to the authors of neoliberal policies as well as out to those who take them up as political causes, contrary to even their own best interests.

Up the anthropologist . . . again

What if our goal is not only to understand how the poor and powerless respond to these new landscapes of inequality, but also to understand how these conditions develop in the first place? In her contribution to *Reinventing anthropology*, 'Up the anthropologist', Laura Nader (1972) advocated 'studying up' in order to understand how power is exercised through the decisions and interests of corporate elites and government policy-makers. Nader's call has been widely acknowledged, but less often followed. Some in economic anthropology have done so through commodity-chain analysis, extending the analytical focus from the least powerful segments of the world economy (almost always primary producers) to the consumers who exercise their choices among the array of products available to them.

Commodity-chain analysis has been useful for elucidating the polar ends of global economic structures, but it has been less effective at illuminating through ethnography the network of traders, certifiers, wholesalers and supermarket executives whose decisions set the terms of trade between primary producer and retail consumer. It seems that the more they probe the settings and processes of decision-making among corporate executives and public office-holders the more their enquiries are deflected, and the more they ascend into the realm of corporate power and government policy the harder it is for them to gain access to subjects for interviews, much less opportunities for participant observation. Paradoxically, though, these agents may create conditions in which ethnographic research is facilitated at the source of the commodity chain.

In my research with Fairtrade banana producers in the Eastern Caribbean (Moberg 2014, 2016), my enquiries were inadvertently facilitated by the certification require-ments binding farmers to the Fairtrade market. Under the guise of 'transparency,' the world's largest Fairtrade labelling entity, Fairtrade International (FLO), required that producers make their farms and packing sheds accessible to all visitors. This was intended to permit inspections and auditing by FLO officials, who could conduct visits even when farmers were not present. Similarly, FLO required farmers to main-tain extensive records of their agricultural inputs, to be provided on demand when auditors arrived, usually unannounced, to conduct an inspection. In this context of continuous surveillance, my (pre-arranged) visits were seen as far less intrusive. In short, certification requirements made the visiting ethnographer a sympathetic and even welcome presence in comparison to the gatekeepers who usually descended on their farms. Also, my visits afforded producers an opportunity to vent their frustra-tions with a system that most regarded as less than fair, which was revelatory given the rhetoric of democracy and equity that pervades Fairtrade advocacy aimed at consumers in the developed countries who are concerned with social justice.[5]

If the certification requirements of the FLO made farming operations an ethno-graphic open book, such openness was not practised by FLO personnel. Enquiries about FLO decision-making were typically rebuffed or answered with references to public FLO documents. On Dominica, I was prevented from observing interactions between farmers and the company agents who inspected the fruit they delivered for sale, despite the FLO's stated commitments to transparency. Attending man-agement meetings as an observer, I was told, was out of the question. Having conducted years of research both in conventional banana industries in Central America and Fairtrade production in the Eastern Caribbean, I found no difference between them in the opacity of policy-making that linked producers to consumers. The secrecy that I experienced as a field worker mirrored the experiences of many farmers, who could not understand why gatekeepers might suspend them from access to Fairtrade markets or the fact that there was no procedure that they could use to appeal suspension.

Many anthropologists who have attempted to penetrate policy-making and man-agement in corporations have encountered similar impediments. Herein lies a widely assumed, if occasionally exaggerated, hindrance to Nader's call to study up. Assessing the impact of *Reinventing anthropology* two decades after its publication, Hugh Gusterson (1997: 115) observed that anthropologists had finally broken the long disciplinary taboo on research close to home in Western societies. They had achieved less success, however, at accessing the realms of the powerful: '[W]e have very few ethnographic descriptions of how America looks to the rich. Indeed there seems to be a kind of glass ceiling for ethnographers, with the consequence that the ethnographic literature on the U.S. leaves the upper reaches of the social system largely in shade.'

Yet there is nothing intrinsic about the anthropological endeavour that makes elites more inaccessible than relatively powerless people, though many researchers assume that such is the case. Cris Shore (2002: 1), who studied the European Commission in Brussels, pointed out the irony in this assumption: '[W]hat could be more elitist than anthropology itself, a profession steeped in the traditions and practices of Western middle-class academics, most of whom possess doctorates from the most exclusive universities, and whose scholarly output is aimed primarily for . . . other Western, middle-class intellectuals?' Anthropologists are much more likely to share social backgrounds, educational credentials and forms of cultural capital with elites than with more marginalised people.

This is obvious to researchers who have worked in places where they are socially identified with dominant groups and must go to great lengths to establish rapport with less powerful people. Commonly anthropologists in the field maintain some dependence on locally powerful individuals. These relationships and shared backgrounds often colour the resulting ethnographic analyses, as close readings of these accounts can reveal. The editors of *African political systems* (Fortes and Evans-Pritchard 1940) gratefully acknowledged the support of district officers in gaining entrée to African societies; was it a coincidence, then, that their views of political processes meshed closely with the assumptions of colonial administrators? Talal Asad (1972) argued that the transactional model of politics that Frederick Barth developed from his study of the Swat Pathan owed much to the views of the well-educated, cosmopolitan landlord class with whom Barth spent much of his time in the field. In his ethnography of Puerto Rican street-level drug dealers, Bourgois (1996) said that only his harassment by police dispelled people's belief that he was a narcotics officer. And in my research among immigrant banana workers in Belize (Moberg 1996), estate owners generally assumed that I, a well-educated White foreigner, would share their views of non-White workers. While anthropologists seeking closer rapport with marginalised groups can find such local identifications irksome, they also point to a potential to enter otherwise closed corridors of wealth and power.

Earlier elite studies (Marcus 1983; Shore and Nugent 2002) have outlined the similar ways in which dominant groups operate in the economic and political realms, even in radically different societies. To be understood by themselves and others as an elite, their members must 'develop three C's: consciousness, cohesion and conspiracy' (Shore 2002: 4). Common to such groups in Western and non-Western settings alike is their contradictory nature. Arguably the founder of elite theory in political philosophy, Machiavelli noted long ago that the powerful and would-be powerful embrace unmitigated self-interest in belief and behaviour, but typically do so through collective and endogamous channels. Members of elite groups tend to be marked as socially distinct in their cultural capital, as Pierre Bourdieu observed, and in the patterns of kinship, marriage and alliance that perpetuate their dominance in business and politics. Not surprisingly, anthropologists such as Abner Cohen (1981) and Lloyd and Suzanne Rudolph (1984) have found among elites counterparts to the kinship norms thought to govern tribal societies. J. McIver Weatherford (1985) pursued similar enquiries in his ethnographic research among members of the US Congress, revealing dense networks of kinship and alliance among what he called *Tribes on the Hill*.[6]

Earlier studies reveal how elites perpetuate their social dominance, but recent work by economic anthropologists also shows how elite decision-making guides expansion and crisis in contemporary capitalism. Working in a Wall Street investment firm, Karen Ho compiled extensive interviews with executives whose actions intimately affect the trajectory of the broader economy. Her *Liquidated* (2009) documents a high-risk work culture among investment bankers whose recruitment and professional advancement reward short-term but unsustainable financial returns. While bubbles and subsequent downturns often are seen as natural market processes, Ho suggests that they also are intrinsic in the reward structure facing Wall Street decision-makers, creating a broader economic cycle of frenetic expansion punctuated by crisis. Complementing Ho's ethnography, Gillian Tett, a journalist who trained as an anthropologist, documented how credit-derivative obligations, an esoteric investment vehicle pioneered by J.P. Morgan during the 1990s, inspired riskier strategies in subsequent years. Among these was the investment industry's reliance on credit default swaps tied to a subprime mortgage boom in the US housing market. By 2007, a few Wall Street analysts recognised the disastrous implications of these strategies, but for most this realisation came too late to avert economic collapse. From her insider's perspective, Tett was one of the few journalists to warn of the meltdown of 2008 that became the Great Recession. Her *Fool's gold* (2009) laid out the perverse short-term and unsustainable investment incentives (of the sort mentioned by Ho) that fuelled the most severe contraction in the world economy since the 1930s.

For many anthropologists, however, gaining such intimate access to the sites of elite decision-making is less feasible. Corporations are notoriously opaque about their operations and trade secrets, complicating access to the workplace for researchers who are not directly affiliated with the company themselves.[7] Just as multi-sited ethnographies eschew long-term residence in single locales in order to capture the workings of broad political and economic forces, studying up may require that researchers abandon traditional community-based field work. To replace it, Gusterson (1997: 117) suggests 'polymorphous engagement' based on 'interacting with informants across a number of dispersed sites, not just in local communities, and sometimes in virtual form; and . . . collecting data eclectically from a disparate array of sources in many different ways'. In his study of scientists employed at Livermore Laboratory, a centre of nuclear weapons development in the US, Gusterson was excluded from contact with his informants at their actual places of work. Instead, he

> socialised informally with scientists from the laboratory in local churches, social clubs, bars, hiking groups and so on. However, polymorphous engagement also involved an eclectic mix of other research techniques: formal interviews of the kind often done by journalists and political scientists; extensive reading of newspapers and official documents, and careful attention to popular culture. (Gusterson 1997: 116)

Conversations with nuclear scientists outside the workplace revealed how they struggle to reconcile their professional lives with their personal beliefs (some are devoutly religious, and a surprising number are politically liberal) while distancing themselves from the dire implications of their work with a dark, sardonic humour. Within another, similar context behind the secretive veil of defence, David Price (2004) has drawn on access to declassified (if often heavily redacted) documents through the Freedom of Information Act and public archives to illustrate the workings of the CIA, FBI and other agencies as they confronted perceived enemies, among whom were many anthropologists suspected of Leftist sympathies during the Cold War.

Conclusions

Just a handful of anthropologists have conducted research among Deplorables, who have contributed to the ascendancy of Right-wing populism. Nor have many really penetrated the elite sites of decision-making that guide global patterns of accumulation, investment and crisis. Deplorables and elites could not appear more dissimilar in their outlooks, cultural capital and class membership. Downwardly-mobile working-class Whites and corporate and investor elites remain divided in other ways as well, notably on the merits of internationalism as a political stance and globalism as economic strategy. Yet they are inextricably bound, some as the authors and others as the enablers of contemporary neoliberalism.

Policies of deregulation, privatisation and the dismantling of social safety nets have defined the neoliberal agenda since the 1970s, have long been a hallmark of conservative and centre-Right parties in Europe and have been aggressively pursued by the more Right-wing Republican Party in the US. Ironically, those who direct such agendas are rarely perceived as elites by the White working people whose votes make such policies possible. In the US, 'elite' has instead become synonymous with liberal entertainers and intellectuals who are often believed to be dismissive toward the White working class and at the heart of imagined conspiracies to undermine it in favour of less deserving non-Whites. Much of the power of elites rests on their ability to divert the attention of White voters to such illusory threats to their well-being. In other words, contemporary elites maintain power much as Shore identified, with his three Cs. They conceal themselves and the resources they command from much of the rest of society.

Research among the elite authors and working-class enablers of neoliberalism entails challenges that anthropologists have avoided for a generation or more. With the shift to a moral framework in anthropology since the 1970s, many have felt compelled to adopt a posture of either sympathy or denunciation in their work, depending upon the subjects of their study. Those whose moral stance diverges from that of the researcher are often consigned to the category of the 'repugnant Other', as Eduardo Dullo (2016) calls them, and are either decried or ignored as potential subjects of research. Yet recent scholarship such as Hochschild's work among Louisiana Whites, much of it from outside anthropology, points to how researchers can foster an empathic understanding of those whose values they do not share. The task here is to return to an older, naturalistic model of social enquiry, that of *Verstehen*, associated with Max Weber. That takes informants' perceptions and explanations of their behaviour seriously as a starting point and builds backwards to the institutions and cultural forces that give rise to them.

The challenge for an anthropology of neoliberal elites is more daunting methodologically and ethically. Given their frequent closure to outside enquiry, impediments to physical access can be as formidable as securing permission for research purposes. The principles of informed consent would foreclose most research within the corporations or state institutions in which elites operate and wield their power. In a few cases, anthropologists and other social scientists have been given licence to conduct enquiries within such institutions as the World Bank, the European Commission and General Motors, but these entities have usually retained some veto power over the researcher's resulting publications. Business anthropology, as such research is usually called, typically serves the interests of corporations rather than the researcher's academic discipline or general public. The solution to these problems involves a broader and more diffuse notion of the field than is traditional. Cultivating relationships with individual members of elite groups rather than focusing on a field site associated with a specific locale, as Gusterson described, can accomplish both the anthropologist's obligations of informed consent and autonomy in matters of enquiry and publication. These methods, it may be noted, more closely resemble journalism than traditional social or cultural anthropology.

Today's neoliberal social order has been decades in the making, corresponding to the time in which anthropologists have often elevated their political perspectives over analytical priorities. Responding to the challenges of *Reinventing anthropology*, researchers over the last four decades have redefined their agendas to embrace liberation and solidarity with the oppressed Other. Given that ethnic, national, racial and sexual minorities are more exposed to everyday and institutional violence today than in the recent past, this mission remains a valid priority for anthropologists seeking to understand how neoliberalism operates. But the oppression experienced by vulnerable groups must not be taken as an exogenous variable or its perpetrators considered as marginal to the anthropological project. An anthropology of the Deplorable must start with the structural economic and cultural conditions in which Deplorable beliefs and policies flourish. It must examine the multiple paradoxes that arise as members of downwardly-mobile and demographically-declining groups react to their new-found precarity. And it must study up to interrogate the powerful individuals and organisations poised to take advantage of their economic insecurities and cultural anxieties. This will take us into unfamiliar and, for many of us, unfriendly territory, but it is a terrain in which many of our fellow citizens conduct their lives and politics. In the end, if we want to render that terrain familiar and inviting, so that we can work towards a world that we wish to be, we must first understand the world that is given to us.

NOTES

1 Scheper-Hughes has amassed decades of activism with grassroots organisations that are grounded in explicitly moral concerns. Her plea that anthropologists express solidarity with marginalised people in their research finds a counterpart in the 'preferential option for the poor' emphasised in liberation theology. These conjoined research and political goals are described in her experiences with a Catholic Worker community advocating for the homeless in California (Scheper-Hughes 2017).
2 This has become a contentious term in recent anthropology. Some journal editors now proscribe the use of 'subject' in reference to anthropologists' informants, encouraging authors to instead refer to them as 'collaborators' or 'interlocutors'. The intended effect is a levelling of the anthropologists' ethnographic authority with that of the people they set out to describe.
3 At least one stunned participant in the roundtable wanted to rename it 'What the F**k Happened?'
4 Cooper relates the story of an older unemployed man who held up a bank, patiently waited for his own arrest and then petitioned the court for a sentence to enable him to remain in prison until he was eligible for his Social Security and Medicare benefits.
5 These resentments are largely unknown to consumers, whose knowledge of the Fairtrade system is mostly based on the advertising of Fairtrade NGOs and the supermarkets that carry the products.
6 'The Hill' is a common American term for the US Congress, which is located on Capitol Hill.
7 In Belize, one banana company manager explained his reluctance to provide information about board meetings and corporate policy by saying that people feared that I might be spying for a rival firm.

References

Asad, Talal 1972. Market model, class structure and consent: A reconsideration of Swat political organisation. *Man* 7 (1): 74–94.
Bangstad, Sindre 2017. Doing fieldwork among people we don't (necessarily) like. *Anthropology News* (28 August). www.anthropology-news.org/index.php/2017/08/28/doing-fieldwork-among-people-we-dont-necessarily-like/ (accessed 1 October 2017)
Bourgois, Philippe 1996. *In Search of Respect: Selling Crack in El Barrio.* New York: Cambridge University Press.
Carrier, James G. 2012. Anthropology after the crisis. *Focaal* 64: 115–28.
Cohen, Abner 1981. *The Politics of Elite Culture.* Berkley: University of California Press.
Collins, Jane, Micaela di Leonardo and Brett Williams (eds) 2008. *New Landscapes of Inequality: Neoliberalism and the Erosion of Democracy in America.* Santa Fe: School for Advanced Research Press.
Cooper, Marianne 2014. *Cut Adrift: Families in Insecure Times.* Berkeley: University of California Press.

D'Andrade, Roy 1995. Moral models in anthropology. *Current Anthropology* 36 (3): 399–408.

Dullo, Eduardo 2016. Seriously enough? Describing or analysing the Native(s)'s point of view. In *After the Crisis: Anthropological Thought, Neoliberalism and the Aftermath* (ed.) James G. Carrier, pp. 133–53. London: Routledge.

Fortes, Meyer and E.E. Evans-Pritchard (eds) 1940. *African Political Systems*. London: Oxford University Press.

Gingrich, Andre and Marcus Banks (eds) 2006. *Neo-Nationalism in Europe and Beyond: Perspectives from Social Anthropology*. Oxford: Berghahn Books.

Gusterson, Hugh 1997. Studying up revisited. *PoLAR* 20 (1): 114–19.

Ho, Karen 2009. *Liquidated: An Ethnography of Wall Street*. Durham, NC: Duke University Press.

Hochschild, Arlie R. 2016. *Strangers in Their Own Land: Anger and Mourning on the American Right*. New York: New Press.

Holmes, Douglas R. 2001. *Integral Europe: Fast-Capitalism, Multiculturalism, Neofascism*. Princeton, NJ: Princeton University Press.

Hymes, Dell (ed.) 1972. *Reinventing Anthropology*. New York: Random House.

Kalb, Don 2009. Conversations with a Polish populist: Tracing hidden histories of globalization, class, and dispossession in postsocialism (and beyond). *American Ethnologist* 36 (2): 207–23.

Marcus, George 1983. Elite as a concept, theory, and research tradition. In *Elites: Anthropological Insights* (ed.) G. Marcus, pp. 7–27. Albuquerque: University of New Mexico Press.

Miller-Idriss, Cynthia 2009. *Blood and Culture: Youth, Right-Wing Extremism, and National Belonging in Contemporary Germany*. Durham, NC: Duke University Press.

Moberg, Mark 1996. *Myths of Ethnicity and Nation: Immigration, Work, and Identity in the Belize Banana Industry*. Knoxville: University of Tennessee Press.

Moberg, Mark 2014. Certification and neoliberal governance: Moral economies of fair trade in the Eastern Caribbean. *American Anthropologist* 116 (1): 1–16.

Moberg, Mark 2016. Market's end: Fair-trade social premiums and development in Dominica. *American Ethnologist* 43 (4): 677–90.

Nader, Laura 1972. Up the anthropologist: Perspectives gained from studying up. In *Reinventing Anthropology* (ed.) Dell Hymes, pp. 284–311. New York: Random House.

Price, David H. 2004. *Threatening Anthropology: McCarthyism and the FBI's Surveillance of Activist Anthropologists*. Durham, NC: Duke University Press.

Reilly, Katie 2016. Read Hillary Clinton's 'basket of deplorables' remark about Donald Trump supporters. *Time* (10 September). http://time.com/4486502/hillary-clinton-basket-of-deplorables-tran script/ (accessed 20 October 2018).

Rudolph, Lloyd and Suzanne Rudolph 1984. *India: The Modernity of Tradition*. Chicago: University of Chicago Press.

Salisbury, Richard 1968. Anthropology and economics. In *Economic Anthropology: Readings in Theory and Analysis* (eds) Edward E. LeClair, Jr and Harold K. Schneider, pp. 477–85. New York: Holt, Rinehart, and Winston.

Scheper-Hughes, Nancy 1995. The primacy of the ethical: Propositions for a militant anthropology. *Current Anthropology* 36 (3): 409–40.

Scheper-Hughes, Nancy 2017. Anthropologist as court jester: Civil disobedience and the People's Café. *Boom California* (7 February). https://boomcalifornia.com/2017/02/07/anthropologist-as-court-jes ter-civil-disobedience-and-the-peoples-cafe/ (accessed 15 November 2017)

Scott, James C. 1985. *Weapons of the Weak: Everyday Forms of Peasant Resistance*. New Haven: Yale University Press.

Shore, Cris 2002. Introduction: Toward an anthropology of elites. In *Elite Cultures: Anthropological Perspectives* (eds) C. Shore and Stephen Nugent, pp. 1–21. London: Routledge.

Shore, Cris and Stephen Nugent (eds) 2002. *Elite Cultures: Anthropological Perspectives*. London: Routledge.

Shoshan, Nitzan 2016. *The Management of Hate: Nation, Affect, and the Governance of Right-Wing Extremism in Germany.* Princeton, NJ: Princeton University Press.

Tett, Gillian 2009. *Fool's Gold: How the Bold Dream of a Small Tribe at J.P. Morgan was Corrupted by Wall Street Greed and Unleashed a Catastrophe.* New York: Free Press.

Vance, J.D. 2016. *Hillbilly Elegy: A Memoir of a Family and Culture in Crisis.* New York: Harper.

Weatherford, J. McIver 1985. *Tribes on the Hill: The US Congress Rituals and Realities,* revised edition. New York: Bergin & Garvey.

Index